Social Studies Excursions, K-3
Book Three

Social Studies Excursions, K-3

Book Three: Powerful Units on Childhood, Money, and Government

JANET ALLEMAN AND JERE BROPHY
With Contributions by Barbara Knighton

HEINEMANN
Portsmouth, NH

Heinemann
A division of Reed Elsevier Inc.
361 Hanover Street
Portsmouth, NH 03801–3912
www.heinemann.com

Offices and agents throughout the world

Library of Congress Cataloging-in-Publication Data
Alleman, Janet.
    Social studies excursions, K–3 / Janet Alleman and Jere Brophy with contributions by Barbara Knighton.
        p.   cm.
    Includes bibliographical references.
    Contents: Bk. 3. Powerful units on childhood, money, and government.
    Book One: ISBN 0-325-00315-7 (pbk.)
    Book Two: ISBN 0-325-00316-5 (pbk.)
    Book Three: ISBN 0-325-00317-3 (pbk.)
    1. Social sciences—Study and teaching (Primary). I. Brophy, Jere E.
  II. Knighton, Barbara. III. Title.

LB1530 .A44 2001
372.83'044—dc21   00-054121

Editor: Danny Miller
Production: Lynne Reed
Cover Design: Darci Mehall, Aureo Design
Cover Illustrations: Mark E. Speier and Christian T. Speier
Compositor: Drawing Board Studios
Manufacturing: Steve Bernier

Printed in the United States of America on acid-free paper
07 06 05 04 03 VP 1 2 3 4 5

Contents

· ·

Contents

Series Preface

. . . .

This series contains three volumes, each of which includes detailed plans for social studies units intended for use in the primary grades. The unit plans provide a substantive content base and learning and assessment activities designed to help primary-grade teachers provide their students with a powerful introduction to social education. Like the major primary-grade social studies textbook series, these units focus on cultural universals—basic human needs and social experiences found in all societies, past and present (food, clothing, shelter, communication, transportation, family living, childhood, money, and government). However, unlike the units found in the major textbook series, the units in this series are structured around powerful ideas and designed to develop those ideas in depth and with attention to their applications to life outside of school. Consequently, they are suitable for use as substitutes for, or elaborations of, material on the same topics found in the textbook series.

Such elaboration is needed because the textbooks produced for use in the early grades are primarily picture books that do not provide sufficient content to support a powerful social studies program. Concerning government, for example, textbooks typically include a few pages on the topic in units on schools, neighborhoods, or communities. Pages on school rules or voting might be located within the unit on schools; pages on community helpers (services) or on taxes might be located within a unit on community. A lesson here or there on the U.S. government or patriotic symbols and songs might be woven into a unit on our country that addresses location, our country's leaders, what makes states special, and natural resources. Texts rarely introduce the topic by making personal connections to children, such as by illustrating how government functions and services are very much a part of their lives. While citizenship and core democratic values are expressed in every social studies textbook, it is not uncommon to find these topics treated as sidebars—isolated rather than woven into the narrative in meaningful ways. In contrast, our government unit explores multiple facets of this cultural universal in depth, beginning with citizenship within the classroom community. As the unit continues, it addresses the geographic, economic, and cultural reasons that have led various past and present societies to develop governmental structures and services to provide for needs and wants that people cannot provide for on their own. Students emerge from the unit with connected understandings about how the government is very much a part of their lives and serves to protect them and keep them safe. Students also learn that the government can't do it all and, therefore, volunteers are in high demand.

The series has been developed primarily for preservice and inservice primary-grade teachers who want a more substantive and powerful social studies program than the major textbook series can support. Each volume contains plans for three instructional units intended to support instruction for forty to sixty minutes per day for three to four weeks. Units are divided into lessons that elaborate the content base in detail and include plans for suggested learning activities, assessment tasks, and follow-up home assignments. The home assignments are not conventional worksheets but instead are activities calling for students and their parents to engage in conversations or other enjoyable activities connected to the unit topic. Along with the unit plans as such, each volume includes information about how and why the units were developed, suggestions about how teachers might adapt them to their students and local communities, and tips about planning and implementing the units from the authors and from Barbara Knighton, the teacher who has had the most experience teaching the units to her students.

Besides teachers who will use the units directly with their own students in their own classrooms, the volumes in this series should be useful to several other audiences. State- and district-level staff developers and social studies curriculum coordinators should find the volumes useful as bases for workshops and presentations on making primary-grade social studies more powerful and more in line with national and state standards. Each unit develops a network of powerful ideas (basic social understandings) about the topic and provides opportunities for students to apply these ideas in their lives outside of school. The instructional content and processes reflect the guidelines of the National Council for the Social Studies and related professional organizations.

Finally, the volumes should be useful to professors and others conducting preservice and inservice teacher education relating to social studies in the primary grades. Using materials from this series, instructors can show teachers how the cultural universals addressed in the early social studies curriculum can be developed with a focus on powerful ideas and their applications, so as to create a social studies program that reflects reform standards. Also, by assigning preservice teachers to teach one or more lessons from these units, instructors can provide opportunities for their students to experience what it is like to develop big ideas in depth and to begin to build habits of good professional practice.

Since the 1930s, there has been widespread agreement among primary-grade curriculum makers and teachers that cultural universals are appropriate topics for introducing students to social studies concepts and principles. Given this "wisdom of practice," we believe that instructors will find that the approach taken in this series (i.e., retaining the cultural universals as unit topics but developing them much more coherently and powerfully) makes more sense as a response to criticisms of the contemporary primary-grade social studies textbooks than commonly suggested alternatives that call for shifting to something else entirely (e.g., a primary focus on history or on social issues). We elaborate this point at the end of the first chapter in each volume.

Acknowledgments

. . . .

The units presented in this series could not have been developed without the assistance of a great many people. Most prominent among them is Barbara Knighton, the teacher who first makes our unit plans come to life in her classroom and provides us with many suggestions for improving them. We also wish to acknowledge and thank Gina Henig, Barbara's colleague, who also has provided us with useful feedback and suggestions; the principal, parents, and students associated with the school at which Barbara teaches; Carolyn O'Mahony and Tracy Reynolds, who interviewed students before and after they experienced the units; and June Benson, who transcribed the audiotapes of the class sessions and the interviews. We also wish to acknowledge and thank the College of Education at Michigan State University for its support of the research and development that led to these units and the Spencer Foundation for its support of a related line of research on what K–3 students know (or think they know) about topics commonly addressed in early elementary social studies. Finally, we thank Danny Miller for his feedback on Book Three and Lynne Reed for her invaluable editorial work on all three volumes in the series.

Social Studies Excursions, K-3
Book Three

1

Background
How and Why We Developed the Units

This is the third in a series of three volumes in which we present plans for instructional units on cultural universals—basic human needs and social experiences found in all societies, past and present—designed to be taught in the primary grades (K–3). The units primarily reflect the purposes and goals of social studies, but they do include some science content. They also integrate language arts by including writing assignments and reading and discussion of children's literature. The units may be used as supplements to (or substitutes for) the primary-grade textbooks in the major elementary social studies series.

This third volume includes plans for units on childhood throughout history and across cultures, economics/money, and government. Book 1 contains plans for units on food, clothing, and shelter. Book 2 contains plans for units on communication, transportation, and family living. Each unit has been developed to stand on its own as an independent module, so there is no inherent order in which they need to be taught.

The units have been taught successfully to first and second graders, and they can be adapted for use in kindergarten and third grade. This is because all students, even kindergarteners, have had a variety of personal experiences with cultural universals and are ready to learn more. At the same time, however, what primary-grade students know (or think they know) about these topics is spotty, mostly tacit, and frequently distorted by misconceptions, so even third graders can benefit from opportunities to learn most of what is included in these units. In schools where the complete set of units is taught, the primary-grade teachers

Integrate science & LA w/ social studies concepts

Culture can be taught at any age but it does have to be struct.

will need to coordinate their planning to determine which units will be taught at which grade level.

The Need for a Powerful Content Base in Early Social Studies

In most American elementary schools, the primary-grade social studies curriculum addresses three major goals: (1) socializing students concerning prosocial attitudes and behavior as members of the classroom community, (2) introducing them to map concepts and skills, and (3) introducing them to basic social knowledge drawn mostly from history, geography, and the social sciences. Even though all three of these instructional goals and related content emphases are featured in state and district curriculum guides for elementary social studies, they are not equally well addressed in the resource materials commonly made available to elementary teachers. The major textbook series generally do a good job of providing appropriate content and learning activities for developing students' map concepts and skills. They are more variable in what they offer as a basis for socializing students as citizens of the classroom community (and subsequently, successively broader communities).

A good selection of ancillary resources is available to support primary-grade teachers' planning of experiences designed to help their students learn to interact respectfully, collaborate in learning efforts, resolve conflicts productively, and in general, display prosocial attitudes and democratic values in their behavior as members of the classroom community. Unfortunately, good instructional resources are not readily available to support primary-grade teachers' efforts to help their students develop basic knowledge about society and the human condition. There is widespread agreement among critics of the major elementary social studies series that the content presented in their primary-grade texts is thin, trite, and otherwise inadequate as a foundation for developing basic social understandings. (These criticisms are reviewed in detail in Brophy & Alleman, 1996, and in Larkins, Hawkins, & Gilmore, 1987.)

The social studies curriculum for the elementary grades is usually organized within the expanding communities sequence that begins with a focus on the self in kindergarten and gradually expands to address families in Grade 1, neighborhoods in Grade 2, communities in Grade 3, states and geographic regions in Grade 4, the United States in Grade 5, and the world in Grade 6. However, the categories in the expanding communities sequence refer primarily to the levels of analysis at which content is addressed, not to the content itself. That is, although there is some material on families in first grade, on neighborhoods in second grade, and on communities in third grade, the topics of most instructional units are the human social activities that are carried on within families, neighborhoods, and communities. These activities tend to be structured around cultural universals (food, clothing, shelter, communication, transportation, government, etc.).

Despite problems with the textbook series, we believe that the cultural universals traditionally addressed in the primary grades provide a sound basis for developing fundamental social understandings. First, they are basic to the human condition. Human activities relating to these cultural universals account for a considerable proportion of everyday life and are the focus of much of our social organization and communal activity. Furthermore, children begin accumulating direct personal experiences with most cultural universals right from birth, so that by the time they begin school, they have developed considerable funds of knowledge and experience that they can draw upon in constructing understandings of social education concepts and principles.

If cultural universals are taught with appropriate focus on powerful ideas and their potential life applications, students should develop basic sets of connected understandings about how the social system works, how and why it got to be that way over time, how and why it varies across locations and cultures, and what all of this might mean for personal, social, and civic decision making. The units in this series provide a content base capable of supporting this kind of powerful social studies teaching.

As we've noted, such a content base is needed because it is not provided in the major publishers' elementary social studies textbook series. The primary-grade texts in these series (especially the K–2 texts) are better described as picture books than textbooks. Their pages often contain rich collages of color photos relating to the unit topic, but these photos are accompanied by little or no text—a sentence or two at most. The photos are potentially useful as instructional resources if students are induced to process them with reference to powerful ideas, but the texts typically do not convey such ideas to students. Nor do the accompanying manuals convey them to teachers or provide guidance concerning how the photos might be used as bases for powerful social studies teaching.

For example, a lesson on government might have several pages of photos showing the current president (and perhaps several past pesidents), the White House, the Capitol building, the Supreme Court building, the flag, and various other things symbolizing the United States as a country or its government in particular (the American bald eagle, the Declaration of Independence, the U.S. Constitution, postal workers or vehicles, military personnel or weapons, and so on). However, the text on these pages might say little or nothing more than, "Our nation's government protects and works for all of our people." Students will not get much out of exposure to such collages unless they are helped to process what they are seeing with reference to powerful ideas (in this case, ideas about why governments are needed and what functions they perform). We believe that instruction on government in the primary grades can provide much more substantive information than identification of leaders, locations, and symbols associated with government, yet remain less abstract and more functional for students than the kinds of lessons found in civics and political science textbooks for higher grades (e.g., how a bill becomes a law, comparisons of presidents with prime ministers).

We think that attention should focus on governments as needed not only to establish and maintain an orderly society but also to address a broad range of human needs and wants. The basic idea is that governments provide needed infrastructure and services that are too big in scope, expense, and so on for individual families to provide for themselves. Other basic ideas include: different levels (federal, state, local) and branches (executive, legislative, judicial) of government have different responsibilities and perform different functions, and people pay taxes to fund their governments' activities. With exposures to ideas such as these, students can begin to understand government and appreciate its relevance to their lives, developing basic sets of connected ideas instead of just acquiring familiarity with a few isolated facts and symbols.

Teaching Cultural Universals for Understanding, Appreciation, and Life Application

Our development of instructional units on cultural universals has been guided by several sets of principles. One set reflects an emerging consensus about what is involved in teaching school subjects for understanding, appreciation, and life application. Reviews of research on such teaching (e.g., Good & Brophy, 2003) suggest that it reflects the following ten principles:

1. The curriculum is designed to equip students with knowledge, skills, values, and dispositions that they will find useful both inside and outside of school.

2. Instructional goals emphasize developing student expertise within an application context and with emphasis on conceptual understanding of knowledge and self-regulated application of skills.

3. The curriculum balances breadth with depth by addressing limited content but developing this content sufficiently to foster conceptual understanding.

4. The content is organized around a limited set of powerful ideas (basic understandings and principles).

5. The teacher's role is not just to present information but also to scaffold and respond to students' learning efforts.

6. The students' role is not just to absorb or copy input but also to actively make sense and construct meaning.

7. Students' prior knowledge about the topic is elicited and used as a starting place for instruction, which builds on accurate prior knowledge but also stimulates conceptual change if necessary.

8. Activities and assignments feature tasks that call for critical thinking or problem solving, not just memory or reproduction.

9. Higher-order thinking skills are not taught as a separate skills curriculum. Instead, they are developed in the process of teaching subject-matter knowledge within application contexts that call for students to relate what they are learning to their lives outside of school by thinking critically or creatively about it or by using it to solve problems or make decisions.

10. The teacher creates a social environment in the classroom that could be described as a learning community featuring discourse or dialogue designed to promote understanding.

integrating & scaffolding thinking skills w content knowledge

These principles emphasize focusing instruction on big ideas that are developed in depth and with attention to their applications. In identifying big ideas to feature in our units, we sought an appropriate balance among the three traditional sources of curriculum: (1) knowledge of enduring value (including but not limited to disciplinary knowledge), (2) the students (their needs, interests, and current readiness), and (3) the needs of society (the knowledge, skills, values, and dispositions that our society would like to see developed in future generations of its citizens).

Teaching for Conceptual Change

Related principles come from research on teaching for conceptual change. Students' prior knowledge about topics sometimes includes naive ideas or even outright misconceptions that can cause the students to ignore, distort, or miss the implications of new information that conflicts with their existing ideas. Teachers who are aware of common misconceptions can plan instruction to address these directly. This involves helping students to recognize differences between their current beliefs and the target understandings, and to see the need to shift from the former to the latter. Such instruction is often called *conceptual change teaching*.

Kathleen Roth (1996) developed an approach to conceptual change teaching that she applied to science and social studies. She embedded the conceptual change emphasis within a more comprehensive "learning community" model of teaching school subjects for understanding. This approach emphasizes eliciting valid prior knowledge that instruction can connect with and build upon, not just identifying misconceptions that will need to be addressed. Our instructional units have been designed accordingly.

Background

These efforts also were informed by a series of studies that we have conducted on K–3 students' knowledge and thinking about cultural universals. These studies yielded a great deal of information about accurate prior knowledge that most students are likely to possess as they begin each unit, as well as about important knowledge gaps and common naive ideas or misconceptions that will need to be addressed during the instruction. These findings are noteworthy because some proponents of alternative curricula have claimed that there is no need to teach about cultural universals in the primary grades because children learn all that they need to know about them through everyday experiences. This claim was made in the absence of relevant research. Our studies speak directly to this issue.

We have found that the knowledge about cultural universals that children accumulate through everyday experiences is limited, disconnected, and mostly tacit rather than well articulated. Also, it frequently is distorted by naive ideas or outright misconceptions. We do not find this surprising, because most of children's experiences relating to cultural universals are informal and do not include sustained discourse structured around key ideas. In any case, it is now clear that primary-grade students stand to benefit from systematic instruction about these topics. A summary of our key findings concerning each of the cultural universals is included in the introduction to its corresponding instructional unit.

NCSS Standards

Our unit development efforts also were informed by two definitive standards statements released by the National Council for the Social Studies (NCSS) during the 1990s: one on curriculum standards and one on powerful teaching and learning. The curriculum standards are built around ten themes that form a framework for social studies (see Figure 1). The publication that spells out these standards elaborates on each theme in separate chapters for the early grades, the middle grades, and the secondary grades, listing performance expectations and potential classroom activities that might be used to develop the theme (National Council for the Social Studies, 1994). The NCSS subsequently sponsored publication of a collection of readings illustrating how the ten themes might be addressed in elementary social studies teaching (Haas & Laughlin, 1997) and a survey of children's literature published in the 1990s that relates to these themes (Krey, 1998).

Along with its curriculum standards, the NCSS released a position statement identifying five key features of powerful social studies teaching and learning (see Figure 2). The publication that elaborates on these five key features frames them by stating that social studies teaching is viewed as powerful when it helps students develop social understanding and civic efficacy (National Council for the Social Studies, 1993). Social understanding is integrated knowledge of the social aspects of the human condition: how these aspects have evolved over time, the variations that occur in

Ten themes serve as organizing strands for the social studies curriculum at every school level (early, middle, and high school); they are interrelated and draw from all of the social science disciplines and other related disciplines and fields of scholarly study to build a framework for social studies curriculum.

I. Culture
Human beings create, learn, and adapt culture. Human cultures are dynamic systems of beliefs, values, and traditions that exhibit both commonalities and differences. Understanding culture helps us understand ourselves and others.

II. Time, Continuity, and Change
Human beings seek to understand their historic roots and to locate themselves in time. Such understanding involves knowing what things were like in the past and how things change and develop—allowing us to develop historic perspective and answer important questions about our current condition.

III. People, Places, and Environment
Technical advancements have ensured that students are aware of the world beyond their personal locations. As students study content related to this theme, they create their spatial views and geographical perspectives of the world; social, cultural, economic, and civic demands mean that students will need such knowledge, skills, and understandings to make informed and critical decisions about the relationship between human beings and their environment.

IV. Individual Development and Identity
Personal identity is shaped by one's culture, by groups, and by institutional influences. Examination of various forms of human behavior enhances understandings of the relationship between social norms and emerging personal identities, the social processes that influence identity formation, and the ethical principles underlying individual action.

V. Individuals, Groups, and Institutions
Institutions exert enormous influence over us. Institutions are organizational embodiments to further the core social values of those who comprise them. It is important for students to know how institutions are formed, what controls and influences them, how they control and influence individuals and culture, and how institutions can be maintained or changed.

VI. Power, Authority, and Governance
Understanding of the historic development of structures of power, authority, and governance and their evolving functions in contemporary society is essential for emergence of civic competence.

VII. Production, Distribution, and Consumption
Decisions about exchange, trade, and economic policy and well-being are global in scope, and the role of government in policy making varies over time and from place to place. The systematic study of an interdependent world economy and the role of technology in economic decision making is essential.

VIII. Science, Technology, and Society
Technology is as old as the first crude tool invented by prehistoric humans, and modern life as we know it would be impossible without technology and the science that supports it. Today's technology forms the basis for some of our most difficult social choices.

IX. Global Connections
The realities of global interdependence require understanding of the increasingly important and diverse global connections among world societies before there can be analysis leading to the development of possible solutions to persisting and emerging global issues.

X. Civic Ideals and Practices
All people have a stake in examining civic ideals and practices across time, in diverse societies, as well as in determining how to close the gap between present practices and the ideals upon which our democracy is based. An understanding of civic ideals and practices of citizenship is critical to full participation in society.

Source: National Council for the Social Studies. (1994). *Curriculum Standards for Social Studies: Expectations of Excellence* (Bulletin No. 89). Washington, DC: Author.

FIGURE 1   Ten Thematic Strands

Meaningful

The content selected for emphasis is worth learning because it promotes progress toward important social understanding and civic efficacy goals, and it is taught in ways that help students to see how it is related to these goals. As a result, students' learning efforts are motivated by appreciation and interest, not just by accountability and grading systems. Instruction emphasizes depth of development of important ideas within appropriate breadth of content coverage.

Integrative

Powerful social studies cuts across discipline boundaries, spans time and space, and integrates knowledge, beliefs, values, and dispositions to action. It also provides opportunities for students to connect to the arts and sciences through inquiry and reflection.

Value-Based

Powerful social studies teaching considers the ethical dimensions of topics, so that it provides an arena for reflective development of concern for the common good and application of social values. The teacher includes diverse points of view, demonstrates respect for well-supported positions, and shows sensitivity and commitment to social responsibility and action.

Challenging

Students are encouraged to function as a learning community, using reflective discussion to work collaboratively to deepen understandings of the meanings and implications of content. They also are expected to come to grips with controversial issues, to participate assertively but respectfully in group discussions, and to work productively with peers in cooperative learning activities.

Active

Powerful social studies is rewarding but demanding. It demands thoughtful preparation and instruction by the teacher, and sustained effort by the students to make sense of and apply what they are learning. Teachers do not mechanically follow rigid guidelines in planning, implementing, and assessing instruction. Instead, they work with the national standards and with state and local guidelines, adapting and supplementing these guidelines and their instructional materials in ways that support their students' social education needs.

The teacher uses a variety of instructional materials, plans field trips and visits by resource people, develops current or local examples to relate to students' lives, plans reflective discussions, and scaffolds students' work in ways that encourage them to gradually take on more responsibility for managing their own learning independently and with their peers. Accountability and grading systems are compatible with these goals and methods.

Students develop new understandings through a process of active construction. They develop a network of connections that link the new content to preexisting knowledge and beliefs anchored in their prior experience. The construction of meaning required to develop important social understanding takes time and is facilitated by interactive discourse. Clear explanations and modeling from the teacher are important, but so are opportunities to answer questions, discuss or debate the meaning and implications of content, or use the content in activities that call for tackling problems or making decisions.

Source: National Council for the Social Studies. (1993). A Vision of Powerful Teaching and Learning in the Social Studies: Building Social Understanding and Civic Efficacy. *Social Education, 57,* 213–223.

8   FIGURE 2   Five Key Features of Powerful Social Studies Learning

different physical environments and cultural settings, and emerging trends that appear likely to shape the future. Civic efficacy is readiness and willingness to assume citizenship responsibilities. It is rooted in social studies knowledge and skills, along with related values (such as concern for the common good) and dispositions (such as an orientation toward confident participation in civic affairs).

Along with publishing the statement on powerful teaching, the NCSS has made available a multimedia teacher education resource. It is a professional development program that includes print materials and videotapes for use by district-level staff developers working with teachers to revitalize local social studies programs (Harris & Yocum, 1999).

In developing our units, we did not begin with these NCSS standards. Instead, we began with lists of powerful ideas that might anchor networks of social knowledge about the cultural universal under study. As unit development proceeded, however, we used the NCSS content and teaching standards as guidelines for assessing the degree to which the unit was sufficiently complete and well balanced. No individual lesson includes all of the ten content themes and the five features of powerful teaching, but all of these content and process standards are well represented in the plans for the unit as a whole.

We have found that units planned to develop connected understandings of powerful ideas consistently meet the NCSS standards (as well as state standards). Our units include embedded strands that address history, geography, economics, culture, government, and decision making. However, the units were developed as pandisciplinary (or perhaps we should say, predisciplinary), integrated treatments of the topic, not as collections of lessons organized around the academic disciplines treated separately.

Key Characteristics of the Units

In summary, we emphasize teaching for understanding (and where necessary, conceptual change) by building on students' prior knowledge and developing key ideas in depth and with attention to their applications to life outside of school. The unit plans provide a basis for three to four weeks of instruction, depending on the topic and the degree to which the teacher includes optional extensions. All of the units feature six common components:

1. The units begin with focus on the cultural universal as experienced in contemporary American society, especially in the students' homes and neighborhoods (this includes eliciting students' prior knowledge and helping them to articulate this mostly tacit knowledge more clearly). Early lessons use familiar examples to help students develop understanding of how and why the contemporary social system functions as it does with respect to the cultural universal being studied.

2. The units consider how the technology associated with the cultural universal has evolved over time. Lessons on this historical dimension illustrate how human responses to the cultural universal have been influenced by inventions and other cultural advances.

3. The units address variation in today's world in the ways that the cultural universal is experienced in different places and societies. Along with the historical dimension, this geographical/cultural dimension of the unit extends students' concepts to include examples different from the ones they view as prototypical. This helps them to place themselves and their familiar social environments into perspective as parts of the larger human condition (as it has evolved through time and as it varies across cultures). In the language of anthropologists, these unit components "make the strange familiar" and "make the familiar strange" as a way to broaden students' perspectives.

4. The units include physical examples, classroom visitors, field trips, and especially, children's literature selections (both fiction and nonfiction) as input sources.

5. The units include home assignments that call for students to interact with parents and other family members in ways that not only build curriculum-related insights but engage the participants in enjoyable and affectively bonding activities.

6. The units engage students in thinking about the implications of all of this for personal, social, and civic decision making in the present and future, in ways that support their self-efficacy perceptions with respect to their handling of the cultural universal throughout their lives. Many lessons raise students' consciousness of the fact that they will be making choices (both as individuals and as citizens) relating to the cultural universal under study. Many of the home assignments engage students in decision-making discussions with other family members. These discussions (and later ones that they often spawn) enable the students to see that they can affect others' thinking and have input into family decisions.

Our units address many of the same topics traditionally taught as part of the expanding communities curriculum. However, they are designed to be far more powerful than the ostensibly similar units found in contemporary textbooks. They focus on the elementary and familiar in that they address fundamental aspects of the human condition and connect with experience-based tacit knowledge that students already possess. However, they do not merely reaffirm what students already know. Instead, they help students to construct articulated knowledge about aspects of the cultural universal that they have only vague and tacit knowledge about now. They also introduce students to a great deal of new information, develop connections to help them transform scattered items of information into a network of integrated knowledge, and stimulate them to apply this knowledge to their lives outside of school. For more information about the rationale underlying the units, see Brophy and Alleman (1996).

Developing the Unit Plans

In developing unit plans, we began by generating a list of big ideas about the cultural universal that might become the major understandings around which to structure the unit. The initial list was developed from three major sources: (1) social studies education textbooks written for teachers, standards statements from NCSS and other social studies–related professional organizations, and the writings of opinion leaders and organizations concerned with education in history, geography, and the social sciences; (2) ideas conveyed about the cultural universal in elementary social studies texts and in fictional and nonfictional literature sources written for children; and (3) our own ideas about which aspects of the cultural universal are basic understandings that students could use to make sense of their social lives. As we developed and discussed this basic list of key ideas, we revised it several times. In the process, we added some new ideas, rephrased existing ones, combined those that appeared to go together, and sequenced them in a way that made sense as a list of lesson topics for the unit.

Once we were satisfied with the listing and sequencing of big ideas, we began drafting lesson plans. We elaborated the big ideas in considerable detail and considered ways in which they might be applied during in-class activities and follow-up home assignments. We also shared tentative plans with Barbara Knighton and other collaborating teachers. Barbara critiqued what was included and contributed specific teaching suggestions, such as identifying places where she might bring in some personal possession to use as a prop, read a children's literature selection that we had not considered, or add a learning activity.

Sequencing the Lessons

Typically, a unit begins with consideration of the cultural universal as it is experienced in the contemporary United States, and especially in the homes and neighborhoods of the students to be taught. Subsequent lessons bring in the historical dimension by considering how human response to the cultural universal has evolved through time. Later lessons bring in the geographical, cultural, and economic dimensions by considering how human response to the cultural universal has varied in the past and still varies today according to local resources and other aspects of location and culture. Still later lessons bring in the personal and civic efficacy dimensions by involving students in activities calling for them to consider their current and future decision making with respect to the cultural universal and to address some of the social and civic issues associated with it. Finally, a review lesson is developed as a conclusion to the unit.

Looking across the unit as a whole, the sequence of instruction:

1. Begins by building on students' existing knowledge, deepening it, and making it better articulated and connected (to solidify a common base of valid prior knowledge as a starting point).
2. Broadens their knowledge about how the cultural universal is addressed in the context most familiar to them (contemporary American society).
3. Extends their knowledge to the past and to other cultures.
4. Provides opportunities to apply what they are learning to present and future decision making as an individual and as a citizen.
5. Concludes with a review.

Our Approach Compared to Alternatives

We have noted that our response to the widely recognized content problem in primary-grade social studies is to retain cultural universals as the unit topics but develop these topics much more thoroughly than they are developed in the textbook series, and with better focus on big ideas. Others have suggested different responses. We briefly mention the major alternative suggestions here, both to explain why we do not endorse them and to further explain our own position.

Cultural Literacy/Core Knowledge

E. D. Hirsch, Jr. (1988) proposed cultural literacy as the basis for curriculum development. He produced a list of more than five thousand items of knowledge that he believed should be acquired in elementary school as a way to equip students with a common base of cultural knowledge to inform their social and civic decision making. We agree with Hirsch that a shared common culture is needed, but we question the value of much of what he included on his list of ostensibly important knowledge. Furthermore, because it is a long list of specifics, it leads to teaching that emphasizes breadth of coverage of disconnected details over depth of development of connected knowledge structured around powerful ideas.

Subsequently, educators inspired by Hirsch's book have used it as a basis for developing the CORE curriculum, which encompasses science, social studies, and the arts. The social studies strands are built around chronologically organized historical studies, with accompanying geographical and cultural studies. First graders study ancient Egypt and the early American civilizations (Mayas, Incas, Aztecs). Second graders study ancient India, China, and Greece, along with American history up to the

Civil War. Third graders study ancient Rome and Byzantium, various Native American tribal groups, and the thirteen English Colonies prior to the American Revolution. Because it is divided by grade levels and organized into World Civilization, American Civilization, and Geography strands, the CORE curriculum is a considerable improvement over Hirsch's list of assorted knowledge items as a basis for social studies curriculum in the primary grades. However, it focuses on the distant past. We think that cultural universals have more to offer than historical chronicity as a basis for introducing students to the social world. Also, we believe that an approach that begins with what is familiar to the students in their immediate environments and then moves to the past, to other cultures, and to consideration of the future constitutes a better-rounded and more powerful social education than an exclusive focus on the past that is inherently limited in its applicability to students' lives outside of school.

History/Literature Focus

Kieran Egan (1988), Diane Ravitch (1987), and others have advocated replacing topical teaching about cultural universals with a heavy focus on history and related children's literature (not only fiction but myths and folktales). We agree with them that primary-grade students can and should learn certain aspects of history, but we also believe that these students need a balanced and integrated social studies curriculum that includes sufficient attention to powerful ideas drawn from geography and the social sciences. Furthermore, we see little social education value in replacing reality-based social studies with myths and folklore likely to create misconceptions, especially during the primary years when children are struggling to determine what is real (vs. false/fictional) and enduring (vs. transitory/accidental) in their physical and social worlds. Thus, although fanciful children's literature may be studied profitably as fiction within the language arts curriculum, it is no substitute for a reality-based social studies curriculum.

Issues Analysis

Many social educators believe that debating social and civic issues is the most direct way to develop dispositions toward critical thinking and reflective decision making in our citizens (Evans & Saxe, 1996). Some of them have suggested that primary-grade social studies should deemphasize providing students with information and instead engage them in inquiry and debate about social policy issues. We agree that reflective discussion of social issues and related decision-making opportunities should be emphasized in teaching social studies at all grade levels. However, we also believe that a heavy concentration on inquiry and debate about social policy issues is premature for primary-grade students whose prior knowledge and experience relating to the issues are quite limited.

In this first chapter we have presented the rationale for our approach to primary-grade social studies, identified six key components that are common to all of our units, and described how we developed the units and assessed their effectiveness through classroom tryouts. In Chapter 2 we will share experienced-based suggestions about how to prepare to teach the units and bring them to life in your classroom.

2

Implementation
Preparing for and Teaching the Units

Preparing to Teach the Units

Based on our experiences with Barbara Knighton and other teachers, we suggest the following as steps that you might take in planning to incorporate our units into your curriculum. (Barbara also has some tips to pass along, which she does in the introductions to each unit and each subsequent lesson.)

Initial Planning and Scheduling

We suggest that you begin by reading through the unit several times to familiarize yourself with its goals, resources, content, and activities. Then begin making plans for how to fit the unit into your schedule; how to gather the needed instructional resources and arrange for potential classroom visitors or field trips; and how to adapt the unit to your grade level, your students' home cultures, and your local community.

We have organized each unit as a series of "lessons," but you should expect considerable variation in the time needed to complete these lessons. The content and activities that we have included within a given lesson are grouped together because they develop a common set of connected big ideas, not because they are expected to take a particular amount of time to complete. Some lessons may require two or three class sessions (or more, if your sessions are very short).

To maximize the coherence of the units, we recommend that they be taught forty to sixty minutes each day, five days per week, for three to four weeks. This probably exceeds the amount of time that you ordinarily allocate to social studies as a daily average, although you probably allocate at least that much time to science and social studies combined. If you are not doing so already, we recommend that you adopt a practice followed by Barbara and many other primary-grade teachers: Instead of teaching both science and social studies each day for twenty to thirty minutes, alternate these subjects so that you teach only social studies for three to four weeks for forty to sixty minutes per day, then shift to science for the next three to four weeks for forty to sixty minutes per day. This will simplify your instructional planning and classroom management, as well as make it possible for you to provide your students with more sustained and coherent instruction in both subjects.

Adapt Plans to Your Students

You should also consider whether the plans might need to be adapted to suit your grade level. If you teach in kindergarten or first grade, you may want to omit or plan substitutes for certain activities, especially those that call for writing. (Alternatively, you could provide extra support for your students' writing, such as by posting words that they are likely to want to use but not know how to spell.) If you teach second or third grade, you may want to plan some application activities that go beyond those currently included in the unit. You are in the best position to judge what to teach your students about the topic and how they might best apply what they are learning in and out of school. However, in making any changes or additions to the unit plans, keep the major goals and big ideas in mind.

Think about ways to adapt or enhance the unit to connect it to your students' home cultures and to resources in your local area. Do some of your students' parents work in occupations related to the cultural universal? If so, this might provide opportunities for fruitful classroom visits (by the parents) or field trips (to their work places). Do some of your students come from cultures that feature traditional artifacts related to the cultural universal (ethnic foods, clothing items, etc.)? If so, these students or their parents might be invited to bring the items to class and explain them. Are there stores, factories, museums, government offices, historical landmarks, and so forth located in your area that relate to the cultural universal? If so, you might exploit these potential instructional resources by obtaining information or materials from them, by arranging for people who work there to visit your class, or by arranging for your class to visit the sites. When your class is receiving a presentation from a parent or other visitor, or is visiting a site, you can use your own comments and questions to help guide the presentation and connect it to the unit's big ideas. (If possible, provide presenters with a list of these big ideas ahead of time.)

Gather Resources

You will need to gather the resources needed to teach the unit. Most of these are materials already available in the classroom or common household items that you can bring from home, but some are children's literature books that you will need to purchase or borrow from a library. If you are unable to obtain a recommended book, you may wish to search for a substitute, enlisting the help of local librarians if possible. Before including a book in your plans, however, read through it to make sure that it is suitable for use with your students and worthwhile as a resource for developing one or more of the unit's big ideas. Also, consider how you will use the book:

Will you read it all or only certain parts?

Will one copy be enough or should you try to get a copy for each table of students?

If you read from a single copy, will you leave the students in their seats and circulate to show illustrations, or will you gather them in a closely compacted group on a rug and show the illustrations to the whole group as you read?

Will the book be left in some designated place following the reading so that individual students can inspect it?

If you are considering supplementing or substituting for the children's literature selections identified as resources for the unit, we have a few guidelines to suggest based on our experiences to date. First, children's literature (as well as videos, CD-ROMs, and other multimedia resources) can be useful both as content vehicles and as ways to connect with students' interests and emotions. Nonfictional children's literature is most useful in teaching about how and why things work as they do and how and why they vary across cultures. Fictional sources are more useful for reaching children's emotions, as in reading and discussing stories about homeless people or about a child who volunteers at a soup kitchen.

However, not all children's literature selections that are related to a unit's topic are appropriate as instructional resources for the unit. For example, we originally intended to use the book *Woodrow, the White House Mouse* (Barnes & Barnes, 1998) because it offers cleverly written material about the executive branch of the government. In pilot testing our unit, however, we realized that students were distracted by the mice and other fancifulness associated with the story about the president and his activities. We therefore recommend substituting *The Story of the White House* (Waters, 1991) and encourage teachers to show the pictures and retell the story using language appropriate to the grade level. *Woodrow, the White House Mouse* can be used during a subsequent literacy lesson, followed by a "minds on" activity calling for students to distinguish fact from fiction. This learning opportunity also can serve as an informal social studies assessment.

Problems such as these frequently lead us to drop children's literature selections from our unit plans. In some cases, their deficiencies are obvious (e.g., content or illustrations that are so dated as to be misleading, or that focus on the exotic and convey ethnic stereotypes instead of helping students to appreciate cultural variations as intelligent adaptations to time and place). However, some deficiencies are more subtle and recognized only when problems occur as they are used during class (e.g., the language is too difficult or fanciful, or the content or illustrations tend to derail the class from key ideas into side issues). When such problems appear in nonfictional selections, some of the books still can be used by presenting their most useful parts and omitting the rest. However, fictional selections usually have to be either read all the way through or omitted entirely.

Add Learning Activities

You also may wish to supplement or substitute for some of the learning activities or home assignments included in the unit plans. We believe that any activity considered for inclusion in a unit should meet all four of the following basic criteria: (1) goal relevance; (2) appropriate level of difficulty; (3) feasibility; and (4) cost effectiveness.

Activities have goal relevance when they are useful as means of accomplishing worthwhile curricular goals (i.e., intended student outcomes). Each activity should have a primary goal that is important, worth stressing, and merits spending time on. Its content base should have enduring value and life-application potential. This criterion is typically met when the activity is useful for developing one of the big ideas that anchor the unit's content base.

An activity is at the appropriate level of difficulty when it is difficult enough to provide some challenge and extend learning, but not so difficult as to leave many students confused or frustrated. You can adjust the difficulty levels of activities either by adjusting the complexity of the activities themselves or by adjusting the amount of initial modeling and explanation and subsequent help that you provide as you engage the students in the activities.

An activity is feasible if it can be implemented within whatever constraints apply in your classroom (space and equipment, time, student readiness, etc.). An activity is cost effective if the learning or other benefits expected to flow from it justify its costs in time and trouble for you and your students and in foregone opportunities to schedule other activities.

In selecting from activities that meet these primary criteria, you might consider several secondary criteria that identify features of activities that are desirable but not strictly necessary:

1. Along with its primary goal, the activity allows for simultaneous accomplishment of one or more additional goals (e.g., application of communication skills being learned in language arts).
2. Students are likely to find the activity interesting or enjoyable.
3. The activity provides an opportunity to complete a whole task rather than just to practice part-skills in isolation.
4. The activity provides opportunities for students to engage in higher-order thinking.
5. The activity can be adapted to accommodate individual differences in students' interests or abilities.

Along with these criteria, which apply to individual activities, we suggest additional criteria for the set of activities for the unit taken as a whole:

1. The set should contain a variety of activity formats and student response modes (as another way to accommodate individual differences).
2. Activities should progressively increase in levels of challenge as student expertise develops.
3. Students should apply what they are learning to current events or other aspects of their lives outside of school.
4. As a set, the activities should reflect the full range of goals identified for the unit.
5. Where students lack sufficient experiential knowledge to support understanding, learning activities should include opportunities for them to view demonstrations, inspect artifacts or photos, visit sites, or in other ways to experience concrete examples of the content.
6. Students should learn relevant processes and procedural knowledge, not just declarative or factual knowledge, to the extent that doing so is important as part of developing basic understanding of the topics.

The key to the effectiveness of an activity is its cognitive engagement potential—the degree to which it gets students thinking actively about and applying content, preferably with conscious awareness of their goals and control of their learning strategies. If the desired learning experiences are to occur, student involvement must include cognitive engagement with important ideas, not just physical activity or time on task. In short, the students' engagement should be minds-on, not just hands-on.

If an activity calls for skills or response processes that are new to your students (e.g., collaboration within a pair or small group, writing in a journal), you will need to provide them with modeling and instruction in how to carry out these processes and with opportunities to practice doing so. In this regard, we recommend that you introduce new processes or skills in the context of applying already-familiar content. Young learners often become confused if they are asked to cope with both new content and new skills at the same time (or they become so focused on trying to carry out the activity's processes successfully that they pay little attention to the big ideas that the activity was designed to develop).

The success of an activity in producing thoughtful student engagement with important ideas depends not only on the activity itself but on the teacher structuring and teacher-student interaction that occur before, during, and after it. Thus, an important part of making an activity successful as a learning experience is your own:

1. Introduction of the activity (communicating its goals clearly and cueing relevant prior knowledge and response strategies).
2. Scaffolding of student engagement in the activity (explaining and demonstrating procedures if necessary, asking questions to make sure that students understand key ideas and know what to do before releasing them to work on their own, and then circulating to monitor and intervene if necessary as they work).
3. Handling of debriefing/reflection/assessment segments that bring the activity to closure (during which you and the students revisit the activity's primary goals and assess the degree to which they have been accomplished).

For more information about designing or selecting learning activities, see Brophy and Alleman (1991).

Plan Your Assessment Component

We view assessment as a basic component of curriculum and instruction that should be an ongoing concern as a unit progresses, not just as something to be done when the unit is completed. Also, the goals of assessment should include generating information about how the class as a whole is progressing in acquiring the intended learnings and about ways in which curriculum and instruction may need to be adjusted in the present or future, not just generating scores that will provide a basis for assigning grades to individual students.

You might begin by assessing your students' prior knowledge before you start teaching the unit. You can use some or all of our interview questions for this purpose (these are provided in the introduction to each unit), or else formulate your own questions. Such preassessment will provide you with useful information, both about valid prior knowledge that you can connect with and about gaps, naive ideas, and misconceptions that you can address specifically as you work through the unit. It may suggest the need for additional physical artifacts, photos, or other props or visuals, or for more extensive explanations of certain points than you had anticipated providing.

To promote accomplishment of this broad assessment agenda, we have embedded informal assessment components within most lessons, and we have included a review lesson at the end of each unit. However, you may want to add more formal assessment components, especially if your students will be participating in state- or district-wide social studies testing. Also, you may want to include relatively formal assessment (i.e., tests that carry implications for grading) as a way to communicate high expectations for student engagement and effort in social studies activities and as a way to convey to students and their parents that you consider social studies to be just as basic a curricular component as language arts, mathematics, and science.

In any case, we recommend that you focus on the major goals and big ideas when planning a unit's assessment components. This includes affective and dispositional goals, not just knowledge and skill goals. It may require you to use alternative forms of assessment instead of—or in addition to—conventional tests. In this regard, bear in mind that a great deal of useful assessment information can be gleaned from your students' responses to ongoing in-class activities and home assignments. These responses frequently will indicate that certain points need reteaching or elaboration because several students are confused about them. For more information about assessment in elementary social studies, see Alleman and Brophy (1997, 1999).

Prepare the Parents

Most of the lessons include home assignments calling for students to interact with parents or other family members by discussing some aspect of how the cultural universal is experienced or handled within their family (and then recording some key information on a brief response sheet to be returned to class and used as data in follow-up discussion). It will be important to alert the parents to this feature of the social studies units and elicit their cooperation in completing the home assignments and seeing that their children return the data sheets the next day. If your school schedules parent orientation meetings early in the school year, this would be a good time and place to explain the social studies program to them in person. In any case, before beginning your initial unit, send the parents an informational letter (see Figure 3). Subsequently, in sending home the data retrieval sheets for individual home assignments, be sure to include sufficient information to enable parents to know what to do as they interact with their child to accomplish the assignment successfully.

Dear Parents,

This year we are taking part in a new exciting way to learn social studies. Our units of study will be based on cultural universals. A cultural universal is something that is common to children around the world, such as childhood, money, and government. By using the cultural universals, we are able to help children first connect the learning to their own lives and then learn more.

 Within each unit, we will look at the many parts of the cultural universal and how it ties to important social studies topics like history, careers, geography, economics, and more. Our hope is to have students who are more excited and motivated to learn about the world within their reach and far away.

 Our first cultural universal will be childhood. During this unit, we will be starting with a discussion of childhood—what it is and what children all over the world have in common. We will also discuss how children are unique. There will be lessons on how childhood has changed over time, how children and their families celebrate, how families support children, how children and their families make choices, and how children's interests and talents can contribute to their avocations and careers. There will also be a lesson focusing on good citizenship that includes being responsible, helping others, and in some small way, making the world a better place.

 As parents, you will be asked to contribute your knowledge in this area as well. Some home assignments might include visiting your family album or picture box and putting together a simple time line with pictures, photos, drawings, and words that tell your child's story from babyhood to present (e.g., baby, toddler, preschool years, and early school years), discussing birthdays and other family celebrations, discussing how children's work has changed just since you and your parents (child's grandparents) were in the early grades, and talking about and listing choices your child helps make at home. Another way you can help with our learning is to ask your child often about our childhood lessons and share your own thoughts about the topics we discuss.

 If you have any questions about this unit or the cultural universals, please feel free to drop me a note or call. Thank you for your help in making our unit successful.

Mrs. Knighton

FIGURE 3 Model Letter to Parents

Some teachers become concerned when they hear about our home assignments. However, we have found that most parents not only cooperate by taking the time needed to complete the requested activities with their children but enjoy doing so, see the activities as valuable, and express considerable enthusiasm for them. There are several reasons for this. First, the assignments do not require any special preparation or demanding work from the parents. Mostly, they involve family members in activities that are nondemanding for the parents, interesting and informative for the children, and enjoyable for both (e.g., talking about what is involved in spending money wisely, about "coming of age" celebrations, about the locations and functions of local community services, and about relatives', friends', and neighbors' jobs in occupations related to childhood, money, or government).

In addition to personalizing the unit's content and providing additional opportunities for students to construct understandings of it and communicate about it, these home assignments engage the parents and children in conversations that support family ties and enhance their appreciation for one another. The children learn many things about their parents' past lives and decision making that help them to know the parents more fully as individuals, and the parents learn a lot about their children's ideas, interests, and capabilities. Parents commonly report that these interactions have helped them (and other family members, such as older siblings) to develop enhanced respect for their child's insights and reasoning abilities, and that interests that the child expressed during these interactions subsequently led to other shared activities. When you communicate with parents about the home assignments, do so in ways that encourage the parents to look forward to experiencing these interesting and emotionally satisfying interactions with their children, not just to "helping them with their homework."

Theory and research on learning suggest that exposure to new information is of most value to learners when it leads them to construct understandings of big ideas that are retained in forms that make them easily accessible for application in the future. This is most likely to occur when learners have opportunities not just to read or hear about these big ideas but to talk about them during interactions with others. The home assignments embedded in our units create important extensions to the discourse that occurs in the classroom by providing opportunities for your students to engage in additional knowledge construction at home during content-based interactions with parents and other family members.

The home assignments allow students to connect what they learn in social studies class to their lives outside of school. We want students to be able to use the social knowledge and skills that they are learning whenever these are applicable. Doing this consistently requires, along with accessible knowledge and skills, self-efficacy perceptions and related beliefs and attitudes that orient students toward drawing on their social learning and using it to inform their thinking and decision making about personal, social, and civic issues. Our home assignments (and the subsequent topic-related interactions that they tend to engender) will help both your students and their family members to appreciate the students' developing capabilities for engaging in informed discussions about the social world, reasoning about the trade-offs embedded in potential alternative courses of action, and developing plans or making decisions accordingly. Typically, self-efficacy perceptions become enhanced as students begin to discover and appreciate their own growing expertise and as family members begin to display increased respect for their knowledge and informed opinions.

For more information about out-of-school learning opportunities in social studies, see Alleman and Brophy (1994).

Arrange for Pairing with Older Students

A few of the suggested in-class activities call for pairing your primary-grade students with older, intermediate-grade students who come to your class for the occasion and act as mentors helping your students to meet the activity's requirements. Pairing with older mentors is especially helpful for kindergarten or first-grade students whose writing skills are limited. During these activities, the mentors help the younger students to generate and clarify responses to questions, then record the responses. Ideally, each pair of students will engage in sustained conversation about the questions, and the older students will develop and explain their own answers to the questions along with helping the younger students to do so.

Both students typically benefit from these pair activities. The older students tend to enjoy and take satisfaction in helping the younger students to develop their thinking, and the younger students benefit from the presence of a partner who provides both needed assistance in carrying out the activity and an authentic and responsive audience for their ideas. An added bonus is that the warm affective tone of these interactions tends to carry over and contribute to a positive interpersonal climate in the school as a whole.

If you want to include these mentor/pair activities, you will need to make arrangements with one or more intermediate-grade teachers. (Ordinarily it is best to work with a single intermediate-grade class, both to simplify the planning involved and to make it possible for the same pairs of students to work together throughout the year.) Initially, this will require explaining the general purpose and nature of these activities and negotiating agreement on a general plan. Subsequently, prior to the implementation of each pair activity, the teachers will need to prepare their respective classes for participation by explaining (and, perhaps, modeling or role-playing) what will be accomplished during the activity and how each of the participants is expected to fulfill his or her role.

Establish a Social Studies Corner or Learning Center

If you have room in your classroom, we recommend that you develop a social studies corner or interest center. At minimum, this should include a wall display of key words, photographs, student products, and so forth connected to the unit topic, along with a collection of related books and other materials that students can inspect during free times in class or take home at night. Ideally, the social studies area would be a more complete learning center, equipped with a table, some chairs or a rug, maps and a globe, and physical artifacts for students to inspect; activities for them to complete; or opportunities for exploration or enrichment using print materials, CD-ROMs, or other learning resources. The area should also include materials previously used during lessons that your students might wish to inspect at their leisure, such as children's literature selections or photos or artifacts that connect people, events, places, or institutions in your community to the cultural universal under study.

Because each of our units includes a historical dimension, we recommend that you display a time line along one of the walls of your classroom. The units typically address human responses to the cultural universal "long, long ago" (cave dweller days), "long ago" (seventeenth or eighteenth centuries, or Native American/Pilgrim/pioneer days), and "today" (especially in the contemporary United States). Your time line might be composed of connected sheets of construction paper that stretch for five to fifteen feet horizontally, with key words and photos or symbols depicting developments in human responses to each cultural universal that characterize each of these three time periods (and perhaps others in between, such as the early twentieth century).

Additional items can be added to the time line (on a new row) each time a new social studies unit is taught. These can be occasions for looking across units to revisit some of the big ideas, especially common threads such as development over time and variation across locations and cultures in human response to cultural universals. Ideas about what to display on the time line can be found in the historical text and charts included in each unit.

Teaching the Units

Our units are built around featured big ideas that are elaborated in some detail, sometimes in language that you might use to present information to your students. This format makes these sections easier to follow by eliminating phrases such as "Explain to your students that . . . ." However, their script-like appearance is not meant to imply that you should use them as scripts by reading or reciting them to your students. They are meant only as background information to inform your lesson planning. Ordinarily you would explain or elicit this information as you develop the content with your students, but not read or recite it directly from our lesson plans. You will also need to adapt the material to your students and your local situation by placing it into a context that includes your own and your students' experiences, photos and artifacts from your local community, and references to current events and local connections.

In the process, bring the unit to life by showing or telling your students about your own past or present involvements with the cultural universal (e.g., "As a child, my favorite game was _____"; "Here's a photo of me when I was a toddler"). Barbara Knighton uses this personalized approach to great advantage in her classroom. Her students are fascinated to learn details about her personal life and background, and the modeling she provides as she shares this information encourages her students to share productively about topic-relevant aspects of their own lives. This kind of sharing also enhances the authenticity and life-application potential of the material, especially when the teacher explains the reasons for personal decisions (e.g., about creating a family budget, deciding whether to pay cash or use a credit card, volunteering for a worthy cause, etc.).

Another way for you to personalize and communicate enthusiasm for the content is to share your own responses to the in-class activities and home assignments. This will provide you with additional opportunities for modeling engagement with the big ideas and contributing responses that will stimulate your students' thinking. In this regard, it is important to make sure that your students carry out the home assignments in collaboration with their parents or other family members and bring back the completed data sheets the next day, and that you follow up by displaying the data and leading the students through a discussion of its meanings and implications (typically at the beginning of the next day's social studies period). Students should understand that you view the home assignments as an integral part of social studies, that you expect them to complete the assignments faithfully and return the data sheets the next day, and that the information on these data sheets will be reviewed and discussed as part of the next lesson.

In developing unit content with your students, you will need to find an appropriate balance between showing/telling key ideas, trying to elicit these ideas through questioning, and providing opportunities for your students to discover them through their engagement in activities and assignments. Traditional ideas about teaching emphasized transmission approaches in which teachers (or texts) do a lot of explaining and students are expected to remember or copy this input and retrieve it later when answering recitation questions or filling out worksheets. More recent ideas about teaching emphasize social constructivist methods, in which teachers focus more on asking questions and leading discussions than on showing/ telling, and students are expected to collaborate in constructing knowledge as they discuss issues or debate alternative solutions to problems.

Exclusive reliance on transmission approaches is unwise because it bores students and unwittingly encourages them to emphasize low-level rote memorizing strategies instead of processing what they are learning more actively. However, exclusive reliance on social constructivist approaches also is unwise. It can be inefficient and confusing, especially if the students do not have much accurate prior knowledge and therefore end up spending a great deal of their class time carrying on discussions that are based on false premises and laced with naive ideas and misconceptions. Counterproductive discussions of this kind often occur when primary-grade students (who are still undergoing cognitive development) are prematurely asked to discuss topics about which their prior knowledge is limited, poorly articulated, and distorted by naive ideas or misconceptions. Consequently, we recommend that you begin most units and lessons with instruction designed to establish a common base of accurate knowledge (relying more heavily on showing and telling at this stage) and then gradually shift into more emphasis on questioning and discussion as students' expertise develops.

Even when doing a lot of showing and telling to establish a common base of knowledge, however, try to avoid extended "lecturing." Use more of a narrative (storytelling) style to develop explanations, and spice your presentations with frequent references to examples from your own life, your students' lives, or current events. Also, break up extended "teacher talk" segments and keep your students actively involved by asking questions, pausing to allow students to discuss a point briefly with partners or table-mates, or asking them to indicate understanding (or readiness to provide an example) by raising their hands, touching their noses or ears, and so on. Bear in mind that although your students usually will lack articulated knowledge about the topic, they will have personal experience with many of its aspects. You can keep making connections to this experience base as you develop big ideas, both to enhance the meaningfulness of the content for your students and to keep them actively involved as the lesson progresses.

On days when you will be making a home assignment, be sure to leave enough time at the end of class to go over the assignment with your students. Explain and model how they should present it to their families and show how they might respond to one or two of the questions on the data sheet. Your students should go home feeling confident that they know what the assignment requires and how they (working with family members) will respond to it.

Also, do the home assignment yourself. This allows you to "bring something to the table" the next day when you summarize and lead discussion of the data. In addition, it communicates through modeling the importance of the home assignments and some of the thinking involved in applying social studies learning to our lives outside of school; it alleviates potential concerns about invasion of privacy (because you are sharing your life, too); and it helps your students and their families to get to know you as a person in ways that promote positive personal relationships.

Unit 1: Childhood

Introduction

To help you think about childhood as a cultural universal and begin to plan your teaching, we have provided a list of questions that address some of the big ideas developed in our unit plans (see Figure 1). The questions focus on what we believe to be the most important ideas for children to learn about childhood: ways in which children around the world are similar and different; individual characteristics of the student that make him or her different from all other children; why we have schools for children; why children in some countries work in fields or factories most of the time but children in our country go to school most of the time; schooling in other countries; how schools in Japan or in Kenya differ from our schools; how pioneer children spent their days; pioneer children's schooling and recreation; toys and games used in other countries; toys or games used in Japan or in Kenya that are different from our toys or games; what birthdays are; how birthdays are celebrated in other parts of the world; birthdays before the invention of calendars; why some birthdays are more important than others; things that children are not allowed to do until they reach a certain age; differences between babies and young children and between young children and older children; things that young children sometimes believe that older children do not believe; the purposes and nature of advertising directed toward children; laws that the government has passed to help protect children; special talents that the student possesses that might be used later in a job or career; things that the student could do to help others, practice good citizenship, and help get rid of the problem of discrimination; and choices that students make in their lives.

1. Today we're going to talk about children and childhood. Children all around the world are the same in some ways and different in others. How are all children around the world the same?

2. What are some ways in which children around the world are different?

3. Some things about each child are special. What are some special things about you that make you different from all other children?

4. Children usually go to school. Why do we have schools for children?

5. In some countries, children work in fields or in factories most of the time, but in our country, children go to school most of the time. Why is that? . . . If your family wanted you to stop going to school and start working to earn money, could you do that? [If relevant, probe to see if student understands that there are laws forbidding child labor.]

6. Today, children all around the world go to school. Do you know about schools in any other countries? [If yes] Are the schools in _____ different from ours?

7. What about in Japan—are Japanese schools different from ours? . . . Do Japanese children do anything different in their schools than you do in your school?

8. What about in villages in places like Kenya in Africa—are African schools different from ours? . . . Do African children do anything different in their schools than you do in your school?

9. Here is a picture showing life back in the pioneer days, when most people lived in log cabins and worked on farms. How do you think pioneer children spent their days when they were your age? . . . What was their typical day like?

10. Did pioneer children go to school? What were their schools like? Did they do anything different in their schools than you do today in your school?

11. Even back in the pioneer days, children played and entertained themselves with toys and games. Did pioneer children entertain themselves differently than children do today? . . . Why?

12. Today, kids play with toys and games all over the world. Do you know of a country where kids play different games than in our country? [If yes, probe for description and explanation.] . . . Do you know of a country where kids play with different toys than you play with here? [If yes, probe for description and explanation.]

13. Do Japanese children have different games than American children? . . . Do Japanese children play with different toys than American children?

14. Do African children have different games than American children? . . . Do African children play with different toys than American children?

15. In our country we celebrate birthdays. What are birthdays? [If necessary, ask: "What does it mean when you have a birthday?"]

16. What do you know about children in other parts of the world and how they celebrate their birthdays?

17. Did people have birthdays before calendars were invented? [If yes] How did they know when to celebrate their birthday? [If no] Then how did they know how old they were?

18. Are some birthdays more important than others? [If yes, ask for explanation about which birthdays are especially important and why.]

19. Children aren't allowed to do certain things until they reach a certain age, like sixteen. What are sixteen-year-olds allowed to do that younger children aren't allowed to do? . . . What about eighteen—what are eighteen-year-olds allowed to do that younger children are not?

20. Children include babies and little kids and bigger kids like yourself. What are some differences between babies and little kids? . . . When do you stop being a baby and start being a little kid? . . . What are some differences between little kids and bigger kids like yourself? . . . When do you stop being a little kid and start being a bigger kid?

21. Young children sometimes believe things that aren't true because they don't know any better. What are some of those things that young children believe? . . . What are some things that kids your age know that younger children don't know?

22. Many companies advertise their products on television to try to get you to buy them, like cereals. What are some things that cereal companies do to try to get you and your family to buy their cereals?

23. What are some laws that the government has passed to help protect children?

24. Do you have any special talents or interests right now that you might use in your job or career when you grow up?

25. What are some things that you can do even as a child to help others and practice good citizenship, either here at school or in your community?

Continues

FIGURE 1. (Continued)

26. Some people suffer from discrimination—they are treated badly because they are different. What can you do as a child to help get rid of this problem of discrimination?

27. None of us can do everything, so we all have to make choices in our lives, even children. What are some kinds of choices that you make in your life?

To find out what primary-grade students know (or think they know) about these topics, we interviewed twelve students, six in first grade and six in second grade, stratified by gender and achievement level. You may want to use some or all of our interview questions during pre-unit or pre-lesson assessments of your students' prior knowledge. For now, though, we recommend that you jot down your own answers before going on to read about the answers that we elicited in our interviews. This will sharpen your awareness of ways in which adults' knowledge about childhood differs from children's knowledge, as well as reduce the likelihood that you will assume that your students already know certain things that seem obvious to you but may need to be spelled out for them.

If you want to use some of these questions to assess your students' prior knowledge before beginning the unit, you can do this either by interviewing selected students individually or by asking the class as a whole to respond to the questions and recording their answers for future reference. If you take the latter approach, an option would be to embed it within the KWL technique by initially questioning students to determine what they <u>k</u>now (or think they know) and what they <u>w</u>ant to find out, then later revisiting their answers and recording what they <u>l</u>earned. An alternative to preassessing your students' knowledge about topics developed in the unit as a whole would be to conduct separate preassessments prior to each lesson, using only the questions that apply to that lesson (and perhaps adding others of your own choosing).

Children's Responses to Our Childhood Interviews

Students had difficulty answering the first question about similarities among children around the world. Only four gave accurate answers (all eat food; all have same body parts; all need food and water; and all have clothes, shoes, food, and houses), and two of these also gave incorrect answers (all have same skin color and wear the same outfits; all have the same pets). Two of the other students were unable to respond and another gave an incorrect answer (they all play the same sports).

The remaining five students could only identify ways that children "might" be the same: know the same songs, have friends with the same name, have the same hair or skin color (two students), be twins (two), have the same music or sports preferences, have the same appearance or eat the same food, and have the same views on school.

In contrast, all twelve students were able to identify ways in which children differ. Eight mentioned skin color (although none used the word *race*), and a ninth said that people "look different." Other responses mentioned by more than one student included differences in foods (five), wealth or material possessions (three), hair color (three), sports (two), languages (two), and clothes (two). Unique responses included differences in need for glasses; countries; eye colors; running speed; preferences for colors, books, music, sports, or games; looks; birthdays; handicaps; and access to schooling. The student who mentioned handicaps had a handicapped sibling.

These responses are typical of young children's self-descriptions in that they focus on physical appearance or specific behavioral preferences or activities, without reference to more abstract qualities such as happiness or generosity. The responses also replicate earlier findings indicating that children typically find it easier to identify differences than similarities when asked to draw comparisons.

When asked what makes them special, students tended to mention facial features (four), musical or sports talents or skills (three), prized toys or pets (three), having many friends (two), and unique family connections (mother is a school principal, father has many tattoos). Unique responses included not riding his scooter in the winter (when other kids do); living in a different house; possibly having something different to eat tonight for dinner; sometimes loses her teeth; and has traveled to Kentucky. Once again, these responses mostly reflect physical appearance or behavioral activities rather than more abstract personal traits.

When asked why we have schools, all twelve students said that children need to learn knowledge and skills that will be needed in the future: reading (four), thinking (four), mathematics (two), writing (two), science, music, and learning how to teach by observing the teacher. Four students mentioned preparation for jobs and one mentioned preparation for high school and college. Unique elaborations included the following: teachers want children to go to school; we learn to make friends at school; we learn to be better people; and we learn to be safe and to respect others, including people from other countries.

When asked why there are no schools in some places in the world, nine students could not respond. Two said that these are places where people are very poor and do not have money to build schools, and the other said that we go to school in our country because that is how the president wants it (implying that the presidents of some other countries have different ideas).

When asked if they would stop going to school if they could, all twelve students said no. Eight simply repeated that children need to get prepared for the future. Three said that children their age are too young to get a job. One of these added that she had only a few pennies in her piggy bank, not enough to buy a job (many young children think that jobs must be purchased). Another student said that she would prefer to stay in school because it is more fun than working in the fields, and the one who said that children go to school in our country because that is how the president wants it said that she would stay in school because we all should listen to the president.

Among students who said that children need to stay in school to learn, some were thinking of relatively immediate effects of dropping out, not just future effects. One said that if he stopped going to school, he wouldn't keep learning things that other kids his age were learning. Another said that if he stopped going to school, he would sit around watching cartoons all day and not get smarter like other kids. In general, the students showed good understanding of the fact that schools are established for their benefit. Apparently, even students who are lethargic in school or frequently grumble about requirements understand that learning what is taught in school is in their best interest.

When asked about schooling in other countries, eleven students could not respond and the twelfth gave a good but suspect answer. She claimed to have been in schools in Africa and China, describing them as similar to ours (in teaching ABCs and other school subjects) but said that the people in these schools speak Spanish and talk a lot about dancing and music.

All but one student generated some kind of response when asked how Japanese schools are different from American schools. Six said that a different language is spoken there (although one identified this language as French and another as Spanish). One added that children dance and sing in a circle with an X in the middle in Japanese schools, and another said that they eat rice at all of their meals. Otherwise, the students gave "might" guesses: in Japan, they might have bigger or smaller schools, different lunch or recess schedules, no music, different rooms, different subjects, a different calendar, or one-room schools (for lack of money to build larger ones).

The students generated similar responses when asked how African schools differ from American schools. One said that these schools are no different from our own, but four mentioned language differences, four suggested that the quality of the buildings or of the students' clothes or equipment was not as good, and three mentioned possible differences in the size or type of organization of the school. Except for language differences, these were mostly "might" guesses. So were most of the unique responses: different homework, using brown paper rather than white paper, smaller beds, no lunch boxes, one recess instead of two, a bigger school or a combination school and college in the same building, a smaller school with no afternoon program and no combined first/second-grade classrooms, different arts and crafts, either less or more time in the school day, different activities (they don't have dominoes there), different foods for lunch or snack, and different clothes (ragged for lack of money for better clothes).

The students' responses concerning schooling in other parts of the world were mostly guesses. They found it easier to respond when asked about specific places (Japan, Africa) than about the world in general. This pattern has appeared in several of our interviews. Although several mentioned possible differences in the sizes of school buildings, none said anything about the materials from which the buildings were constructed or the design of schools or classrooms. Several suggested that African schools might suffer for lack of comparable resources to spend on education, whereas only one raised this possibility in talking about Japanese schools.

When asked about the typical day of pioneer children, one student could not respond and another depicted these children as spending the day with their families (without elaboration). The other ten depicted pioneer children as working all day or at least most of the day. The jobs they described were mostly accurate: feed pigs, clean house, build furniture, sweep, make bread, gather or hunt for food, gather wood, tend fire, churn butter, stir honey, work in fields, and help mother prepare meals. One student mentioned that pioneers had no electricity and another said that they had no television.

When asked if pioneer children went to school, eight students said that they could not because there were no schools then (or at least, none in the wilderness where they lived). The other four students described schooling generally similar to ours. However, in elaborating, one said that pioneer schools had fewer toys and less "stuff," so students did more work there and had less time for lunch; a second said that their school was different in some ways such as not using the same calendar; a third said that their studies were mostly similar but they did "French or something"; and the fourth said that pioneer schools didn't have "specials" (field trips?) for lack of money to pay for them.

When asked about pioneer children's toys and games, one student said that things were no different then, four said that they were different but couldn't explain, and the other seven explained with general accuracy. Comments included that pioneers had to make their own toys "from animals and stuff"; pioneer children didn't have much time to play or much stuff to play with; they played with string, played tag or tic-tac-toe, or wrote in the dirt with sticks because they didn't have chalk or slates or paper; they played tag or hide-and-seek but had no board games; they just had wooden toys that they found or made at home; and they just had homemade toys such as paper dolls.

These responses about life in the past are typical of children in that they reflect a pervasive presentism—a tendency to judge the past not in its own terms but in comparison with the present, and thus to emphasize what people in the past were lacking. However, they were mostly accurate as far as they went, indicating that even first and second graders possess some information about pioneer life (either from units taught at school or from children's literature, television, and videos).

When asked if there are other countries where children play with different toys or games, none of the children said no. One did not know, three said yes but could not give examples, two said yes but then gave examples only of toys or games played in the United States, two said that in some places they have only homemade toys, and four gave examples that are or at least could be considered valid. The latter responses included the following: Chinese girls play with dolls but boys play with kites; Canadian children use different skateboards and ramps than we do; China has different Pokemon characters than we have; and in some countries they play a "Jado" game (couldn't explain the game or name the country). Of the two students who spoke of homemade toys, one couldn't specify a country but described balls made from animal skins and the other said that Chinese children don't have board games and have to find "a trash can or something" and make a game with it.

Concerning Japan, five students said that Japanese children play with different toys or games but could give no examples, two gave examples only of toys or games played in the United States, and none gave valid examples of toys or games played in Japan. One student could not respond and the other four said that Japanese children lack certain American toys or must play with homemade toys. Comments included that some of them live in the wild and have no money to buy toys; they make toys out of animals, but we get ours out of a box; they don't have bikes and scooters like we do; and they have some used toys donated from the United States, plus they make their own from garbage cans or old wood chips or something like that.

Concerning Africa, one student said that African children play with the same toys and games that American children do, one didn't know, four said that African children use different toys or games but could not give examples, and one said that African children play with rounded dice. The other five students said that African children lack certain American toys or must play with homemade toys. Comments included the following: it is boring there because they don't have many games; there is no money to buy toys or stores that sell them; they don't have Connect Four games or much other stuff; they play tag in the rain forest, build stuff with leaves using sticky stuff to hold it together, or play with dragons; and they don't have board games and have to make toys out of garbage and dolls out of paper.

Responses to these questions indicated that the students possessed little information about toys or games in other countries. In addition, in contrast to earlier questions about schooling in other places, these questions about toys and games in other places elicited several indications of chauvinism (or at least, of the notion that Japan, Africa, and presumably most other places in the world are not very developed economically and thus are unable to offer their children opportunities to purchase the wide range of manufactured toys and games sold in American stores). Like the responses to most questions about life in the past and in other parts of the world in most of our interviews, these responses indicate that primary-grade students stand to benefit from a broad range of instruction about life in the past and in other places (especially instruction that underscores that people are generally more similar than different).

When asked to define birthdays, one student said that you get a year older, four said that you celebrate or get presents, and the other seven said both of these things. No student used the term *anniversary;* instead, they talked about getting older or celebrating the day you were born. One said that some people do not celebrate birthdays because their parents do not believe in such celebrations (this student's family practiced a religion that includes this prohibition). Another said that your birthday is "the day that you were born but in the past," and two mentioned that when you get a year older, you qualify to go on to the next grade at school.

When asked about birthdays in other countries, six students were unable to respond, two described birthday parties like those held in the United States, and the other four said that other countries celebrate birthdays too, but each in its own way. The latter students envisioned the following celebrations: do something, but probably not have cake or ice cream; sing in a different language and make the cake from different ingredients; maybe have presents but not cakes; and if they were poor, they might have a party at home, but if they had more money, they might have something at a hotel or go on a treasure hunt or something. These were minor variations on familiar forms of birthday celebrations. No one mentioned anything specific about forms of celebration occurring in other countries (although in some of our other interviews, students have made reference to piñatas).

When asked if people had birthdays before calendars were invented, one student could not respond, four said no, one said yes but couldn't explain, and six said yes and attempted an explanation. The explanations all suggested that the people (or their parents) would have to "think really hard," "remember," or "keep track of the days in their head." Two of these students suggested mechanisms that the people could use to help them remember: keep a running tally of months and days (J1, J2, etc.) or draw boxes with thirty or thirty-one days to them and just cross them out one at a time. Even the latter responses construed the problem as a limitation on memory capacity, without taking into account that people had not yet developed the concept of a year as a full revolution in the relationship between Earth and the Sun. The students understood that people could mark days, but did not yet understand that they couldn't mark weeks, months, or years as we define them today.

When asked if some birthdays are more important than others, one student said that your twenty-first birthday is special because you become an adult. Otherwise, five students said no, one said yes but could not explain, and the other five could not respond or said such things as birthdays are more important in certain countries (without being able to explain) or his dad's birthday is especially important because his mom buys his dad special stuff. Thus, the idea that certain birthdays mark important rites of passage was not immediately salient to the students, although some of their responses to subsequent questions indicated awareness of this.

When asked what sixteen-year-olds are allowed to do that younger students cannot, one student could not respond but eight said drive, two said drink, and three said visit with friends or travel far away on their own. Other responses included the following: do more things with computers, buy things on their own at stores, go to high school, wear slit skirts, sit in the front seat in cars, and walk in the streets instead of having to stay on the sidewalks. Although there were a few errors in certain details (e.g., it is not legal to drink at sixteen), the students had generally accurate ideas about things that teenagers can do that children are not allowed to do.

When asked what eighteen-year-olds are allowed to do that younger children cannot, one student could not respond, four said drink, three said drive, three said smoke, two said go to a college, and three said make their own decisions about such things as snacks, decorating your room, or doing what you want. Other responses included the following: go to scary movies, cuss without getting whipped, date and kiss, travel to distant cities, get a job, have your own money to use in stores, move into your own place (even in a different state), go to gyms or health clubs, get tattoos, and wear makeup and clothing of your own choice. Again, despite a few incorrect details, it is clear that the students had images of freedoms allowed eighteen-year-olds. It is noteworthy (but probably not surprising) that these responses focused on making their own decisions and participating in activities often viewed as vices, rather than on assuming adult responsibilities such as higher education, marriage, voting, or military service.

When asked about differences between babies and young children, five students mentioned size differences, three said that babies cry, and three said that babies cannot yet walk. Other responses: babies don't like to watch television and children do; babies are gentle and we can hug them but they can't hug us; children are stronger than babies; babies don't have hair yet; babies are more vulnerable to broken bones; babies can't ride roller coasters yet; babies spend a lot of time napping, cannot play outside alone, and cannot swim without floaties; babies don't do much other than cry, move around, and drink milk, but children can run, play, and hop; children can do more things; and children have different toys, can paint their nails, drink from cups rather than bottles, and can play outside or go to friends' houses.

When asked when a child stops being a baby and starts being a young child, three students said when the baby has a birthday and another said when the baby becomes one year old. The remaining responses ranged from two years old to five years old, with most concentrated in the three- to four-year-old range.

When asked about differences between younger children and older children like themselves, one student could not respond and six mentioned size differences. In addition or instead, students also mentioned that bigger kids get to go to more places; little kids can be bad; bigger kids can be bossy and little kids nicer, and bigger kids are in higher grades in school; little kids can't ride roller coasters; bigger kids go to sports practices, do more things, and use computers; bigger kids have longer hair; bigger kids go to different schools; and bigger kids know how to paint their nails and drink from cups rather than bottles. Many of these responses were similar to those given to the previous question about differences between babies and young children.

When asked when a child stops being a little kid and starts being a bigger kid, three students said "on your birthday" but didn't specify a particular age. One said that your parents tell you because they see that you stop crying as much and you get bigger. The remaining students gave ages or age ranges, with several clustered at ages 4 to 5 but two at ages 6 to 9 and two at ages 10 to 13. We were surprised at the range of ages mentioned as markers between babies and little children and between little children and bigger kids. We wonder if the differences might be related to birth order differences, with oldest children tending to identify younger transitional ages (because they feel like bigger kids) and younger siblings tending to specify older transition ages (because they look forward to privileges enjoyed by their older siblings).

When asked about things that younger children believe that older ones no longer believe, five students mentioned believing in ghosts, monsters, or people coming to get you in the middle of the night. Other mistaken beliefs included if they break glass, they will get in trouble; the blue cup holds more water than the green cup (he fooled his younger brother about this one time); angels and tooth fairies; things depicted in cartoons are real; fear of the dark; they really are eating or drinking when they use binkies (pacifiers); things depicted in horror movies are real, Jaws is a real shark, and sharks fear humans and won't eat them; maybe people like them but maybe they don't; and they don't think that God is real or they believe in other gods rather than the real God. Some of these responses touched on the conservation of volume, the distinction between intentional and accidental property destruction, and other children's concepts studied by child development researchers, but most of them dealt with fictions deliberately conveyed to children by their parents or by the producers of children's literature and entertainment.

When asked what older children know that younger children don't yet know, one student could not respond; four mentioned academic skills of reading, writing, or mathematics; three mentioned manners or morality (not scratching on walls or ripping off posters, going to school the right way and knowing right from wrong, and knowing how to act at restaurants); and two mentioned safety knowledge (being careful around glass, the stove, or when reaching up over a counter; not tasting things when you don't know what they are and being careful with knives or hot curling irons). Unique responses included the following: there are no ghosts or monsters; how to ride bikes and scooters; knowing about homework and knowing that you have to be sixteen to drive; and knowing that there are no ghosts or people coming to take you away in the night. In general, most of what the students said about differences between babies and younger children and between younger children and older children was accurate.

When asked what cereal companies do to try to get children to buy their cereal, three students could not respond, six mentioned putting prizes in the box, four mentioned showing advertising depicting the cereal as good tasting or "cool," and two mentioned advertising low prices or sales. However, one who mentioned advertising low prices and one who talked about glowing depictions of the product went on to say that these claims may be lies—that what you find when you get to the store is not always the quality of product or the price that you have been led to expect. Other responses: make commercials and show them on television; and put up signs at the store, in commercials, or on the cereal box itself. Most of the students were not yet very aware of advertising directed at children, but some of those who were aware had already developed skepticism about the claims made in this advertising.

When asked about laws that protect children, four students could not respond and four mentioned laws against underage smoking or drinking. Other responses included the following: not allowed to drive until age 16; bikers must wear helmets; laws against picking up children and taking them away in cars and laws forbidding children to do things that are not safe; laws requiring children to stay in school until they finish learning; laws forbidding children to have guns; required fire alarms and seat belts; and laws specifying that schools must have principals prepared to intercept potential child molesters and call the police to arrest them. In addition to the two comments about laws forbidding child molesting or kidnapping, two other students spoke of house or school rules against getting into a stranger's car or getting out of the house immediately if there is a fire. The eight students who were able to respond to this question showed good awareness of child safety and protection issues, although they sometimes confused informal admonitions or rules with formal laws.

When asked if they had any special talents that might be useful later in a career, four students could not respond, three said no, two mentioned football or basketball skills, and three mentioned language arts skills. Of the latter, one said that he was a good reader and could become a lawyer, another that she enjoyed writing stories and could become a children's story writer, and a third that she was good at drawing and wanted to become an artist. These responses were good as far as they went, but were limited to five of the twelve students.

When asked what they could do to practice good citizenship, two students were unable to respond. However, the rest gave responses that talked either about generally doing good and respecting others or about helping someone (especially a younger child) with something specific. These responses included the following: if they need help with spelling or are stuck in the road; help others, like if they are hurt in an accident, pull them out of the car and away from danger; help younger children learn to read; help younger children find a game on the computer; ask their parents to respond to television ads calling for sponsoring third-world children in need; do good things, respect others, and grow up to be a cop; help younger students cross the street, go and get their mom if they get hurt, and help make their food; do your job because that will help others to do theirs; help new classmates learn what we do in our class; and donate old clothes and toys to the poor. These responses were accurate and mostly realistic.

When asked what they could do to help get rid of discrimination, three students could not respond, three mentioned Martin Luther King Jr. and spoke of imitating him by growing up to fight unjust laws and telling people to get along, and five spoke of being nice to people who are discriminated against or treating them well (make them feel at home, don't treat people differently by skin color, be nice to them and become their friend, learn to be fair, be their friend, be nice to people who think they are stupid because they are different). In addition, three students spoke of interceding directly: talk to people who are discriminating and tell them that they shouldn't do it (and if they are little, tell their parents what they did); confront them directly by telling them that they are acting mean when they disparage people of other races (this student claimed to do this with her own father); and first ask them not to do that "because it hurts my feelings and I don't want anybody to get killed, because I like these people," and if necessary, say, "Don't do that or you'll be in big trouble by the president." We find it encouraging that most of these young students already possessed specific ideas about avoiding discrimination in their own behavior, and that some of them said that they would confront discrimination by others when they encountered it.

The last question asked students about choices that they make in their lives. One student couldn't respond, three mentioned food choices, two television program choices, and three choices of what to do during literacy time at school. Surprisingly, eight students mentioned choices regarding deportment or following rules (not doing dangerous things, doing the right thing, saying no to offers of cigarettes, choosing to be quiet and be a good listener, doing what you are asked to do at school, not saying bad words or lying, being helpful to classmates, and getting good grades). We think that these responses reflect the fact that in recent years, the language of choice and responsibility has been incorporated into many of the socialization messages directed at children by their parents and teachers. Other choices included when to play the drums at home; which classmate to sit by during free times; things to buy at the store; where to sit; to stick up for himself against bullies; and a joint decision with her mother that she would eat breakfast at the baby-sitter's house rather than her own house on school days.

Across the interview as a whole, the children's responses usually were accurate as far as they went, but often indicative of very limited knowledge about the topics addressed in the questions (especially questions about childhood in the past or in other countries).

Overview of the Childhood Unit —Barbara Knighton

The childhood unit focuses on the idea that all people share some common experiences as they grow from a child to an adult. This unit in particular is wonderful for promoting the ideas of diversity and tolerance. As you learn and talk about children growing, it is easy to see that everyone is unique. I found that students became excited about finding unique qualities in themselves and others. At the same time, we were also focusing on accepting the differences and looking for ways to connect with others no matter how different they are.

This unit is a terrific companion to the family unit, partly because it takes a closer look at information that was introduced during the family unit. Children were interested in learning more about topics like birthdays, games, toys, family rules, and chores. If you do this unit after the family unit (even if a year has elapsed), the students can make connections to prior learning and will enjoy extending the learning from their favorite topics.

A pleasant bonus was the relationship building that occurred between parents and students after different home assignments. Many parents commented that they enjoyed spending time talking with their children about their birth and growing up. Parents also had opportunities to talk about their own childhoods and even began making plans with their children for experiences in the coming years.

This unit offers many opportunities to share information about children around the world. I relied heavily on books from our library to show photographs of actual children and their lives. It became commonplace for our lunchtime and other casual conversations to include talking and wondering about children in other countries.

The big ideas featured within each lesson will help you to stay on topic during these lessons. Because they are "experts" about childhood, your students will want to share lots of information and stories. Be sure to review all the big ideas before teaching each lesson to help you keep them on task and moving forward.

Lesson 1

Elements of Childhood

Resources

- Photos, pictures, drawings depicting children around the world in the various stages of childhood (include examples secured from your students' families that reflect their children's childhoods)
- Time line to focus on stages of childhood, accompanied by a blank time line
- Photos, pictures, and drawings illustrating the teacher's childhood
- Time lines and photos or pictures of children at various stages in their development for a triad activity

Children's Literature

Marzollo, J. (1998). *How Kids Grow*. New York: Scholastic.

General Comments

To launch the unit, collect the instructional resources and display visual prompts to generate interest in the topic. Post questions (written on wide strips of paper) around the room and on the bulletin board. Here are some sample questions that could be included:

> What is childhood?
> What do children all over the world have in common?
> How are children unique?
> How were the lives of children long ago different from yours today?
> What roles do adults play in children's development?
> How does government help children?

General Purposes or Goals

To help students: (1) understand what childhood is, including the stages (infancy, childhood, adolescence or baby, toddler, preschool years, early school years, and pre-teenage years); (2) understand the needs of children; and (3) understand and appreciate that children everywhere experience changes in their physical growth, ability to communicate their emotions, attitudes, behaviors, and so on.

Main Ideas to Develop

- Childhood includes the early stages of development in every individual's life.
- Children everywhere experience many physical, behavioral, and intellectual changes in their early years.

Teaching Tips from Barbara

Prior to beginning this unit, I sent home a note requesting pictures of children. Families sent in both photos and magazine pictures, which we sorted into different sets depicting stages of development. The pictures were used as both a guide to filling out the Early Life Stages Chart (see Table 1) and props for the time line activity. My students were very motivated to complete the activity because they were in the pictures themselves!

Starting the Lesson

Pose questions regarding childhood. Sample questions might include What is childhood? What is unique about every child? What do children everywhere have in common? How are the lives of children different today from those of children in the past? What roles do children play?

After preliminary discussion of these questions, show the class a bulletin board that you have begun as a way to stimulate interest in learning about childhood. Included might be photos you have secured from their families that reflect their childhood. They would also love to see pictures of your childhood. Elicit from students other questions about childhood that they want to discuss during the unit. Write their queries on strips of paper and add them to the bulletin board display.

Suggested Lesson Discussion

Childhood can be described as a series of substages in a person's development. This is universal throughout the world. Parents everywhere play a vital role in their children's development. One of the chief concerns of parents is to help their children develop normally in terms of the skills or traits that their culture values. Normal development usually includes learning to communicate, getting along with other people, acting responsibly, and so on.

Other skills and traits are valued only by certain societies. For example, in developed countries such as the United States, children go to school and are expected to read and write, whereas in some developing parts of the world, children never attend school, never learn to read or write, and instead do farm chores, work in the fields, herd animals, and do other chores. However, school is becoming more valued in underdeveloped places.

[Using a time line and photos, describe your childhood. Use the information in Table 1 as a guide for describing and graphically representing your story. Underscore your stages of development, including infancy, childhood, and adolescence or baby, toddler, preschool years, early schools years, and preteen years.]

Children everywhere experience changes in their physical growth, ability to communicate, behavior, thought processes, emotions, and attitudes.

[As a means of concluding the lesson and preparing for the next lesson, read the book *How Kids Grow,* which describes changes that children everywhere experience. Encourage your students to listen and look for ways that children change as they get older.]

Activities

At the conclusion of the storylike presentation of *How Kids Grow*, ask students to group in triads and share the most interesting ideas they learned in the lesson. Then elicit ideas from the groups and write them on the board.

After the discussion, provide each triad with a blank time line and a set of pictures of children at various ages or stages of their development. Ask them to organize the pictures according to the changes children everywhere go through as they move from babies to preteens or adolescents. Share the results. (Refer back to your Early Life Stages Chart.)

Summarize

- Childhood includes the early stages of development in every individual's life.
- Children everywhere experience changes in their physical growth, ability to communicate, thought processes, emotions, ability to accomplish tasks, and so on.

Assessment

Have the students provide the correct signal (thumbs up versus thumbs down) for each item in the following quiz.

1.	Thumbs down	Children are toddlers *before* they are babies.
2.	Thumbs down	Preteens are younger than babies.
3.	Thumbs up	I was a toddler *before* I was a preteen.
4.	Thumbs up	I was a toddler *after* I was a baby.
5.	Thumbs up	Children in Nigeria go through similar changes to the ones children in the United States experience.
6.	Thumbs down	Children in Mexico have different basic needs from children in the United States.
7.	Thumbs down	Only children in the United States experience behavioral changes in their early years.
8.	Thumbs down	Only children in Japan experience physical changes in their early years.

Home Assignment

Encourage students to share with their families what they have learned about their teacher's childhood as well as about children in general. Encourage them to look at their family album or picture box and put together a simple time line with pictures, photos, drawings, and words that tell the child's story from babyhood to present (e.g., baby, toddler, preschool years, and early school years). In the next few days, create a display of the individual time lines to serve as the stimulus for an expanded and enriched discussion regarding childhood as a cultural universal.

Dear Parents,

We are beginning a new unit titled Childhood. We want to encourage your family to look at the family album or picture box and put together a simple time line with pictures, photos, drawings, and words that tell your child's story from babyhood to present (e.g., baby, toddler, preschool years, and early school years). A display of the individual time lines will be created in our classroom. The display will serve as a stimulus for an expanded and enriched discussion regarding childhood as a cultural universal. Thank you for your assistance!

Sincerely,

FIGURE 2   Model Letter to Parents

Table 1 Early Life Stages Chart

	PHYSICAL QUALITITES AND SKILLS	COMMUNICATION OF EMOTION	ATTITUDES	BEHAVIOR
Infant (birth to 18 months)	Begin as a baby weighing a very few pounds. Babies may be born with hair. Often they lose their hair and new hair grows in. Their eye color may change. They learn to sit up/stand.	Cry when they need something. By eighteen months they have ten- to twenty-word vocabulary.	Babies (infants) learn to smile and laugh when they are experiencing pleasant things. Learn to wave bye-bye.	Sleep a lot. Learn to feed themselves, walk or run a short distance. Can stack blocks.
Toddler (18 months to 3 years)	Toddlers learn to walk. Acquire several teeth.	Learn to build sentences. Most two-year-olds use one or two words for an entire thought. Imitate sounds.	Toddlers learn to get into trouble and often get upset if things don't go their way.	Toddlers improve all the skills listed above for infants.
Preschool (3 to 5 years)	Often grow slim and tall.	Exhibit feelings of jealousy, anger. Like to pretend.	Like to look at picture books. Like to listen to words.	Learn toilet training. Begin to learn about respect, truthfulness. Begin to learn standards of behavior.
Early School (5 to 8 years)	Develop physical dexterity/fine motor skills.	Begin to realize they can solve problems. Learn to read and write.	Children begin to form a self-image—favorable or unfavorable—often depending on attitudes of parents.	Children begin to realize they have choices in their actions. Children begin to feel guilt as well as shame if they behave wrongly.
Preteen (8 to 13 years)	Physical growth increases sharply. Begin to grow heavier/taller, puberty begins. Nine-year-old boys range from 56 to 81 pounds.	Often argue with adults.	Peer group plays a very important role.	Peer pressure comes into play. Most learn to control aggression by preteen years.
Teen (13 to 19 years)	By fourteen, most boys are heavier and taller than girls their age.	Sometimes they argue with adults, want to avoid adults because they feel devalued—want independence.	Teens highly regard the opinions of their peers.	Peer pressure continues.

Lesson 2

Specialness

Resources

- Teacher's childhood story, represented by photos on a time line
- Teacher's photos illustrating preteen or adolescent, teenager, young adult, and adult, emphasizing unique features
- Teacher's footprint or handprint and/or other data that identified him or her in the hospital nursery
- Teacher's family picture
- Pictures and photos of children who look and dress very differently
- Magazine and catalogs to cut up for Activity
- Copies of Figure 4: Important Information Sheet About Me

Children's Literature

Lewis, D., & Lewis, G. (1995). *When You Were a Baby*. Atlanta: Peachtree.

Middleton, D. (1999). *Dealing with Discrimination*. New York: Rosen.

General Comments

The focus of this lesson will be the uniqueness of all children (who also have many things in common). Its richness will depend on input from the children and their families.

General Purposes or Goals

To help students develop knowledge of, understanding of, and appreciation for: (1) childhood around the world—similarities and uniquenesses; and (2) factors that contribute to specialness or uniqueness: inheritance, culture, environment, and so on.

Main Ideas to Develop

- Childhood is universal.
- Children everywhere go through a series of changes in their development (from infancy to adolescence) and they experience many changes physically, emotionally, behaviorally, intellectually, and so forth.
- While children all over the world are alike in many ways, each one is unique (e.g., fingerprints, footprints, voice, cells in the body, face, the way she or he thinks, feelings about things, talents, etc.).
- Discrimination is treating someone badly because he or she is different from you.
- Even as young school children, we can help get rid of discrimination.

- Prejudice is a negative opinion formed without knowing all of the facts.

Unit 1
Childhood

Teaching Tips from Barbara

I divided this lesson into two parts. The first part involves children being born and growing and being unique. This part connected hand in hand with health lessons in our Human Growth and Development unit. We were able to meet the curriculum requirements for both areas in this one lesson. The second day I focused on the discrimination part of this lesson. I took the "I can help fight discrimination" part of the assessment and turned it into a class project. We wrote a pledge together listing ways to fight discrimination. We then published the list and everyone signed it. It became a living document that helped to direct our relationships and behavior.

Starting the Lesson

Share the results of the home assignment. Discuss similarities of all the students in the class (e.g., they all have gone through the stages of childhood—baby, toddler, preschool, early school years). Compare your time line with those of the students, underscoring the idea that even though you are older, you too experienced the same stages that they are experiencing. Explain that they will go through additional stages, just as you have (e.g., preteen or adolescent, teenager, young adult, etc.). Show pictures and photos of these stages. Underscore the idea that children everywhere go through these stages in development.

Suggested Lesson Discussion

[Read *When You Were a Baby* by Lewis and Lewis.] Babyhood occurs throughout the world. Some babies have green eyes while others have blue or brown eyes. Some babies have red hair; some have brown or black hair; and some have very little hair. Some have very fair skin and others have darker skin. Families are special groups of people who love and usually take care of their babies. Every child who is born is already a part of a family. Some babies have older brothers and sisters. Some babies will grow up to be big brothers or sisters. Some families have grandmothers, grandfathers, aunts, and uncles. No family is exactly like yours.

While all children begin as babies, each is special. [Return to your time line accompanied by the visuals and words, only this time, emphasize your unique features. Show photos of your family members, pointing out some of your inherited features (specially shaped nose, eye color, hair color and texture, etc.). Show your footprint, handprint, or other data that identified you in the hospital nursery. Continue by explaining how you are unique within the context of other family members (e.g., you have an older sister who is blonde like your aunt. She is also very musical while you were much more athletic as a child, etc.).]

[Then continue by showing pictures of children who look and dress very differently than your students do and introduce the concept of discrimination.]. *Discrimination* means treating people badly just because they look or act different. Sometimes only a person's feelings are hurt, but often the results are much worse. Sometimes people get teased, or left out at games or parties. Sometimes they are physically injured. Unfortunately, the more different from others a person looks, speaks, or acts, the more likely it is that he or she will be treated unfairly. [Share the book *Dealing with Discrimination* by Middleton. As you read it, encourage the students to listen for examples of discrimination.]

Disliking others for no good reason is called *prejudice*. When we act on prejudice we often miss out on getting to know others, learning from them, and possibly developing friendships.

[Talk about the examples of discrimination that were highlighted in the book you read. Then discuss other examples that class members may have experienced and the personal feelings associated with them. As a class, discuss what members can do to stop discrimination and show that differences are valued.]

Activity

Using a class discussion format, have students complete a chart like the following one to illustrate the key points of the lesson with words and pictures gleaned from magazines and catalogs. Encourage sketches and drawings to fill in the gaps.

CHILDREN ALL OVER THE WORLD ARE ALIKE	CHILDREN ALL OVER THE WORLD ARE UNIQUE
Begin as babies	Handprint
When they are born, they are already members of a family	Footprint
Have eyes, ears, hair, etc.	Eye shape
Need adults to take care of them when they are babies	Nose shape
	Family members—no two families are alike

After completing this activity, as a class write a group journal entry that begins, "We can help get rid of discrimination by _____."

Summarize

- Childhood is experienced around the world.
- Children all over the world experience many of the same changes, yet every child has unique features.
- Prejudice is a negative opinion formed about someone without knowing or examining all the facts.
- Discrimination is treating someone badly because she or he is different from you.
- Even as school children in the early grades, we can help get rid of discrimination.

Assessment

Have each student complete a narrative and provide illustrations that respond to the following statements.

1. Children everywhere are like me in the following ways:
2. I am unique in the following ways:
3. I can help fight discrimination (treating someone badly because he or she is different) by:

Home Assignment

The goal is to think about sameness and specialness or uniquenesses of children. Encourage students to discuss what they learned about sameness and specialness regarding childhood around the world. Then, have the family complete the Important Information Sheet About Me. The results will be shared with classmates.

Dear Parents,

We are learning about specialness. Attached is an Important Information Sheet About Me that we would like your child to complete with a family member's assistance. The results will be shared during our social studies class. Thank you for your help!

Sincerely,

FIGURE 3   Model Letter to Parents

IMPORTANT INFORMATION SHEET ABOUT ME

Please complete the survey with at least one member of your family. Be ready to share the results with the class.

I am unique because _____

_____

_____

Here are pictures of my early childhood:

BABY	TODDLER	PRESCHOOL	EARLY SCHOOL YEARS

Some things my family wants to share about me:

    Examples:

    I weighed _____ when I was born.

    My first word was _____.

    My favorite toy when I was a baby was _____.

We encourage family members to have a conversation about specialness and to list several examples of your child's specialness.

Figure 4   Important Information Sheet About Me

© 2003 by Janet Alleman and Jere Brophy from *Social Studies Excursions, K–3: Book Three*. Portsmouth, NH: Heinemann.

Lesson 3

A Day in the Lives of Children Around the World

Resources

- Globe
- Photocopies of pictures of children around the world as portrayed in the book *Wake Up, World!*
- Pen pal data and Internet access

Children's Literature

Ajmera, M., & Ivanko, J. (1991). *To Be a Kid.* Watertown, MA: Charlesbridge.

Ajmera, M., & Versola, A. (1997). *Children from Australia to Zimbabwe.* Watertown, MA: Charlesbridge.

Hollyer, B. (1999). *Wake Up World: A Day in the Life of Children Around the World.* New York: Henry Holt.

General Comments

This lesson underscores how early elementary school children all over the world have much in common but may seem different because of availability of resources, climatic conditions, cultural identity, and other factors. It relies heavily on *Wake Up, World! A Day in the Life of Children Around the World.* If this book is not available, other materials can be substituted. For example, *Children from Australia to Zimbabwe* is a viable option.

General Purposes or Goals

To help students understand and appreciate: (1) certain ways in which childhood around the world is very different, even though all children have much in common; (2) the many factors that contribute to childhood around the world and why it is experienced differently; and (3) how they can apply what they learn about childhood to their own lives—and more ably explain the reasons for their experiences.

Main Ideas to Develop

- Children's lives around the world are alike in many ways, yet different in other ways.
- Differences in children's lives are based on culture, geographic conditions, economic resources, personal choices, and so on.

Teaching Tips from Barbara

The students enjoyed finding similarities between their lives and those of other children. I copied pictures of the children from the book *Wake Up,*

World! and marked on the globe the places where these children lived. This added to students' interest and understanding of the information.

Starting the Lesson

Discuss the results of the home assignment.

Begin this lesson by asking students how they think children's lives around the world are alike or different. List their responses. Then introduce *Wake Up, World! A Day in the Life of Children Around the World*. Make copies of the eight photos of the children described in the book and attach them to the appropriate locations on the globe.

Optional   Establish a pen pal Internet e-mail exchange with a class in some other part of the world or with children in many places. This would be a perfect place for volunteers to provide support for instruction.

Suggested Lesson Discussion

In certain ways childhood around the world is very different. Yet children everywhere have much in common. [As you read *Wake Up, World!*, ask students to listen for likenesses and differences between the lives of children in other parts of the world and those of children in your classroom.]

All over the world, children live with their parents, brothers and sisters, and sometimes with other relatives. Some families also include pets. Children all over the world usually begin their mornings by eating breakfast. Many help with family chores, and most get ready for school by washing, brushing their teeth, and getting dressed.

Depending on where they live, children make the trip to school in different ways. Some walk while others ride a train, ride a bus, or go in a car.

School is very important for children around the world. Children in America learn about children in other countries while they are learning about us. Schools differ in what they look like and in the availability of resources for learning.

Children throughout the world find enjoyment in playing. Some create their own games and make their own toys, while others have lots of opportunities to use technology and engage in activities that involve expensive play equipment.

Children around the world share their lives with their families, friends, and others who live in their communities. They help out in a variety of ways: taking care of animals, cleaning their rooms, picking up toys, folding laundry, setting the table, caring for younger brothers and sisters, preparing meals, and so on.

Every place in the world has special foods. Families have different ways of cooking and eating the foods. Some families have lots of choice in the foods that they eat, while others eat the same foods almost every day. Some children have access to desserts daily while for others, a sweet is available only on special occasions.

Children everywhere go to bed. The types of beds they sleep in and the bedtime practices vary, but at night children everywhere rest their bodies and minds.

[At the conclusion of the story, revisit their initial responses to the question. Then, as a class, make a chart comparing the lives of children in other parts of the world and children in your classroom.]

LIKENESSES IN CHILDREN'S LIVES	DIFFERENCES IN CHILDREN'S LIVES
Children everywhere have the same basic needs: food, shelter, clothing. Children all over the world enjoy playing. Children all over the world go to school.	Children eat different foods, live in different kinds of homes, and often on special occasions wear different kinds of clothing. Some children do not have toys, so they play with sticks, stones, old bicycle wheels, etc. Children read and write at school in different languages.

Activity

Describe the activities of a child from another part of the world using the information found in *Wake Up, World*. (Summaries follow.) Select countries and cultures considering the demographics of your class, places that your students have been exposed to in literature, places in the news, and so on. Show a picture of the child. Have each table discuss where the child might live, what his or her cultural heritage might be, and what could be said about his or her family's available resources. During the interactive discussion, reiterate that differences are often due to culture, geographic conditions, economic resources, personal choices, and other factors.

India   This child helps his mother make flat bread called *chapattis*, outside the kitchen. He also helps his father with house repairs. His own job is feeding and milking the goats every day. He walks to school in a nearby village. The walk is very hot and dusty and most of the children go barefoot. He loves art class. He also loves soccer.

France   This child speaks French. She also learns English at school. Often she rides her bicycle to a nearby bakery early in the morning to pick up a long loaf of crusty white bread called a *baguette* for her family. She learns a lot about vineyards and wine by listening to her family talk about the weather, seasons, and prices they can get for grapes. Her favorite sports are cycling and soccer.

Brazil This child sleeps in a hammock. When she awakens, she has a bucket shower every morning. After her shower she has breakfast, which consists of coffee mixed with manioc flour. She feels lucky that she can go to school. Not every village has a school. Her school has few instructional materials besides a few books and a blackboard. Her school subjects include reading, writing, math, and geography. She loves to play soccer.

Vietnam This child lives in a very small apartment with his family. He shares a bed with his brother, mother, and father. The family sleeps, eats, and watches television all in the same room. He also has to do his homework in this room—usually as he lies on the bed. One of his jobs is to wash rice for his mother to cook with fish and vegetables for breakfast. Then he walks to school. He only attends half days because in his country there are not enough teachers or schools for all the children to go to school full time. He loves to play badminton and soccer.

Village in Ghana This child lives in the country. He usually sleeps on a mat, which he shares with other family members. When it's hot the family sleeps outside. Often he gets up early with his father to let the animals out of their walled yard to graze in the open during the day. He washes in the bucket of water he has carried from the well, then gets dressed in shorts and a shirt, eats breakfast, and walks a couple of miles to the school. One of his favorite after-school activities is playing in the dirt and making toys out of the claylike soil. After the objects dry in the sun, the children are able to play with them. The family does not have money to buy toys and there are no stores in the area where toys are sold. Soccer is another favorite activity of his.

Optional Share *To Be a Kid* by Ajmera and Ivanko. The brilliant photographs convey the idea that children everywhere have much in common, including creative play and a love for family and friends.

Summarize

- Children around the world participate in many of the same activities (e.g., eat, sleep, play, go to school, help family members, etc.).
- Children do different things or do the same things in different ways because of their cultural heritage, their location or climatic conditions, available resources, their personal choices, and so on.

Assessment

Describe an activity in the life of a child and have students give "thumbs up" if it is an activity common to the children in your classroom and "thumbs down" if it is uncommon or does not happen at all in your community. Encourage students to give reasons for their responses.

1. Thumbs up   Playing soccer after school
2. Thumbs down   Bathing in a wooden tub or with a bucket
3. Thumbs down   Herding, feeding, and milking goats or cows before going off to school
4. Thumbs down   Gathering firewood for mother to use when she cooks dinner over the wood-burning stove
5. Thumbs down   Making your own toys out of sand, mud, water, pieces of wood, or recycled parts of old bicycles or cars
6. Thumbs up   Bathing in a bathtub or taking a shower
7. Thumbs up or down   Riding a bus, a train, or a car to school
8. Thumbs up   Playing basketball after school
9. Thumbs up or down   Bicycling to a nearby bakery to pick up a loaf of bread for breakfast
10. Thumbs down   Helping mother wash clothes at the river
11. Thumbs up or down   Learning English as well as another language at school
12. Thumbs down   Going to bed in a hammock
13. Thumbs down   Walking barefoot on dirt roads to get to school
14. Thumbs down   Watching your father shave outside using a small bucket of water from the river

Home Assignment

Encourage the students to share with their parents some of the information they have learned about children's activities around the world. Then as a family, they should select a place in the world they would like to investigate in order to learn more about the typical activities of a child there. Encourage them to use the Internet and other library sources to gather data. Students should be prepared to share the information at an upcoming class session.

Dear Parents,

Your child has been learning that children around the world participate in many of the same activities (e.g., eat, sleep, play, go to school, help family members, etc.); however, they may do these things in different ways based on their cultural heritage, geographic location or climatic conditions, their family's available resources, and their personal choices.

    We encourage you as a family to select a place in the world to investigate. Use encyclopedias, books, videos, and/or the Internet to learn more about the activities of a child in that place, noting similarities with and differences from children in our community. The information will be shared during an upcoming social studies lesson. Thank you!

                    Sincerely,

Figure 5   Model Letter to Parents

Lesson 4

Birthdays

Resources

- Pictures of children in various parts of the world celebrating their birthdays
- Fairy bread (treat from Australia)
- Artifacts depicting the teacher's birthday celebrations
- Globe
- Fruit and vegetable candy and paper flowers from Brazil
- Kelewele (fried plantain chunks from Ghana)
- Cake with candles, powdered sugar pancakes, tarts, lemonade from the Netherlands
- Piñata from Mexico
- Pictures that depict children living in places where birth dates are not recorded
- Cassette tape of "Happy Birthday" song in multiple languages (The book *Happy Birthday, Everywhere* includes pronounciations of the term in multiple languages, recipes for birthday foods, and descriptions of special birthday decorations and games.)

Children's Literature

Arnold, G. (1987). *Everybody Has a Birthday*. New York: Franklin Watts.

Erlbach, A. (1997). *Happy Birthday, Everywhere*. Brookfield, CT: Millbrook.

Kindersley, B., & Kindersley, A. (1997). *Celebrations*. New York: D. K. Publishing.

Perl, L. (1984). *Candles, Cakes, and Donkey Tails*. New York: Clarion.

General Purposes or Goals

To help students understand and appreciate: (1) that children around the world all have birthdays although they have some very different celebration customs; (2) that there are parts of the world where birthdays go unnoticed; and (3) games, foods, and customs of other cultures (they might want to add some of these activities to their own birthday celebrations).

Main Ideas to Develop

- Children around the world all have birthdays, although they may have very different celebration customs from ours.
- There are places in the world where birth dates go unnoticed and instead people have group birthdays when everyone becomes one year older (e.g., Chinese New Year).

- There are places in the world where a single special day (such as All Saints Day) is the occasion for celebrating everyone's birthday.

Teaching Tips from Barbara

This was one of the children's favorite lessons in the whole unit. Students were excited and intrigued by the ideas and different ways to celebrate birthdays. If you plan ahead, parents can help out with the ingredients for the birthday treats like fairy bread, fried bananas, and tarts. This activity provided for a wonderful, authentic link between social studies and writing. I had my students write a letter to their mom or dad asking for a particular way to celebrate their next birthday. The students talked about this information throughout the year and well into the next.

Starting the Lesson

Begin the lesson by discussing the results of the home assignment.
Then play a tape of the song "Happy Birthday" sung in several different languages.

Suggested Lesson Discussion

For most children, their birthday is one of their favorite days of the year. It is a time for looking back over the past year and planning for the next. [Show pictures and artifacts and describe how you celebrate your birthday. Then elicit input from the students. List all of the customs, games, and foods that they mention.]

Long, long ago, birthdays were considered dangerous because they marked a change in a person's life. It was feared that this might cause evil spirits to do harm. So, people believed that if friends and relatives visited them on their birthday, they would be protected. Using noisemakers at a birthday party was probably done to scare away the evil spirits.

Candles on a cake is another custom that started long, long ago. People believed that many gods lived in the sky, so they thought that the rising smoke would send their prayers to the gods so they would be answered. Today, blowing out candles is a modern version of this ancient custom.

Even among your class members, there is some variety regarding birthday celebrations. Children of different cultures have different birthday customs. [Select four to six parts of the world and describe birthday celebrations. Point out each place on the globe. Allow the students to look at pictures, sample the food, and play a game typical of the culture. (See *Happy Birthday Everywhere.*)]

Australia Greeting: Happy Birthday

Many Australian families prepare barbecues for birthday parties. The children eat something called fairy bread. This special treat is buttered bread covered with colored sugar sprinkles.

Brazil   Greeting: Feliz Aniversario (feh-LEEZ ah-ni-ver-SAH-ree-yoe)

Brazilian families decorate their homes with brightly colored banners and paper flowers. They serve colorful candies shaped like fruits and vegetables.

Ghana   Greeting: Medzi dzigbe njkeke nyuie na wo (I wish happy birthday to you) (mehd-ZEE gih-BAY nuh-KAY-KAY new-EH nah woe)

Children having birthdays in Ghana wake up to a special treat called *oto* (AH-toe). It is mashed potato and eggs fried in palm oil. Later in the day, children have a birthday party similar to ours. They might eat stew and rice and a dish called *kelewele* (kelly-welly), which is fried plantain chunks. Plantains are similar to our bananas.

The Netherlands   Greeting: Van Harte Gefeliciteerd (Hearty Congratulations) (van har-TEH geh-fell-ih-CIH-teared)

Birthdays are very important to Dutch families. Most homes have a birthday calendar in the bathroom. Its purpose is to remind everyone in the house about their friends' and relatives' special days. Relatives usually visit on children's birthdays.

Many Dutch children have a cake with candles much like ours. They usually have pancakes sprinkled with powdered sugar. They also eat small tarts and drink lemonade or hot chocolate.

Mexico   Greeting: Feliz Cumpleaños (Happy Birthday) (feh-LEEZ coom-plee-ON-yoes)

Children in Mexico invite lots of friends to their birthday parties. Every party features a piñata. It's a decorated bag or jug usually shaped like an animal. It is filled with candies, small toys, and coins. The piñata hangs from the ceiling. Children are blindfolded. They attempt to break the piñata with a stick. When it breaks, everyone rushes for the goodies.

Other Countries   There are places in the world where birth dates are not recorded and/or go unnoticed and instead people have group celebrations. [Show pictures that depict these places (e.g., desolate village in Tanzania or a family living in Outer Mongolia.] There are also places where other celebrations (e.g., All Saints Day) replace birthdays except on legal documents such as passports and drivers' licenses.

[We encourage you to be culturally sensitive and feature traditions celebrated by the children in your classroom. For example, if you have a child from India, you will want to include content and objects reflective of his or her culture.]

Activity

Pair/Share—Ask students to think about all they have learned about birthdays and decide on one thing they would like to add to their next party.

Summarize

- Children all over the world tend to view their birthdays as special days of the year.
- Games, decorations, foods, and activities vary according to cultural and individual preferences.
- There are parts of the world where birth dates either go unnoticed or are simply not recorded because of absence of calendars and connections to other parts of the world.

Assessment

Have each student write a description of what she or he will plan for his or her next birthday party. Students should include at least one thing they would like to incorporate from another culture and be able to explain why.

Home Assignment

Encourage students to share with their families what they have learned about birthday celebrations around the world. Surfing the Internet would yield a lot of additional information. Ask students to discuss what new features they would like to add to their birthday celebrations next year based on what they learned in school.

Have family members describe how they celebrated their birthdays when they were children. Encourage them to write their responses for sharing during the next social studies lesson.

Dear Parents,

Your child is prepared to share what we have learned about birthdays around the world. In many places, the customs are different from those typically found in our community. There are parts of the world where birth dates go unnoticed and instead people have group birthdays when everyone becomes one year older (e.g., Chinese New Year). Ask your child to talk about one new feature he or she would like to add to his or her birthday celebration based on what we have learned about other children's customs. Then, please describe how you celebrated your birthday as a child. The results will be shared during our next social studies lesson. Thank you!

Sincerely,

FIGURE 6   Model Letter to Parents

Lesson 5

Rites of Passage

Resources
- Word cards: Bar Mitzvah, Bat Mitzvah, Confirmation, Sweet Sixteen Party, Graduation
- Time line that represents the years of childhood (from birth to age 18)
- Pictures and photos of bar mitzvahs, bat mitzvahs, first communion ceremonies, confirmation ceremonies, sweet sixteen parties, graduations
- Resource people who can talk about their "coming of age" parties (preferably teenagers)
- Artifacts depicting a celebration that you as the teacher experienced in "coming of age"

Children's Literature
Ajmera, M., & Versola, A. (1997). *Children from Australia to Zimbabwe*. Watertown, MA: Charlesbridge.

Dineen, J. (1995). *Rites of Passage*. Philadelphia: Chelsea House.

Margolis, B. (1990). *Rehema's Journey*. New York: Scholastic.

Patrick, D. (1993). *Family Celebrations*. New York: Silver Moon.

Sita, L. (1999). *Coming of Age*. Woodbridge, CT: Blackbirch.

General Comments
The intent of this lesson is to give the students a flavor of what "coming of age" means for various cultural groups, keeping in mind that not all families within a given group celebrate these occasions.

General Purposes or Goals
To help students understand and appreciate what "coming of age" means and how some families within certain cultural groups celebrate it.

Main Ideas to Develop
- People all over the world celebrate major happenings in their lives.
- Many families celebrate when a boy or girl is no longer a child.
- When a child comes of age, it means he or she has taken an important step toward growing up. A young adult now has both new rights and new responsibilities.
- Some "coming of age" celebrations are religious.
- The age at which a person becomes an adult varies around the world.

Teaching Tips from Barbara

It works best to begin with rites of passage that are familiar to your students and their families. One year, I had several students participating in their first communion during this unit, so I began with that. Another year we were doing this unit in May, so graduation was our starting place. During this lesson, I found it important to remind myself frequently about the big ideas. It can be fascinating to look at other cultures, but the big ideas focus on "coming of age" most of all (not the details of the ceremonies).

Starting the Lesson

Discuss the results of the home assignment. Begin the lesson by posing the question, "When are you no longer a child?" Encourage students to think quietly for a moment and put a finger on their forehead when they have an idea to share. List the responses on the board. Then show pictures and photographs that illustrate how various families interpret "coming of age" and celebrate the event. As the students observe the pictures, ask them if they have ever participated in one of these celebrations. If possible, invite some teenagers to the class to share stories about their "coming of age" parties (e.g., bar mitzvah, bat mitzvah, sweet sixteen party, graduation, etc.), bringing photos, clothing, and other artifacts to help explain the event.

If you as the teacher have experienced one of these events, be sure to share your story with the class. Show photos and artifacts to bring the event alive for the students. As you share descriptions of rites of passage, refer to them on a time line that spans birth to age 18.

Suggested Lesson Discussion

Many families celebrate when a boy or girl is no longer a child. [Read the story "Zak and the Battling Aunts" in *Family Celebrations*.] Zak's celebration is called a *bar mitzvah*. [Write this term on a large word card and attach to the board.] It is a religious celebration for male Jewish children when they reach about thirteen years of age. [Ask the students to listen for how the family celebrated this important event.]

Jewish children study Hebrew for a number of years because the Torah (Jewish bible) is written in that language. On the day of the bar mitzvah, the boy gives his first public reading from the Torah. Additionally, he gives a speech and says a prayer as a way of demonstrating what he has learned from years of study. After the religious ceremony, friends and relatives attend a party in his honor. After the bar mitzvah, the boy is recognized as an adult and as a responsible member of the Jewish community and faith.

Jewish girls in some families celebrate in similar ways; however, they call the celebration *bat mitzvahs*. [Write this term on a large word card and attach to the board.] A girl celebrates this event at age 12. [Add word cards with the names of the other special events for "coming of age" as you provide explanations.]

Some children around the world whose families are Christian take part in a religious ceremony called *confirmation.* Children dress up for this very important event. In the United States, the girls usually wear white dresses and the boys usually wear suits. In some countries, children wear colorful costumes that represent their native dress. The ceremony suggests that the child has become an adult. It is a time for the church to formally initiate and accept the individual into church membership. This ceremony usually takes place at about age 12 or 13. It is believed that the child is old enough to understand his or her faith and to be a responsible member in the church. Responsibility includes practicing the behaviors expected of church members (e.g., going to church, living according to the laws of the church, giving time and money to help others, etc.).

The people of several African countries have a variety of customs associated with "coming of age." For example, the Pokot people of Kenya have a ceremony called *sapana.* The highlight of the festivity is the giving of a mud cap to the boy, whose head has been shaved. This is a sign of adulthood. The mud cap is put on carefully and then painted. It can be worn only during dry weather when the mud is baked hard in the sun. Pokot girls leave the village to learn about adulthood from some of the older women. When they return, their faces are disguised with chalk. A ceremonial feast including eating and dancing follows and serves as a welcome into adulthood. As adults, they are expected to respect their elders; take care of younger members; as young men, protect members from harm; and as young women, perform the duties of wives.

In east Africa the Masai have community celebrations welcoming thirteen- to seventeen-year-olds into adulthood. The boys' heads are shaved; they are given ritual baths; their faces are painted; and they build their own houses in a special compound where they will live as junior warriors. They are expected at this age to be responsible (e.g., to protect other members of their cultural group and exhibit bravery).

Other cultural groups engage in activities unique to their group (although not necessarily practiced by all members) to recognize the passage from childhood to adulthood. [Share select sections of *Coming of Age* and underscore the idea that cultures all over the world note and celebrate the cycles of life. Countries represented in the book include Brazil, England, India, Israel, Japan, Mexico, Nigeria, Puerto Rico, Russia, and the United States.]

Many teenagers in the United States have nonreligious "coming of age" parties. For example, many girls have a sweet sixteen party or participate in a public celebration (e.g., cotillion). Some families have a party when their son or daughter graduates from high school. Often this party is labeled as an open house and family and friends gather for food and social time after the school ceremony. Typically the student being honored receives gifts from the guests.

Other "coming of age" experiences that most young Americans have include securing a driver's license at age 16, being able to register to vote at age 18, changing from the child to adult price structure for certain services such as movies, and so on. With these changes and transitions to adulthood come more rights but also more responsibilities. For example, young adults have the opportunity to drive cars, but they also are expected to drive carefully and abide by the traffic laws.

Activity

Give each table a word card with the name of a "coming of age" celebration on it and corresponding pictures and photographs. Have the group talk about that celebration as a "coming of age" event. What are the big ideas associated with that type of celebration? Select a student from each table to serve as a spokesperson for sharing the group's ideas with the whole class.

Summarize

- People all over the world celebrate major happenings in their lives.
- Many families celebrate the "coming of age" of their children.
- "Coming of age" is the transition from childhood to adulthood.
- Some "coming of age" celebrations are religious while others are tied to demonstrations of behaviors such as bravery.
- Still other celebrations are related to a specific birthday or completion of high school.
- When a child comes of age it means she or he has taken an important step toward growing up.
- As a young adult, a person has more rights but also more responsibilities.

Assessment

Have each student complete an open-ended story:

Coming of age means _____

_____

_____

Optional   Have students draw a picture to illustrate their response.

Home Assignment

Encourage the students to talk with their families about "coming of age" celebrations and share their open-ended stories and illustrations. Family members who have participated in these events should share photos, artifacts, and personal stories. Encourage families to discuss possibilities of "coming of age" celebrations for their children.

Dear Parents,

Encourage your child to read his or her story regarding "coming of age." If you have experienced "coming of age" celebrations such as confirmations, bar mitzvahs, or graduations, be sure to share your photos, artifacts, and personal stories. If you are planning similar parties for your children in the future, make sure you discuss them. Your child will have an opportunity to share what he or she learned from your conversation during our next class session.

Sincerely,

FIGURE 7   Model Letter to Parents

Lesson 6

Children and Work

Resources

- Time line
- Photos, pictures, and words or phrases illustrating children and work—in the past and present, in both developed and developing countries
- Pictures illustrating after-school chores
- Blank Venn diagrams and packets of pictures and words illustrating children's work in the past and present (one per table)
- Resource people to supervise students experiencing childhood work (e.g., quilting, churning butter, etc.)
- Words or phrases on strips of paper for the pantomime assessment activity

Children's Literature

Kalman, B. (1990). *Visiting a Village.* New York: Crabtree.

Kalman, B. (1991a). *Early Schools.* New York: Crabtree.

Kalman, B. (1991b). *Early Settler Children.* New York: Crabtree.

Kalman, B. (1997). *Nineteenth Century Girls and Women.* New York: Crabtree.

Kalman, B., & Everts, T. (1994). *A Child's Day.* New York: Crabtree.

Weber, V., & Lewis, G. (1999). *Home Life in Grandma's Day.* Minneapolis: Carolrhoda.

Wroble, L. (1997). *Kids in Pioneer Times.* New York: Power Kids Press.

General Comments

The intent of this lesson is to give the students a perspective about work, pointing out that long ago children worked to help their families get everything done. Later, some children worked (in factories, in mines, on farms, and so on) to help support their families. Today, in most places there are laws that protect children from working in factories, and attendance at school is considered children's work. There are places in developing countries where children do not go to school because there is a lack of resources and a need to help their families at home or earn money at a job.

General Purposes or Goals

To help students understand and appreciate: (1) the nature of children's work over time; (2) the role of government in creating and enforcing laws that protect children from working in factories and guarantee them the opportunity to attend school until they are at least sixteen years old in the United States; and (3) reasons that children in some parts of the world still must work to help their families survive.

Main Ideas to Develop

- In pioneer times, children in America worked to help support their families (for example, many children were responsible for farm chores).
- Later, some children in America worked as apprentices to learn from other adults skills that their parents didn't have.
- Still later, some children in America worked in factories to help support their families; however, today there are laws against this.
- In some parts of the developing world, children are still allowed to work in the fields and factories to support themselves and their families.
- Children in America are guaranteed the right to an education that extends through high school. Going to school is considered to be the work of children.
- There are many children throughout the world who still help their families by doing after-school chores.

Teaching Tips from Barbara

My students found this lesson challenging because they continually tried to connect the information to their own work experiences, which were limited. Many felt that the chores that they did daily or weekly qualified as having to work. I helped them to appreciate that people in the more developed parts of the world usually have fewer and easier jobs because of the wealth of resources and high level of technology available, but that long ago, even in America, children did much more strenuous work be-cause families had to satisfy all of their basic needs on their own (and this is still true today in some of the least developed parts of the world). Dis-cussing and exploring the differences between chores and a job at a busi-ness or factory can be an important, essential part of this lesson. As an assessment for this lesson, we created a very simple Venn diagram compar-ing chores long ago with chores today.

Starting the Lesson

Discuss the results of the home assignment. Then show a series of pictures illustrating children at work. Ask students to sort them into two catego-ries: past and present. Encourage them to give reasons for their responses. (Note: Later, students can subdivide the "present" group into present in America and other parts of the developed world and present in some parts of the developing world.)

Indicate that as they listen to your pictorial explanation, they should decide if their preliminary sorting is accurate. Use the pictures and a time line to illustrate the main ideas as you present the interactive narration.

Suggested Lesson Discussion

Long ago, children had lives that were very different from those of boys and girls today. In order to have shelter and enough food and clothing, everybody in the family had to work hard. Children began to do chores almost as soon as they could walk. While parents loved their children, they were very strict and demanded cooperation so that they could get everything done.

Usually the boys worked outside with the men. Together they plowed fields, tamed horses, hunted wild birds, herded, milked and fed the cows and other animals, and carried water from the wells for the animals and the family. Boys helped with the harvest, helped gather fuel by chopping down trees, and so on. Some helped their fathers make furniture. It was not uncommon for boys to get up early in the morning and work until dark. When schools became available, they often attended irregularly (for example, after the crops were harvested in the fall until it was time to plant crops in the spring).

Girls would help their mothers spin thread, weave cloth, make candles, and sew clothing. It was not uncommon for four-year-old girls to have stitched their first quilt square. Girls also churned butter, washed dishes, and helped their mothers prepare meals and preserve foods for use during the long winters. Often the girls were responsible for taking care of their younger brothers and sisters.

Because families had limited resources and technology, they had to do everything for themselves. As time went on, communities began to have people who specialized in providing certain goods or services. Children—usually boys who did not want to be farmers—could leave their parents' houses and live with craftspeople who would teach them trades. A young boy, for example, might become a cooper, who made barrels, or a blacksmith, who made everything from cooking utensils to nails and horseshoes. Girls were expected to stay at home to help their mothers and to learn the skills that they would need later as wives and mothers.

It was not an easy life back then. Families still grew their own food. They worked long and hard hours. The children knew they were doing important work, helping to support the whole family.

In the mid-1700s, things began to change [point out this change on the time line]. Important inventions were made (e.g., cotton gin, steam engine, etc.). Gradually, families who had made clothes at home now went to work in factories. Fuel was needed for steam engines, so coal mines became very busy. As a result, children who had been helping their families at home or working as apprentices started going to work in factories or mines. Factories needed lots of workers because there still wasn't much technology back then and most jobs were done by hand. A worker usually did the same job over and over many times every day.

For a long period of time, children were allowed to work in factories and coal mines. They worked long hours, had little time for breaks, and would often get so tired that they'd fall asleep on the job and have accidents. Yet, managers would complain that the children wanted to play more than work. In some factories there was a whipping room where the children were taken if they didn't do as they were told or if they didn't work fast enough.

Soon adults began to argue about what was happening. Many felt that this was no way for children to grow up, and that the children should be in school. Others argued that working kept the children out of trouble, and that they were learning about hard work and the value of money. Gradually, however, more adults decided that children should not have to go to work at such a young age—and that they should be in school. Laws were passed and today no state in the United States allows children to work in factories, mines, or other places of business. Instead, children are expected to be in school until they are at least sixteen.

Most children do, however, have after-school chores [show pictures] to help out their families at home (e.g., fold clothes, pick up toys, set the table, take out the rubbish). [Read and show pictures from pp. 16–17 of *Home Life in Grandma's Day,* which describe a typical Saturday (cleaning day) in the 1930s and 1940s and the nature of the children's chores. Point out and mark with pictures this period on the time line.]

There still are some children in the world who work in fields or factories. As resources become available and schools are built, this changes. The hope is that children everywhere will have more opportunities to go to school and learn knowledge and skills that will help them to attain success and happiness as adults. [Show pictures that illustrate children's work in parts of the developing world. Also, indicate on the time line that even today in some parts of the world there are children who work on farms, in factories, etc. because of resource limitations. Many of your students' clothes or sneakers, for example, probably were made by children working in Asian factories.]

Most modern jobs don't require backbreaking labor because of technology, but they do require more knowledge and thinking skills, so schooling is even more important than ever. We protect children from hard work and exploitation, but they have the responsibility (as well as opportunity) to learn at school and prepare themselves for their futures as parents, workers, and citizens.

Activity

Provide each table with the same series of pictures and words and a blank Venn diagram. Have students sort the pictures into children's work in the past and present. Encourage them to provide reasons for their decisions. You might want to do the activity twice, first comparing children's work in the past and present in America, and then thinking about children's work today and in the past throughout the world, underscoring that culture, economic resources, and so on influence how and when children work. Explain that what some did for work in the past might be done for pleasure today (e.g., hunting, knitting, etc.). Use the time line to illustrate the changes in children's work over time. Discuss the factors that affect what children do.

Suggested pictures and words include:

Sewing	Churning butter
Knitting	Quilting
Working in a coal mine	Hunting
Working in a factory	Plowing
Repairing a fence	Spinning
Husking corn	Weaving
Making barrels	Chopping wood
Making horseshoes	Attending school

Optional   Under adult volunteer supervision, have students experience childhood work of the past (e.g., quilting, weaving, making candles, churning butter, and so on).

Summarize

- Children's work in America has changed over time.
- In the past, children worked to help support their families.
- Today going to school is considered to be children's work in America.
- There are places even today in the developing world where children still need to work to help support their families.

Assessment

Provide pairs of individuals with a type of children's work to pantomime. Have the class decide what kind of work it is and if it was performed long ago or today or both. Encourage students to explain their responses. Examples are as follows.

- Chop wood
- Hunt
- Fish
- Fetch water from the well
- Herd animals
- Build furniture
- Churn butter
- Spin
- Attend school

- Weave
- Preserve food
- Make candles
- Prepare meals
- Take care of younger brothers and sisters
- Quilt
- Work in factories
- Work in a coal mine

Note: Several types of work are still done by children in some parts of the developing world today because of limited resources. In America, children attend school as their main type of work; however, they might do some of the above tasks after school to help their families. These tasks are referred to as chores. Also, some tasks done in the past out of necessity might be done today as a hobby (e.g., candle making, quilting, hunting, fishing).

As a class, write a group journal entry that explains children and work. Duplicate it for the students to share with their families.

Home Assignment

Encourage a family member to listen to the student as he or she reads the class journal entry that expresses the main ideas learned in school about children and work. Then, the family should discuss how children's work has changed just since the parents and/or grandparents were in the early grades. While they attended school, they probably had more after-school chores. Families should list the differences as well as the similarities between the generations and return the listings to school for a subsequent class discussion.

Dear Parents,

We have been learning about children's work, past and present. We have learned that many changes have occurred in America even since you and your children's grandparents were children. As a family, discuss these changes. Please list them and send them to school with your child so that we can use the responses in our next class discussion. Thank you!

Sincerely,

FIGURE 8   Model Letter to Parents

Lesson 7

Early Schools

Resources

- Field trip to historical site for re-creating a typical school day during pioneer times (optional)
- Time line
- Photos and pictures illustrating family life in pioneer days (e.g., hunting for and gathering food, food preparation, making clothing)
- Pioneer village illustrating types of small businesses found there
- Pictures of early schools (exterior and interior)
- School supplies found in a pioneer school (e.g., slate, ink, quill pen, chalk, birch bark or paper for writing, textbook, etc.) (A local antique dealer could be a great resource.)
- Picture illustrating children walking to school
- Pictures of classroom instruction in a pioneer schoolhouse
- Pictures illustrating disciplinary techniques
- Word cards for card sort activity (a packet of words for each table characterizing schools long ago and schools today)

Children's Literature

Kalman, B. (1991a). *Early Schools*. New York: Crabtree.

Kalman, B. (1991b). *Early Settler Children*. New York: Crabtree.

Kalman, B. (1994). *A One-Room Schoolhouse*. New York: Crabtree.

Weber, V., and G. Lewis. (1999). *School in Grandma's Day*. Minneapolis: Carolrhoda Books.

General Comments

Students will be fascinated to learn about the schools of the past. They will come to realize that while the curriculum had many of the same basic elements of today's schools, the classroom conditions, the instructional materials, and the teaching methods were quite limited.

General Purposes or Goals

To help students understand and appreciate early school life and how it compares with their lives at school today.

Main Ideas to Develop

- Pioneer school children led very different lives than children today do.
- Education in pioneer days was considered a luxury.

- Education in pioneer days was a community effort.
- Early schools were built by members of the community, relied on local building materials, and employed local people as teachers.
- Early schools offered few instructional materials and the instructional practices were limited.

Teaching Tips from Barbara

The time line activity included in this lesson can include a combination of words, drawings, and copied pictures. I was able to find several books in our library, both fictional and nonfictional, with pictures to help show the elements found in schools long ago. Digital pictures taken at a local museum (in place of a field trip if too unmanageable) can also enhance this lesson. At the conclusion of the lesson, we talked about and compared the schools using several categories (e.g., the building itself, the teachers, etc.).

Starting the Lesson

Begin the lesson by having the students share the results of the home assignment. Using pictures and the time line, explain that in pioneer times education was considered a luxury because of the amount of work that needed to be done (e.g., clearing land so houses could be built and crops could be planted). Family members were responsible for hunting for and gathering food, taking care of animals and crops, preparing food, making clothes, and so forth. Initially, the most important lessons that had to be learned related to farming (which crops would grow best in a given kind of soil, when to plant and harvest crops, how to store food, where to find fresh water, and other knowledge and skills for living off the land).

Suggested Lesson Discussion

Gradually, as villages began to develop, people began to realize the importance of math, writing, reading, and other subjects. A local storekeeper needed to be able to do arithmetic in order to keep track of how much he bought and sold and how much profit there was. A farmer needed to know how to sign his name in order to buy land. (The signed deed was the piece of paper that showed proof of his ownership.) In order to keep up on the news of the village, people needed to be able to read newspapers, church bulletins, and other materials. [*Early Schools* by Kalman includes an interesting story describing how one community arrived at a decision to build the first schoolhouse. Read or retell "To Build or Not to Build," pp. 5–7.]

[Show pictures of early schoolhouses.] Early schoolhouses were made of logs; had dirt floors, greased paper windows, narrow wooden tables or desks, and no electricity; and were heated by fireplaces (later by stoves). The school consisted of a single classroom with very young children and much older children all in one class. The rooms were uncomfortable because the heat wasn't spread evenly (hot near the fireplace, cold near the door).

[If possible, secure early school supplies from a local antique dealer and explain that they were very simple. They included charcoal (chalklike for writing), pens made of goose quills, homemade ink (ink powder and water or boiled bark mixed with a chemical called copperas), slates, and birch bark for writing (later paper).]

[Show pictures of children walking to school.] Children lucky enough to attend school had probably been up many hours before coming to school because they needed to do household chores first such as churning butter and feeding the animals. School children typically walked two or three miles to and from school each day. School days tended to be much longer than ours.

[Show pictures that illustrate the typical classroom activities.] The day usually began with prayer, then reading. Students had to wait their turn to work with the teacher because of the wide range of grade levels. Students were expected to recite the alphabet forward and backward, memorize lots of places for geography, and do lots of drills in arithmetic. The emphasis was on perfection and correctness. Students who made too many mistakes could expect to wear a dunce cap and sit in the corner. [Show picture to illustrate.] Spelling was a very important subject and there were matches (contests) every Friday. Grammar, oral reading, handwriting, and drawing were other important subjects. At the end of the day, class was dismissed when all students were silent. Those who had been late for school that day or didn't bring in their homework would have to stay after school. Cleaning blackboards and picking up garbage around the school yard were common punishments.

Common school rules included the following: never make noises or disturb your neighbors at work; bring firewood for the stove whenever the teacher requests it; straighten the benches and tables; sweep the room, dust, and leave everything tidy.

Early schools were places where character was emphasized. Children had many learning experiences that were known as five-finger lessons: truthfulness, honesty, punctuality, cleanliness, and kindness.

As time went on, many changes in education occurred (e.g., boarding schools for boys; finishing schools where girls learned French, dancing, embroidery, manners, etc.; industrial schools for poor children in towns and cities). Instead of paying for their lessons, the children who attended these schools would work at school by making shoes, furniture, or clothes; doing the laundry; serving the food; and so on). Later, trade schools were opened to provide students with opportunities to develop special skills for earning a living. Still later, colleges and universities were started.

[Return to the time line.] By the 1940s, schools had changed considerably since pioneer times, yet were quite different from today's schools. Your great-grandparents or grandparents attended schools during that period. [Share *School in Grandma's Day* by Valerie Weber and Geneva Lewis. It provides an authentic glimpse of schools in middle America at the time.]

[At the conclusion of the interactive discussion about *School in Grandma's Day*, encourage students to talk with grandparents about their educational experiences and opportunities. If photos are available, ask students to bring them to school for inclusion in the unit display.]

[Return to the time line.] Since the 1940s, ballpoint pens have replaced inkwells; light, movable, comfortable chairs have replaced fixed desks; cubbyholes or lockers, rugs, and drinking fountains have been added; white boards and pens have replaced chalkboards and chalk in some schools; school buses bring children to school; and classes are smaller.

Schools continue to change, and the single most recognized change today is the addition of technology, like TVs, VCRs, and computers. For children and adults in America today, educational opportunities are unlimited.

Optional [Prior to this lesson or as a follow-up, take a field trip to a historical site that offers a simulated school day to enhance children's understanding and appreciation for early schooling. Contact your local or state historical society for opportunities available. Use *A One-Room Schoolhouse* by Kalman as a data source. The information and pictures will provide a rich context for the field trip/simulation experience. An alternative would be to use your own classroom for the simulation. Props from an antique dealer would add authenticity.]

Activity

At the conclusion of the lesson, have each table do a card sort, placing in one pile all the words that characterize schools today, and in another pile all words that characterize schools long ago. Discuss the results as a class. Examples of words for card sort: Log Construction; Brick and Concrete Construction; Built by Members of the Community; Built by Contractors; Fireplace Heat; Furnace Heat; Electricity; Candle and Lamplight; Few Books; Computers; Slates; Birch Bark for Writing; Variety of Paper Sources; Dunce Caps; Quill Pens; Charcoal for Writing; Pencils; School Chores; Weekly Spelling Contests; Mostly Memorizing; Reciting Alphabet Backward; Five-Finger Lessons; One-Room Schools; Free Choice Time.

Summarize

- Pioneer school children led very different lives than children today.
- Education in pioneer days was a community effort.
- Early schools were built by members of the community, relied on local building materials, and employed local people as teachers.
- Early schools offered few instructional materials and limited teaching practices.

Assessment

Have each student imagine that she or he is a school child in pioneer times and write a journal entry explaining what classroom life is like, then underline all of the things that are different from classroom life today. Then have students share their responses with the class.

Home Assignment

Encourage children to read to family members their journal entries describing the school life of pioneer children. Then ask family members to discuss which, if any, of those characteristics they would like to see back in our schools today, and why. Have the comments returned to school for an upcoming class discussion.

> Dear Parents,
>
> We have been studying about early schools in America. Your child is prepared to share with you his or her journal entry describing the school life of pioneer children. After listening to the response, please discuss the characteristics of the early schools and why you would or would not like to see one or more of them back in our schools today. Your comments should be returned to school so we can include them in an upcoming class session. Thank you for participating in your child's learning.
>
> Sincerely,

FIGURE 9   Model Letter to Parents

Lesson 8

Today's Schools

Resources

- Materials including photos for developing a profile of the local school
- Map of the local school
- Photos of children in schools around the world
- Photos of children and their schools in a Tanzanian village and a Japanese city
- Blank Venn diagrams or comparison charts and word cards describing the village school in Tanzania and the city school in Japan
- Copies of chart comparing homework practices in the Tanzanian village school and the Japanese city school for the home assignment (see Table 2 for an example)

Children's Literature

Elkin, J. (1987). *A Family in Japan*. Minneapolis: Lerner.

Kalman, B. (1989). *Japan, the People*. New York: Crabtree.

Margolies, B. (1990). *Rehema's Journey*. New York: Scholastic.

General Comments

This lesson will provide an opportunity for students to access knowledge about their local school as they prepare to orient two new classmates, one from a village in Tanzania, and another from a city in Japan.

General Purposes or Goals

To help students understand and appreciate: (1) the emphasis that people around the world place on education; and (2) that schools around the world have common features, yet they may be quite different because of geography, culture, economic resources, and other factors.

Main Ideas to Develop

- When children go to school, they leave their family settings and go to places to learn with children their own age.
- Children travel to school in different ways (e.g., walk, ride a bus, take a train, ride in a car, ride a bicycle, etc.).
- In most countries, the government pays for schools, using tax money collected from people in the community.
- School is important everywhere in the world.

- Some schools have lots of classrooms, books, equipment, and other resources while others have few. In fact, in some places lessons take place out-of-doors because there is a lack of economic resources to build schools.
- In some parts of the world, children have to work to help their families satisfy their basic needs, so they are not able to attend school regularly.

Teaching Tips from Barbara

We began this lesson by creating a comparison chart with categories about schools that we were interested in exploring further. We then used the chart as a guide and searched through our resources to find the information about schools in three places in the world. Be sure to avoid judging schools by what they have or don't have, and focus on descriptions and comparisons in general.

Starting the Lesson

Discuss the responses to the homework assignment. Then have the students imagine that very soon two new classmates will be arriving, one from Japan and one from Tanzania. Explain that your students will have a chance to orient the new students to your school. Explain also that because of the geographic conditions and limited economic resources, the school in Tanzania is much different than yours; however, the Japanese school is much like yours. Economic resources are more readily available in Japan than in most of Africa. As a class, complete a chart that provides a profile of your local school, including items such as the following:

Describe how students travel to school.

Describe the exterior of the school building.

Make a simple map of the interior of the building.

Identify and describe the adults in the building who are paid to help the students.

Describe the school curriculum (school subjects).

Describe the ways in which students in your school learn.

Describe the kinds of learning resources available in your school.

Describe how recess and lunchtime operate.

Describe unique features of your school.

After developing a profile of your school, share descriptions of the schools that the imaginary classmates are coming from (see lesson discussion for discriptions).

Suggested Lesson Discussion

[Using information drawn from *Rahema's Journey* and *A Family in Japan*, compare life for children in two contrasting environments.]

Eleale, from a Village in Tanzania, Africa   Because of a lack of economic resources, the village school is much different from yours. It could be made of mud bricks, sometimes wood, and it might have a tin or thatch roof, depending on the materials that were available. Many children walk two or more miles to get there. Often they are absent because they need to help the family with chores—or perhaps take care of babies while the adults work in the fields.

The floors of the rooms are made of dirt or cement. Rooms have desks, often in rows, perhaps a blackboard and chalk, but no pictures or photos, no videos, no computers, and no library books.

Most of the lessons are taught by the teacher, who uses a single book. Sometimes the students have their own copies, but other times they have to share. Children read, write, and learn math in Swahili or one of the other African languages. They also learn how to plant and care for tea and coffee, bushes, vegetables, fruits, and flowers. Even when they are on vacation from school, they often help weed the school garden. While not all village schools have gardens, those that do sell the fresh vegetables at the market and use the money to buy chalk, pencils, and paper. Many school children in African villages do not have these supplies because their families cannot afford them.

School children help the teacher with the daily chores, which include sweeping floors and keeping the school yard tidy. These schools cannot afford custodians to keep them neat and clean.

If the children get lunch at all, it's a large bowl of rice that they have cooked at school. Sometimes they all eat out of the same bowl.

During recess and after school they use toys that they have created out of mud, twigs, and recycled materials such as bottle caps and old tires.

Once in awhile a visitor from another part of the world stops by. Lots of people go to Africa to go on safari. Meeting these visitors is one way that the children learn about other people. Also, somebody in their village probably has a TV, which is another way they learn about other parts of the world.

Children who attend these village schools have little homework because often they have to share the textbooks and therefore cannot take them home, and their families do not have paper, pencils, magazines, or other instructional materials. Besides, when they return from school they have many chores to do—gathering wood for the fire, feeding the animals, weeding the garden, and so on.

Niko, from a City School in Japan   Most families in Japan have adequate economic resources to see that their children get educated, and they will sacrifice almost anything else to make sure that they do. For example, many Japanese families live in much smaller homes than we do and many do not own cars.

Even at a very early age, Japanese children are tested and compete for positions in the best schools. The buildings look much like ours. Students are expected to all learn the content in the same way and at the same speed. They study hard after school and on the weekends just to keep up with the pace. Many attend cram schools, where teachers called *crammers* drill them until they have learned all the skills and content expected.

Children in Japan usually go to school about eleven and a half months of the year, with a few holidays sprinkled throughout. Many children study even on holidays in order to pass the tests that allow them to continue and/or transfer to even better schools. School subjects are similar to the ones studied in other parts of the world: reading, math, science, social studies, physical education, music, and art. All of the latest instructional materials are available, and students have many opportunities for field trips as part of their science and social studies instruction. Children in Japan are strongly encouraged to take lessons in piano, dancing, and other arts and to participate in extracurricular activities such as martial arts.

Typically, Japanese children travel to their schools by foot or train. They usually wear uniforms (including hats) and carry book bags. The children have responsibility for keeping the classrooms neat and clean. These classrooms are used not only for instruction but also for eating.

Lunch might consist of the traditional foods such as rice, pickled vegetables, and sushi, or it could be something much like our lunch (e.g., spaghetti). In schools, the children wear hats and aprons when they eat (for cleanliness purposes).

Volleyball, baseball, and soccer are among the games enjoyed at recess or after school, but if it's the child's turn to help clean up the classroom and hallway, these forms of fun must wait until the tasks are done.

After school, there is plenty of homework. Children in the early grades probably would have at least an hour's worth of math and reading assignments. Japanese families are very concerned that the children complete this homework. In fact, some moms take courses so they can help their children do so. Some even come to school and take their child's place if the child is sick. Parents are very fearful that their children will get behind in their schoolwork and lose out on later educational opportunities.

After sharing the descriptions of the schools in Tanzania and in Japan, underscore the major ideas of the lesson (e.g., economic resources influence the type of education that is available; education around the world is important, etc.).

Activity

Using the word cards and Venn diagrams or comparison charts, have each table compare and contrast the Tanzanian school with the Japanese school. How are they alike? How are they different? After completing the comparison charts or Venn diagrams, ask students which imaginary student will have to make the biggest adjustment when coming to your school. Have the students discuss this question in triads and then be prepared to share their responses (with accompanying reasons) with the whole class.

Summarize

- Children around the world leave their family settings and go to places to learn with children their own age.
- Education is valued around the world.
- Economic resources play a major role in providing for quality education.

Assessment

Have each child write a journal entry explaining which school (village school in Tanzania or city school in Japan) he or she would like to visit and why. Ask students to include one question he or she still has about the school. (Option: Upper-grade mentors or volunteers could be invited to assist students in finding responses to these questions by using the Internet.)

Home Assignment

Encourage each student to share his or her journal entry with family members. Then have students share a comparison chart that you have prepared about the homework practices in the Tanzanian village school and in the Japanese city school (see Table 2 for an example). Ask families to discuss what families in your community can learn from these faraway schools and which of their ideas your school might incorporate and why. The responses should be shared in an upcoming class session.

Dear Parents,

Your child has been learning about other schools—one in a village in Tanzania and another in a city in Japan. Please encourage your child to share his or her journal entry explaining which of those two schools he or she would like to visit. Then, using the enclosed comparison chart, discuss what families can learn from these faraway schools and which of these ideas we might incorporate into our schools and why (e.g., homework policies, children participating in building cleanup). The responses will be shared in an upcoming class session. Thank you!

Sincerely,

FIGURE 10   Model Letter to Parents

Table 2 Comparison of Tanzanian and Japanese Schools

TANZANIAN VILLAGE SCHOOL	JAPANESE CITY SCHOOL
Little or no homework is assigned because children have to share textbooks so there isn't one for each student to take home at night. There are no worksheets like we use here because they are too expensive.	Every early elementary child is expected to do at least one hour of homework every night. Most children will need to do homework on the weekend as well.
Neither schools nor families have educational supplies for doing the homework. Homes do not have magazines, computers, pencils, paper, etc.	Families would sacrifice almost anything to ensure that their children receive a good education. Families make sure they have all the necessary school supplies.
Children have to help families with the chores when they return home from school.	Children either are busy with homework or taking extra lessons (e.g., art, piano, dance, etc.) after school. Parents make sure homework is completed.
Some people in the village will probably have television so children can watch it and learn about people in other parts of the world.	Television is available in the home; however, children are not allowed to watch it until all of the schoolwork is completed.

What is your reaction to these practices? Which of the practices might you consider? Why?

Lesson 9

Children's Toys and Entertainment

Resources

- Display of your children's favorite toys and/or descriptions of their favorite entertainment
- Time line
- Pictures of children's toys and entertainment across time
- Pictures of county fairs—past and present
- Pictures illustrating parlor games
- Marbles, jacks, jump rope, barrel hoop, wooden toy
- Pair of stilts
- Picture of child using stilts
- Picture of a peddler and his wares
- Pictures or objects—toy horn, pop-up action books
- Resource person—toy collector to show examples of toys that gradually became available for boys and girls
- Adult volunteers to help with demonstrations
- Individual blank Venn diagrams
- Sets of three cards for each student (for assessment)
    - Green card—Today
    - Blue card—Long ago
    - Yellow card—Both
- Copies of Figure 12: Interview Schedule

Children's Literature

Kalman, B. (1991). *Early Settler Children*. New York: Crabtree.

Kalman, B. (1992). *Early Pleasures and Pastimes*. New York: Crabtree.

Kalman, B. (1993). *Visiting a Village*. New York: Crabtree.

Kalman, B. (1997). *Nineteenth Century Girls and Women*. New York: Crabtree.

Kalman, B., & Everts, T. (1994). *A Child's Day*. New York: Crabtree.

Kalman, B., & Schimpky, D. (1995). *Old-Time Toys*. New York: Crabtree.

Lakin, P. (1995). *Play Around the World*. Woodbridge, CT: Blackbirch.

Wroble, L. (1997). *Kids in Pioneer Times*. New York: Power Kids Press.

General Comments

The emphasis of this lesson is on children's toys and entertainment in the past and how play has changed over the years. The intent is that students will begin to realize how resourceful and imaginative children of long ago really were.

General Purposes or Goals

To help students understand and appreciate: (1) changes in entertainment and toys over time; (2) how the availability of resources influences what individuals do and how they do it; and (3) trade-offs associated with modernization (e.g., imagination, creativity, socialization).

Main Ideas to Develop

- Children and their families of long ago often combined work and entertainment.
- Families of long ago made everything themselves, including toys.
- Children long ago used their imaginations in order to have fun.
- Families long ago as well as today enjoyed outings such as fairs.
- Children have always enjoyed playing with other children. (Long ago, they enjoyed races, skipping rope, and parlor games such as blind man's bluff, whereas today much of their time is spent in organized sports. Younger children also enjoy playground equipment.)
- There are places around the world where resources are limited; therefore, children's entertainment and games are still much like those enjoyed by children in America long ago.

Teaching Tips from Barbara

During the week before this lesson, we played some of the early games to prepare children for the lesson. Many of them had never played or even heard of blind man's bluff, jacks, or even marble games. If you decide to allow your students to bring their favorite toys and games to school, set specific guidelines about what is acceptable and what to do with them at school. The homework assignment to interview a parent or grandparent about games he and she had as a child was a favorite for parents (see Figure 12). Several parents mentioned that they enjoyed connecting with their child on a personal level during this assignment.

Starting the Lesson

Discuss the responses to the homework assignment. (Special Note: For this lesson, ask each student to bring his or her favorite toy to school and place it on display. This display will be used during the second part of the class session.)

Suggested Lesson Discussion

[Have two adults demonstrate husking corn. See illustration on p. 28 of *Visiting a Village.*] Long ago, life for children was very different. They spent long hours helping their families do the work needed for providing food, shelter, and clothing. Families made everything themselves, and all members needed to cooperate. Because their lives were so busy fulfilling basic needs, they often mixed work and play. Besides husking bees, there were quilting bees, apple bees, building bees, and other types of bees. Bees were really work parties to complete big jobs. At a bee, people in the community came together to help each other. After the people finished the work, they usually enjoyed a meal together. [Point out on the time line when these activities existed. Show pictures to illustrate.]

[Use the time line and pictures.] Children long ago spent a lot of time with their parents. One of their favorite outings was the county fair that took place at the end of the harvest season. Women and girls would enter their canned or baked goods in contests. Men and boys enjoyed talking about the crops and animals and participating in tall-tale competitions. Often there were horse races for entertainment. Children today often go to similar outings with their families. Today there's a wide range of entertainment available at fairs (e.g., Ferris wheels, roller coasters, live stage performances, etc.).

Children of long ago enjoyed parlor games such as blind man's bluff. In this game the person who was It put on the blindfold. Other children joined hands and skipped in a circle around It. When It called "stop," everyone stopped and stood still. It pointed at a person in the circle, who then joined It inside the circle. It tried to catch the person and identify him or her. If It was successful, the person he or she caught became It. Tag, blind man's bluff, jacks, and marbles were games enjoyed by children long ago. Children found boards and pieces of string as well as hoops from old wooden barrels to be exciting playthings. [Demonstrate playing jacks, jumping rope, rolling a barrel hoop, etc.] While children had limited resources, they used lots of imagination and creativity.

Gradually families set aside a little time for making toys for their children. For example, stilts were popular. [Show a pair of stilts. Have an adult volunteer demonstrate how they function.] Both girls and boys enjoyed them.

[Return to the time line.] Gradually adults began thinking that some toys were better suited for boys and others for girls. For example, toy soldiers, trains, and kites were considered playthings for boys, while dolls and dollhouses were toys designated for girls. In rural areas, people fashioned dolls out of local resources. For example, sometimes dolls' heads were made of dried apples. Even corn husks were used for making dolls. [Show examples.] Most of the early dolls had wooden bodies. Parents encouraged their daughters to play with dolls as a means of practicing motherhood. Girls were also expected to practice their sewing skills by making doll clothes. Long ago, dollhouses [show pictures if possible] were among the most popular and fanciest toys available. Some of the dollhouses looked like fancy homes where children dreamed of living someday.

[Return to the time line.] As more and more people came to America, things became available from outside their communities. These goods were brought by people called *peddlers* [show a picture], who would come to the villages by horse and wagon. Peddlers would come to trade their wares for homemade candles, soap, and cloth that mothers had produced on the loom. Peddlers sold everything from pots and pans to toys and books [show pop-up action books]. Their wagons were like general stores on wheels.

[If possible, invite a toy collector to visit your class and share examples illustrating the range of toys that became available: action and pop-up books, dolls, trains, children's banks, clockwork toys, optical toys (such as a kaleidoscope), chess, checkers, etc.]

Activities

After an explanation of children's entertainment and toys of the past, as a class, list those that children today still enjoy. Students will probably come to realize that while they appreciate and enjoy many of them, they seldom think about them. Instead, they participate in organized sports or use electronic toys. (During upcoming recesses or physical education periods, engage in activities that children enjoyed long ago as a way to enhance students' appreciation for the past.)

Optional   After discussing entertainment and games of the past that we hear about or experience today, turn to the display of students' toys and/or descriptions of their favorite entertainment today. As a class, determine which existed long ago and which were not in existence back then. Discuss the trade-offs associated with toys of the past and toys of today, such as creativity, imagination, socialization, and costs.

Optional   Table talk—Have each table group focus on the questions, "What would you have liked about entertainment and toys if you were a child who lived long ago?" and "What do you like about entertainment and toys today?" After the small-group discussions, have each student move to his or her preferred designated side—long ago or today. Elicit students' reasons, underscoring the trade-offs associated with each.

Summarize
- Children and families of long ago often combined work and entertainment.
- Entertainment and toys have changed over time; however, remnants of the past still exist today.
- As more resources become available, more choices are available to children; therefore, children today have more choices for toys and entertainment.

Assessment

Have each student complete a Venn diagram comparing toys and entertainment of long ago and today. Share and discuss the responses as a class.

Optional   Provide each student with a set of three cards (green card for today, blue card for long ago, and yellow card for both). Name a toy or type of entertainment and ask each student to hold up the appropriate card that corresponds with the toy or entertainment. For example:

FLASH CARD ASSESSMENT

1. Husking bee	blue card/yellow card (quilting and husking bees occur today on very rare occasions)
2. Jump rope	yellow card
3. Stilts	yellow card
4. Dollhouse	yellow card
5. Checkers	yellow card
6. Soccer	green card
7. Baseball	green card
8. Gymnastics	green card
9. Parlor games (e.g., blind man's bluff)	yellow card

Students will realize that children today have many more choices than children long ago did.

Home Assignment

Encourage each student to share his or her Venn diagram or card exercise comparing past and present toys and entertainment with a family member. Then, have students use the Interview Schedule (Figure 12) to talk to parents about toys and entertainment that they experienced as children. How were they similar to or different from those of today? If grandparents or older neighbors or family friends are available for input, students should seek their responses. Discuss the results during the next class session.

Dear Parents,

We would encourage you and your child to discuss toys and entertainment of long ago and today. Please allow your child to interview you, a grandparent, or an older neighbor or friend about this topic. An interview schedule has been provided so that the data can be shared during our next social studies discussion. Thank you for participating in your child's learning.

Sincerely,

FIGURE 11   Model Letter to Parents

INTERVIEW SCHEDULE

Name _____

Name of person interviewed _____

During what period were you a child? _____

What was your favorite type of entertainment? _____

Describe it. _____

_____

_____

What was your favorite toy? _____

Describe it. _____

_____

_____

If you were a child today, do you think it would still be your favorite? _____

Why or why not? _____

_____

_____

FIGURE 12   Interview Schedule

© 2003 by Janet Alleman and Jere Brophy from *Social Studies Excursions, K–3: Book Three*. Portsmouth, NH: Heinemann.

Lesson 10

Children as Consumers

Resources

- A collection of cereal boxes (Select examples that represent childhood as well as adult preferences. Include those that exhibit unique advertising, awards, gifts, etc.)
- Photos of cereal displays at a supermarket
- Collection of cereal advertisements from newspapers and magazines
- Video footage of cereal advertisements aimed at children
- Collection of children's magazines and sample video clips from children's TV shows illustrating the strategic places and times advertisers present their products for children
- Visual depictions of advertising techniques
- Photos or pictures of children in developing countries eating rice or other grain as cereal
- Copies of Figure 14: Data Retrieval Chart: Choices I Make With My Family

General Comments

This lesson will emphasize the role children play in making choices regarding the goods and services that their families purchase. Besides having an emphasis on economics, the lesson promotes personal efficacy as an important by-product of being informed and thus more able to make wise choices.

General Purposes or Goals

To help students understand and appreciate: (1) what it means to be a consumer; (2) how advertisers try to convince children as well as adults that their products are better than the rest; and (3) that children as well as adults make choices, and the more resources that are available, the more opportunities there are for choice making.

Main Ideas to Develop

- A consumer is one who uses goods and services.
- Children as well as adults are consumers.
- Advertising is making a product or service known and appealing to the public so people will purchase it (children as well as adults).
- Children as well as adults make choices regarding purchases.
- The more resources that are available, the more choices there are.

- Factors that influence people's choices include cost, nutritional value (for food items), personal preferences, advertisements, and recommendations from others.

Teaching Tips from Barbara

As a culminating activity, we graphed the reasons my students' families purchase the cereals that they do. When we created the graph, students who hadn't done the home assignment and talked about family choices were motivated to get the job done so they could be on the graph, too.

Starting the Lesson

Begin by discussing the results of the home assignment. Then introduce a scenario that illustrates the child's role in choice making. The scene is a family making a grocery list with cereal as one of the items. The question is, "What kind(s) shall we buy?" Other questions that surface include "Who should make the decisions?" and "On what basis should the decisions be made?" Using puppetry or a role-play, examine the role of children in this family conversation and the factors that need to be considered in making the decisions. Among those that should be addressed are cost, personal preferences, nutritional value, advertisements, and recommendations from others. During the conversation, underscore the ideas that consumers are people who use goods and services and that children as well as adults are consumers.

Suggested Lesson Discussion

[After the introductory scenario, elicit comments from the students regarding their experiences with cereal choices and consumption. Using a display of cereals and photos of stocked grocery store shelves, continue the interactive lesson, focusing on what it means to be a consumer and how important it is to be a wise one.]

[Use the examples from the display to explain and illustrate the factors that wise consumers need to consider.] Buying a cereal that family members won't eat—even if it is the most nutritious or has the best price—would not be a good decision because the product would simply sit on the shelf and ultimately go to waste.

[Examine the cereal boxes.] Price, personal preference, nutritional information, advertisements, and offers of free gifts (e.g., CD-ROMs, trinkets, etc.) are all factors that influence people's choices. [Show photos that illustrate strategies for displaying cereals in the grocery store.] Cereals most preferred by children usually are placed at their eye level (low), whereas those more popular with adults and those with less appeal (and normally with higher nutritional value) are placed higher on the shelves.

[Show magazine and newspaper advertisements as well as video clips to illustrate what cereal companies do to entice children to consider their brands and products.] Advertisers try to convince children (as well as adults) that their products (or services) are better than the rest. [Show examples of strategic places and times that advertisers present their products for children (e.g., children's magazines, children's TV shows, etc.).]

Companies use a variety of advertising techniques to convince their audiences to buy their products [provide a visual display illustrating these techniques]: bandwagon (everyone's doing it); testimonial from a famous person (assumes that others will buy the product out of admiration); transfer (present the product in a beautiful setting to encourage the buyer to associate the feeling evoked by the picture with the product); scientific (create the impression of superiority by using scientific terms or statistics); "just plain folks" (talking down to people or humbling); "more for your money" (claims that consumers will save money or will get more for their money by buying this brand); symbols or logos (uses a symbol or catchy phrase to represent the product); "weasel words" (uses words like *helps, looks like*); compliment the consumer ("you deserve the best," "you are most important"); and appeal (focuses on the consumer's feelings or values).

It is very important to become a wise consumer, to understand how to make wise choices, and not to be easily influenced by advertising. In countries like America, we have a lot of resources, and the more resources that are available, the more choices there are. In developing parts of the world, children as well as adults have limited resources. [Show photos and pictures of children in a village in Tanzania, Indonesia, or Mongolia.] Limited transportation as well as money preclude choices. Families in those countries would feel fortunate to have rice or other grain as cereal. They typically would eat it for more than one of their daily meals if available.

Children in the United States frequently participate in making other choices regarding purchases. [Elicit examples from students regarding other choices they help make (e.g., which clothes or toys to buy, which foods to order when eating at a restaurant, which videos to rent, etc.).] As you grow up and become adults, you will become even more knowledgeable about what to buy and you will make many more decisions that involve much larger amounts of money (e.g., buying a car, renting or buying a home, etc.).

Activity

Give each table group one of the cereal boxes and have the group plan a short skit explaining what to consider before purchasing that particular product. Provide a simple outline for the plan and presentation. For example:

1. Two questions we have about this cereal:

   _____

   _____

2. What we like about this cereal:
3. Besides the need to be willing to eat the cereal, what other things do we need to consider?

Model an enactment. Then elicit volunteers for additional enactments. Debrief each presentation using the main ideas of the lesson. If time is limited, have students present in small groups.

Summarize

- Children as well as adults are consumers who make choices.
- The more resources that are available, the more choices there are.
- Factors that influence people's choices include cost, personal preferences, nutritional value (for food items), advertisements, recommendations from others, and so on.

Assessment

Have students participate in a "thumbs up/thumbs down" quiz. After each item, elicit justification for the response.

1. Thumbs up   We are all consumers because we use goods and services.
2. Thumbs up   Even children need to learn how to be wise consumers.
3. Thumbs up   Advertisers try to influence the choices we make.
4. Thumbs down   Advertisements (including TV commercials) always tell the whole story.
5. Thumbs down   In making our food choices, we need to consider only what we like.
6. Thumbs down   It is usually not important to consider the cost of a good or service.
7. Thumbs up   As children grow into adulthood, they will gain more information about the goods and services they purchase and therefore can make even wiser decisions.
8. Thumbs up   As children grow up, they make choices and decisions that often involve lots of money.
9. Thumbs down   The more resources we have, the fewer choices we can make.
10. Thumbs up   Children can help their families make wise choices about goods such as cereals and toys.

Have each student write a letter to his or her parents that focuses on the factors that children as well as adults need to consider in order to make wise decisions about the goods they purchase. Provide word cards or a list of key words on the display board as cues to encourage students to use more articulated vocabulary to express their ideas.

Home Assignment

Have each student read his or her letter to an adult or older sibling, engage in a family discussion about the importance of making wise choices, and then complete a data retrieval chart (see Figure 14). Encourage students to return the chart to school for sharing with their peers.

Dear Parents,

We have been learning about children as consumers. Your child has prepared a letter to read to you about wise choice making. Please discuss the contents of the letter and then, as a family, complete the enclosed Data Retrieval Chart. We ask that it be returned to school so that we can discuss the response during social studies tomorrow. Thank you!

Sincerely,

FIGURE 13   Model Letter to Parents

DATA RETRIEVAL CHART

Choices I Make with My Family

List the choices about goods or services that you as a child help make.	What factors are involved in the choices?
Example: Videos to rent	a. Are they appropriate for my age group? b. Is there time to watch the video(s)? (Have I finished my homework?) c. Does our family have the money for renting videos? d. Is there someone in the family who can return the video(s) on time?
1.	a. b. c.
2.	a. b. c.
3.	a. b. c.
4.	a. b. c.

FIGURE 14   Data Retrieval Chart

© 2003 by Janet Alleman and Jere Brophy from *Social Studies Excursions, K–3: Book Three*. Portsmouth, NH: Heinemann.

Lesson 11

Adults Provide for Children's Needs

Resources

- Photos, pictures, signs, objects that illustrate how parents or other adults (e.g., teacher, doctor, dentist, government officials) ensure that children's needs are satisfied
- Photos of local agencies that help satisfy children's needs in emergencies
- Photos of adults whose jobs include helping children (e.g., school nurse, police officer)
- Panel of local adults whose jobs involve meeting children's needs (school nurse, dentist, school bus driver, etc.)
- Newspaper articles that highlight concerns associated with child safety and security
- Basket of possibilities for Activity—strips of paper that identify people, places, and types of childhood activities that require protection and assistance (e.g., school nurse = people, food bank = place, and need to wear seatbelt when riding in a car or truck = activity) (see Figure 15 for suggestions)

General Comments

The thrust of this lesson is on protection for children and the roles and responsibilities of adults to ensure that our children's needs are provided for and that they are safe. The children will be reminded to use what they learn to help themselves. They also will find out what they can do if their needs (including security) are not being met.

General Purposes or Goals

To help students understand and appreciate: (1) what adults are expected to do for children; (2) how government helps adults figure out their responsibilities in providing for children's needs (e.g., food, shelter, clothing, safety, etc.); and (3) their role in being responsible for using what they learn in order to take care of themselves.

Main Ideas to Develop

- One of the main roles of parents is to provide the basic needs for their children. These needs include food, shelter, clothing, security/safety, good health, and education.

- Laws are written by the government to help adults figure out how to protect and teach children (e.g., fireproof clothing, safe toys, traffic control).
- There are adults in the community besides parents whose jobs include making sure that children's needs are satisfied.

Teaching Tips from Barbara

Be aware that this lesson can bring out some personal information from children that will need to be handled carefully. Be sure to be extra sensitive to children who live in a nontraditional setting. I chose to spend less time focusing on the ideas about children not getting what they needed. Instead, I mainly discussed things that children need and who provides for those needs.

Starting the Lesson

Discuss the results of the home assignment. Display a series of artifacts including pictures, photos, and signs (e.g., stop sign, bicycle path, pajamas with inflammable label, food with inspection seal, toys in package with inspection seal, small toy with warning label, etc.) that reveal ways in which the United States government attempts to provide for and protect our children. As a class, examine the examples and together list ways children are provided for and protected. Encourage responses that extend beyond the examples exhibited.

Suggested Lesson Discussion

One of parents' major responsibilities is to provide for their children's needs, which include food, shelter, clothing, love and affection, safety, and security. Sometimes there are unusual circumstances and parents are unable to provide for their children. In those situations, families need to get help from local agencies (e.g., food bank, Salvation Army, local churches, etc.). These circumstances may be caused by a flood, fire, the loss of a job, parental illness, or other factors. Some parents cannot take care of their children, so they seek help by finding other adults who will serve as foster parents, or guardians. There might even be situations when children need to talk with their teachers, school social workers, and/or police officers when their needs are not being satisfied. [You as the teacher will want to delete or expand this section based on your students and the local situation. Also, be alert to other places in the curriculum where this content can be integrated meaningfully.]

All children need other adults besides their parents to provide for them, teach them, and keep them safe. Child care centers and K–12 schools are regulated by the government to ensure that the buildings are safe and comfortable and that they provide safe food and water, appropriate instructional materials and equipment, and caregivers and teachers who have the required education and training. [Show photos, pictures, and artifacts to illustrate.]

[Ask students to list other adults besides parents who help them satisfy their needs and protect them. Post the list on the board. Your list might include family members and relatives, baby-sitter, special teachers, dentist, doctor, school bus driver, firefighter, police officer, etc. (Here is an opportunity to invite a panel of local adults whose jobs focus on helping to provide for the needs of children, including good health, safety, and security. The panel members should briefly explain what they do to ensure that children's needs are met. If they chose this work because of something they experienced during their own childhoods, they should incorporate that into their remarks. They should also explain how their work is regulated by the government.)]

Besides all the people and organizations that focus on aspects of childhood, there are many volunteers to help children. There also are many video and book resources to educate them so that they will become more responsible as they grow up. Additionally, every year, June is designated as Safety Month, to remind families and other adults to educate and protect their children. [Show newspaper articles that highlight concerns associated with safety and security and discuss one or more of them.] A recent article in a local newspaper was titled "Don't Wait: Learn How to Protect Your Kids." It emphasized ways to protect children, including buckling up in vehicles, keeping poisons out of reach, learning first aid, having a fire escape plan and practicing it, handling foods properly (e.g., washing hands often, not eating raw meats, etc.), preventing access to weapons in the home, and teaching children how to call for help.

Activity

Place class members in pairs. Have each pair select from the "basket of possibilities" a person, place, or activity that addresses childhood needs, including protection/safety (person = doctor, dentist, teacher; places = social services, food bank, Salvation Army; activity = wearing a seat belt, making sure any weapons in the home are stored securely and not available to children). (See Figure 15 for suggestions on what to include in the basket.) Have each pair discuss how that person, place, or activity helps children. What do they as children need to remember about it? Pairs should be prepared to share with the class. Have each pair (with assistance from upper-grade mentors, if possible) create through pictures and words one entry (reflecting a selection from the basket of possibilities) for a class booklet titled *People, Places, and Activities That Provide for Our Childhood Needs.* Make copies of this booklet for each child to bring home and share with his or her family for the home assignment.

Summarize

- Parents and other adults and organizations help ensure that children's needs are satisfied.
- These needs include food, shelter, clothing, security, safety, good health, and education.
- Laws written by the government help adults figure out how to protect and teach children.
- If these laws are broken, there are provisions to find other people and places to help our children.

Examples of people, places, and activities that you might want to include:

People

    Doctor, pediatrician

    Dentist

    Nurse

    Social worker

    Police officer

    School bus driver

Places

    Habitat for Humanity

    Crisis center

    Salvation Army

    St. Vincent de Paul Society

    Police station

    Local church

    Fire station

    YWCA/YMCA

Activities

    Making sure foods have been properly prepared and stored

    Wearing a seat belt

    Washing hands frequently

    Checking out the fire escape plan

    Making sure that no weapons are accessible to children

    Making sure poisons and medicines are out of reach of children

    Posting telephone numbers to use in case of emergency

    Examining nightclothes to make sure they contain fire retardants

FIGURE 15   Basket of Possibilities

Assessment

Have students complete "I learned" statements, using the word wall to encourage the use of big ideas and show how different words are spelled.

SAMPLE STATEMENTS

1. I learned that parents help satisfy our basic needs by _____
   _____
   _____.

2. I learned that the government writes laws to help adults remember to
   _____
   _____
   _____.

3. I learned that there are many adults including _____, _____,
   and _____who help children by _____.

4. I learned that one very important adult besides my parents is
   _____ because he or she can help me by _____.

5. When I need help, I can talk to _____.

Home Assignment

Encourage each student to share and discuss the booklet titled *People, Places, and Activities That Provide for Childhood Needs*. Then, have family members select one idea from the booklet that they will spend more time on or learn more about and explain why. They can use the following sample format for recording their answer. Have the students return the responses to school for an upcoming class discussion.

> As a family we need to spend more time on developing our fire escape plan because we have recently moved into a new apartment.

> As a family we need to make sure our children wash their hands more frequently because it's flu season and lots of germs are spread by our bodies.

Dear Parents,

We encourage your child to share the class booklet titled *People, Places, and Activities That Provide for Childhood Needs*. Then, as a family, select one idea from the booklet that you will spend more time on or learn more about and explain why. Please write down your answer and return it to school so that we can use it during social studies as part of our discussion. Thank you!

Sincerely,

FIGURE 16   Model Letter to Parents

Lesson 12

Childhood Talents and Interests

Resources
- Local individuals who share special interests and talents
- Materials for the cube activity (photos of each child, crayons, paste, markers, construction paper, boxes or strong paper to make them with)

Children's Literature

Maze, S. (1999). *I Want to Be Series: Chef, Astronaut, Dancer, Engineer, Firefighter, Veterinarian*. San Diego: Harcourt Brace.

Rachelin, A. (1992). *Famous Children, Mozart*. Hauppauge, NY: Barron's.

Sadler, M. (1996). *Inventors*. New York: Harper Collins.

Wood, R. (1995). *Great Inventions*. Sydney, Australia: Weldon Owen.

[Note: Select other children's literature sources that match the historical or contemporary individuals you wish to emphasize in this lesson.]

General Comments

The intent of this lesson is to generate a sense of "I can." Beginning with children's talents and likes can be a good way to build interest in reading and writing, enhance a sense of self-worth, and open their eyes to possibilities for careers and avocations. Many careers involve making a difference for others.

General Purposes or Goals

To help students: (1) understand and appreciate that often the interests people have as children help them decide what they will be when they grow up; (2) understand and appreciate that the talents and interests they have can be used to make a difference in the world—to make our world better; and (3) develop a sense of efficacy.

Main Ideas to Develop
- Childhood interests and talents (sometimes even difficulties) can contribute to careers and avocations as adults.
- Interests and talents are powerful points for entering the world of possibilities for pursuing careers and avocations.
- Often childhood interests and talents, when developed, can make the world a better place.

Teaching Tips from Barbara

In school, children often spend a lot of time focusing on things that they can't do or are trying to learn to do. One of the best parts of this lesson is that you can spend a good amount of time talking about students' strengths. Once you've talked about their strengths, it's quite natural to flow into a discussion about possible jobs or careers, even with the younger children. I also made sure to allow plenty of "chatting time" for my students to talk with one another about themselves. Along with highlighting Thomas Edison, try to discover some athletes, businesspeople, musicians, dancers, artists, and so on that are familiar or from your local area to use as examples.

Starting the Lesson

Begin the lesson by discussing the responses to the home assignment. Then ask students to think about the kinds of things they like to do and the kinds of things they are good at. Share your story regarding your interests and talents. Highlight how you decided to become a teacher—and the interests and unique talents you bring to the profession.

Suggested Lesson Discussion

An interest is something you like to do or learn about, such as providing learning opportunities for children, working with computers, taking care of animals, and so on. One person's interest in taking care of animals might lead to becoming a veterinarian, another's interest in helping take care of young people might lead to becoming a pediatrician.

Many individuals' interests and talents from the past have made a difference for other people in the world. One example I would like to share is a children's book that characterizes Thomas Edison as a child and tells how he used his early interests throughout his life to invent many things that we enjoy today. As a young boy, Edison was very curious, not unlike many of you. He was always asking questions, experimenting, and trying new things. For example, one time his mother couldn't find him. When she finally did, he was in the barn sitting on a hen's nest, trying to see if he could get the eggs to hatch.

Edison was always trying to figure out how things worked. He asked adults all sorts of questions. He was always trying to fix things. He also built machines that people had never thought of before. Soon, he was selling some of his inventions (phonograph and machine that showed moving pictures). With the money he made, he built a special building called a *laboratory* where he could work on his inventions.

One of his ideas was creating a practical incandescent lightbulb. He drew all kinds of pictures that illustrated how he thought it would work. He'd often work all day and all night to figure it out. He continued to ask other people for suggestions. It took him almost two years, but he finally got his lightbulb to work. Can you imagine what life would be like without Thomas Edison's invention?

[Other individuals to showcase during this lesson might include Louis Braille, Wolfgang Mozart, Eleanor Roosevelt, or people that connect to your curriculum. Examine the goals and big ideas from other content areas and special initiatives you are expected to address to determine what selections could provide for meaningful integration. For example, Thomas Edison might fit nicely with the goals of a science unit, whereas Tiger Woods might work well with the multicultural component. Then, introduce one or more local contemporaries whose special interests and talents from childhood are contributing to making the world a better place. The range of possibilities might include a teenager who has displayed unusual talent (e.g., soloist, pianist, dancer, etc.) or a retiree who as a child loved wood carving and is using that talent to make toys for poor children. Encourage your guest(s) to share their life stories with an emphasis on what individuals can do during childhood to pursue their interests and refine their abilities (e.g., read, work with adults to learn more, practice, observe others with similar interests and talents, etc.).]

[If time permits, use the I Want to Be series to push students' thinking about the range of possibilities open to them. *I Want to Be an Engineer* presents careers that children hear about, but cannot visualize (because they rarely if ever get opportunities to observe engineers at work). Show the pictures from the book.] There are many kinds of engineers who will shape the world during the twenty-first century. They work with plans, models, and laboratory testing. If you are curious, like to build things, are interested in taking things apart to see how they work, like to solve problems, and are particularly interested in math and science, you might want to become an engineer. [At the conclusion of the interactive discussion, explain that you will make the book and other similar ones available for students to take home and discuss with their families. Some of their parents might occupy the roles described in the books, and if so, might be invited to talk about their work with the class.]

I Want to Be a Dancer was written for the children who love music and dance and have special interests and talents in the arts. Some of you might be taking private lessons. Not only does dancing provide great opportunities for exercise, but it might become your career. Or, it could become your leisure activity as an adult. Some of you may decide to be a regular attendee of dance performances as an adult. That would be considered your entertainment. [Use the pictures to explain how children get started in this avocation/vocation, the types of dance that individuals pursue, the types of education and training that are needed, how they can become more informed, etc. Encourage students with these interests to share the book with their families. You might ask parents to give you feedback regarding the conversation that centered around this book and the main ideas of the lesson.]

Activity

Have children work in pairs to list characteristics that the talented individuals discussed durring the lesson had in common (e.g., were excited about their activity, worked long and hard, had adult teachers, practiced, read about their interest or talent, never gave up, etc.). As a class, make a list of all of these characteristics.

Summarize

- Childhood interests and talents are windows to adulthood.
- Often childhood interests and talents become adult professions or avocations.
- These interests and talents frequently result in making the world a better place (e.g., helping others, providing enjoyment to others, etc.).

Assessment

Have each child create a cube with one side illustrating each of the following:

Top—the child's photo

Bottom—drawing of the individual that the child imagines he or she will become

Sides:

1. What I am interested in and like to do
2. A talent that I have
3. How I can use my talent or interest to help others
4. Characteristics of a famous scientist or artist that I admire and would like to develop

Ask students to explain how their interests as children can help them decide what they will be when they grow up and/or how their talents and interests can be used to make a difference in the world.

Home Assignment

Have students discuss with their families the childhood interests and talents of the adults they learned about in class and how they use their talents today in the workplace or in helping others on a volunteer basis. Then have each student talk about his or her interests and talents (using the cube) and how these might provide some possible direction for adulthood.

Dear Parents,

We have been discussing childhood interests and talents. Please talk with your child about your childhood interests and talents and how you use them today in the workplace or in helping others on a volunteer basis. Then, talk with your child about his or her interests and talents and how they might provide some possible direction for adulthood. Your ideas will be shared during an upcoming social studies lesson. Thank you.

Sincerely,

FIGURE 17   Model Letter to Parents

Lesson 13

Children Can Make a Difference

Resources

- Word card—Citizenship
- Pictures of citizenship being practiced at home, in the neighborhood, and at school
- Photo of Justin Lebo (p. 51 in *It's Our World Too*)
- Photo of James Ale (p. 74 in *It's Our World Too*)
- Sample copy of a petition
- Display of brief descriptions of possible class "Children Can Make a Difference" projects
- Copies of a survey to elicit family support for class projects (see Figure 18 for example)

Children's Literature

Hoose, P. (1993). *It's Our World Too*. Boston: Little, Brown, & Co.

General Comments

The focus of this lesson is on citizenship, underscoring the idea that even as a child, one can assist in making the world a better place. The range of possibilities is unlimited, beginning with one's family and extending to the community and, in some instances, the world. This lesson will address the what, why, and how of getting involved.

General Purposes or Goals

To help students: (1) develop an understanding of and appreciation for what it means to be a good citizen; and (2) learn the what, why, and how of age-appropriate social actions that they can undertake in their lives outside of school.

Main Ideas to Develop

- Even children can practice good citizenship, which includes being responsible, helping others, and in small ways making the world a better place.
- Children and adults together can give time and sometimes money to promote a cause, provide a service, or work to solve a problem.

Teaching Tips from Barbara

The students were very interested in the real-world examples that I used to begin the lesson. They found the information very motivating for their own fund-raising challenge. We brainstormed a list of possible charities and activities that we could get involved in. Then, the list went home to the families for voting. Be sure to check into the charity or project before you get your class involved. Not all projects turn out to be valuable for school learning purposes. The simplest one we did involved collecting spare change for a nearby shelter. Other, more elaborate projects included selling candy and popcorn and collecting canned goods.

Starting the Lesson

Begin the lesson by reviewing the results of the home assignment. Then ask the students what *citizenship* means. Post the word. After listing their responses on the board, underscore the idea that citizenship includes being responsible and concerned for others. Some of the first places children learn to practice citizenship are at home, in the neighborhood, and at school. (Show pictures to illustrate.) As a class, create a chart listing examples of citizenship that the students have observed or practiced in these arenas.

After discussing citizenship in the categories of home, neighborhood, and school and listing examples, explain that this lesson will emphasize citizenship in the community.

Suggested Lesson Discussion

During this lesson, you will hear two real-life vignettes drawn from *It's Our World Too*. While these children were just a couple of years older than you, we can be thinking ahead and with a little bit of assistance from high school students or our families, we might be able to start a similar project soon.

Justin Lebo *It's Our World Too* (p. 49) [Retold here.]

[Show photo] Since he was ten, he's been building bikes out of used parts that he finds from old junkers. He gives the rebuilt bikes to less fortunate kids whose families can't afford to buy them.

It all started when he went to a garage sale with his mother and he found an old bike for $6.50. His mother helped him load it into the trunk and off they went. He and his father repaired it and it looked brand-new.

Soon Justin forgot about the bike. It wasn't nearly as good as his racing one. However, one day he and his mother went to another yard sale and he got another one and fixed it up, too. Then he realized he wasn't riding either one of them, but he enjoyed the challenge of making something new and useful out of something old and broken.

He thought about what he should do with those bikes. He remembered that when he was younger he used to live near a home for boys whose families couldn't care for them for one reason or another. He found the name of the home in a phone book and offered to donate the repaired bikes.

When Justin and his mother took the bikes to the home, you can just imagine how excited the boys were! Of course, Justin realized there was one problem. Not every boy could have one.

This really bothered Justin. In fact, when he got home, he called the boys home to find out how many boys lived there. He was determined to build enough bikes so every boy had one. Justin and his mother spent most of that summer hunting for cheap bikes. His father spent lots of time helping him repair them.

Then a wonderful thing happened! A neighbor wrote a letter to the local newspaper describing Justin's great project and how he was practicing citizenship in his community. The result was that lots of people got involved by donating old bikes, giving him money to buy parts, and helping him on his project. Since that time, Justin's project has extended and he has brought joy to many kids in his community. The results have made Justin very happy as well.

James Ale *It's Our World Too* (p. 68) [Retold here]

[Show photo] When James was nine, he saw his friend get hit by a car when they were playing ball in the street. It made him wonder, "Why should we have to play in the street when kids in nicer areas of the town have parks?"

He was angry and very sad. His friend wouldn't have gotten hurt if he'd had a safe place to play. As James was thinking about this, he began to look for a possible site for a park. Suddenly it dawned on him. There was a small field right behind the water plant. They could have a playground at one end for the little kids and a basketball court at the other end. It could have some lights. Everybody could use it.

After talking it over with his father and being cautioned that this project would cost money, he decided that in order to make it happen, he would have to plan carefully and be persistent. Soon he telephoned the mayor's office for an appointment. The mayor's secretary took the information, but James worried that she didn't pay much attention because he was a kid. Later the mayor did call him back, but again James felt that she was treating him like a kid. He needed to figure out a way to get her to take him seriously. He went to his computer and typed out a petition calling for a new park, then took it around the neighborhood seeking signatures.

[Show sample petition.] Many people scoffed and made such comments as, "So who's going to listen to you?" and "Sure man, you're gonna get a park!" Even so, he convinced fifty kids to sign.

With his fifty signatures in hand, he called the mayor again and got an appointment. He explained the local situation and described the accident caused by playing in the street. With the help of his parents, he'd done his homework, described his proposed site for the park, and then gave the mayor the petition with fifty signatures of kids who supported his idea. He didn't criticize the mayor or blame the town. Instead, he had a positive plan of action. The mayor responded. Soon the town council and adult members of the community were involved. People expressed their ideas in the local newspaper. Every few days he'd call the mayor's office to see if he could help in any way. He was always polite.

Finally, his work paid off. A council meeting was held and the members voted for the creation of the park. A nine-year-old's proposal (with assistance from adults) had been accepted.

These boys (Justin and James) had certain things in common: Each had a plan; they both found adults as well as other children to help them; they stayed focused on what they wanted to accomplish; they brought pleasure to others; and they enjoyed helping others. [List these characteristics on the board.]

Activity

Have table groups select one of the stories (Justin or James) and plan how they would explain the story to their families, making sure they tell how it shows children practicing citizenship. Role-play and discuss the big ideas associated with each story.

Summarize

- Good citizenship is being responsible and helping others.
- Good citizenship is giving time and sometimes money to make our world a better place.
- You do not have to wait until you are an adult to practice good citizenship.

Assessment

Introduce students to the letters to the editor column in the community and/or school newspaper. Explain that this column provides space for school and community members to share ideas and opinions about things that are important to them. Prior to the individual assessment, designate time for table talk, having students discuss the range of ideas they have for making a difference in their community. Indicate that you want each student to write a short paragraph and draw a picture that informs and encourages readers to realize that kids too can make a difference (upper-grade mentors could be helpful). Examples should represent how they, individually or as a class, would be willing to make a difference. The products should be submitted to the local/school community newspaper with the expectation that at least some will be published. The others should be displayed in a selected public place.

Explain to the students that while Justin and James were a couple of years older and their projects might be difficult at this age, with the assistance from their families and other community volunteers, you will launch a class project so they too can experience "making a difference." Create a survey for families that lists student ideas represented in the assessment products and/or other possible projects, such as (1) collecting used greeting cards and submitting them to a children's organization such as St. Jude's that recycles and sells them to earn money for its hospital; (2) participating in a walk-a-thon and raising money for a specified organization;

SURVEY

Our class wants to show our community how children can make a difference. We would like you to help us. Please rank order the projects listed below, with 1 being your first preference (the one you would be most interested in helping with), 2 being your second choice, and so on.

_____ (Idea suggested as a part of table talk)

_____ (Idea suggested as a part of table talk)

_____ Collect greeting cards for a children's organization that recycles and sells them to earn money for its hospital.

_____ Participate in a walk-a-thon to raise money for an organization that our class will select.

_____ Spend time with us at a nearby extended care facility by reading, singing, and making art projects with the residents.

If you have other suggestions, please include them here.

Thank you!

FIGURE 18   Sample Making a Difference Survey

(3) planning for and spending time at a nearby extended care facility by reading, singing, or making art projects with the residents. (See Figure 18.) Explain to students that with the help of their families, they will choose a project to work on.

Home Assignment

Encourage each student to discuss with family members what he or she learned from Justin and James regarding how kids can make a difference and to share his or her ideas for making a difference as a class or individually. Then as a family, they should complete the survey and return it to school so the class project focusing on children making a difference can be put into action.

Dear Parents,

We have been learning about being good citizens in our community and how even children can make a difference. Your child is prepared to share what he or she has learned about this topic, including ideas that she or he has for doing something locally. In order to have this experience, we would like you to participate. Please complete the enclosed survey and return it to school. We hope to begin our class project soon. Thank you!

Sincerely,

FIGURE 19   Model Letter to Parents

Lesson 14

....

Childhood: Review

Resources

- Students' home assignments from entire unit
- Student journals
- Student time lines
- Other student artifacts created during the unit
- Children's literature sources
- Photographs and pictures used during the unit
- Open-ended statements for the review/lesson
- Student guests (Invite a class that has not experienced the Childhood unit. The students will have an opportunity to learn from their peers who have studied childhood.)

General Comments

To conclude this unit, the students will invite a class that has not studied childhood to come see what your students have learned about this cultural universal. The session will give your students an opportunity to experience authentic assessment and at the same time give another class an opportunity to learn about childhood.

General Purposes or Goals

To provide students with: (1) an opportunity to revisit major understandings associated with childhood that they have been exposed to during the unit; and (2) the opportunity to share with others what they have been learning.

Main Ideas to Develop

- Childhood includes the early stages of development in every individual's life.
- Children everywhere experience many physical, behavioral, and intellectual changes in their early years.
- Childhood is universal.
- Children everywhere go through a series of changes in their development (from infancy to adolescence) and they experience many changes physically, emotionally, behaviorally, intellectually, and so on.
- While children all over the world are alike in many ways, each one is unique (e.g., fingerprints, footprints, voice, cells in the body, face, the way he or she thinks, feelings about things, talents, etc.).

- Prejudice is a negative opinion formed without knowing all of the facts.
- Discrimination is treating someone badly because she or he is different from you.
- Even as young school children, we can help get rid of discrimination.
- Children's lives around the world are alike in many ways, yet different in other ways. Differences in children's lives are based on culture, geographic conditions, economic resources, personal choices, and other factors.
- Children around the world all have birthdays, although they may have very different celebration customs than ours.
- There are places in the world where birth dates go unnoticed and instead people have group birthdays. Each person simply becomes one year older at the same time (e.g., Chinese New Year).
- There are places in the world where a single special day (such as All Saints Day) is the occasion for celebrating everyone's birthday.
- People all over the world celebrate major happenings in their lives.
- Many families celebrate when a boy or girl is no longer a child.
- Some "coming of age" celebrations are religious.
- The age at which a person becomes an adult varies around the world.
- When a child comes of age, it means he or she has taken an important step toward growing up. A young adult has both new rights and new responsibilities.
- In pioneer times, children in America worked to help support their families (for example, many children were responsible for farm chores).
- Later, some children worked as apprentices to learn from other adults skills that their parents didn't have.
- Still later, some children in America worked in factories to help support their families; however, today there are laws against this.
- In some parts of the developing world, children are still allowed to work in the fields and factories to support themselves and their families.
- Children in America are guaranteed the right to an education that extends through high school. Going to school is considered to be the work of children.
- Pioneer school children led very different lives than those of children today.
- Education was considered a luxury in pioneer times.
- Education was a community effort in pioneer times.
- Early schools were built by members of the community, relied on local building materials, and employed local people as teachers.

- Early schools offered few instructional materials and the instructional practices were limited.
- There are many children throughout the world who still help their families by doing after-school chores.
- When children go to school, they leave their family settings and go to places to learn with children their own age.
- Children travel to school in different ways (e.g., walk, ride a bus, take a train, ride in a car, ride a bicycle, etc.).
- In most countries the government pays for schools, using tax money collected from people in the community.
- School is important everywhere in the world.
- Some schools have lots of classrooms, books, equipment, and other resources while others have little. In fact, in some places, because of the lack of economic resources, lessons may take place out-of-doors.
- In some parts of the world, children have to help their families satisfy their basic needs; therefore, they are not able to attend school regularly.
- Children and their families of long ago often combined work and entertainment.
- Families of long ago made everything themselves, including toys.
- Children long ago used their imaginations in order to have fun.
- Families long ago as well as today enjoyed outings such as fairs.
- Children have always enjoyed playing with other children. (Long ago, they enjoyed races, skipping rope, and parlor games such as blind man's bluff, whereas today much of their time is spent in organized sports. Younger children also enjoy playground equipment.)
- There are places around the world where resources are limited; therefore, children's entertainment and games are still much like those enjoyed by children in America long ago.
- A consumer is one who uses goods and services.
- Children as well as adults everywhere are consumers.
- Advertising is making a product or service known and appealing to the public so people will purchase it. (Advertisers try to convince children as well as adults that their products and services are better than the rest.)
- Children as well as adults make choices.
- The more resources that are available, the more choices there are.
- Factors that influence peoples' choices include cost, nutritional value (if food), personal preferences, advertisements, and recommendations from others.

- One of the main roles of parents is to provide the basic needs for their children. These needs include food, shelter, clothing, security/safety, good health, and education.
- Laws are written by the government to help adults figure out how to protect and teach children (e.g., fireproof clothing, safe toys, traffic control).
- There are adults in the community besides parents whose specific jobs include making sure children's needs are satisfied.
- Childhood interests and talents (sometimes even difficulties) can contribute to careers or avocations as adults.
- Interests and talents are powerful points for entering the "world of possibilities" for pursuing careers and avocations.
- Often childhood interests and talents, when developed, can make the world a better place.
- Even children can practice good citizenship, which includes being responsible, helping others, and in small ways making the world a better place.
- Children and adults together can give time and sometimes money to promote a cause, provide a service, or work to solve a problem.

Teaching Tips from Barbara

The format included in the review lends itself nicely to group discussion, pair and share, or perhaps even sharing with another class or an older student. If you work with another class, your children can take on the role of the teacher, instructing another set of students.

Starting the Lesson

Begin the lesson by reviewing the results of the home assignment. Additional class time over the next several weeks will be needed for planning and implementing the "Children Can Make a Difference" project. For the assessment, arrange for the participation of upper-elementary mentors or students from a primary-grade class that hasn't studied childhood. In advance, collect materials from the daily authentic assessments that seemed most important, yielded a depth of understanding, or appeared most challenging. Place the materials at "stations" around the room. Provide student pairs or small groups with a designated guest and a set of open-ended statements to guide their sharing (making mini-presentations to the guests, who will listen and ask questions). The corresponding instructional materials (e.g., time lines, children's literature, pictures, student work, etc.) that were used during the previous lessons should be at the appropriate sites. As part of the preplanning, decide how many sites each pair or group should visit and how much time should be allocated for each mini-presentation at the site (e.g., for

Lesson 1, provide pictures of children doing a range of activities and have the students at the center explain which ones show things that all children have in common, etc. Include the Thumbs Up, Thumbs Down assessment from the lesson.

EXAMPLES OF OPEN-ENDED STATEMENTS TO GUIDE THE SHARING

1. Children around the world have many things in common, which include: _____

    _____.

2. In certain ways, childhood around the world is different because

    _____.

    Examples of these differences include: _____

    _____.

3. The story of children's toys and entertainment in the past includes:

    _____

    _____.

4. In places around the world where resources are limited, children's play and entertainment is _____

    _____.

5. Children's past and present play and entertainment in America are similar in the following ways: _____

    _____;

    they are different in the following ways: _____

    _____.

6. Examples of childhood interests and talents that contribute to careers or lifelong leisure activities include stories such as: _____

    _____.

7. Children all over the world have the same basic needs. These include: _____

    _____.

8. Examples of how different children satisfy their needs include:

    _____

    _____.

9. Key points about children's work in the past include: _____

    _____.

10. In some parts of the developing world even today children still work in fields and factories because _____

    _____.

11. Pioneer schools were different than ours today in the following ways:

_____

_____ .

12. People all over the world celebrate major happenings in their lives. Examples of these "rites of passage" include: _____

_____ .

13. Important points about school children around the world include:

_____ .

_____ .

14. We learned many important things about children around the world and how they celebrate birthdays. These include: _____

_____ .

15. There are parts of the world where birth dates go unnoticed and instead people _____

_____ .

16. All children are unique. By that we mean _____

_____ .

17. Even children can practice good citizenship. By that we mean

_____

_____ .

18. In small ways, even as children, we can make the world a better place. Examples include: _____

_____ .

19. Examples of government regulations that help children include:

_____

_____ .

20. Children make lots of choices. These include: _____

_____ .

21. Children can become more wise consumers by_____

_____ .

As the classroom teacher, you will want to clarify and enhance student responses as needed. If time allows, you might invite peer audience members to ask questions and/or share the most important things they learned.

Unit 2: Money

Introduction

· ·

To help you think about money as a cultural universal and begin to plan your teaching, we have provided a list of questions that address some of the big ideas developed in our unit plans (see Figure 1). The questions focus on what we believe to be the most important ideas for children to learn about money. These include the following: money is a medium of exchange, needed in all but the simplest and most isolated societies; several denominations of coins and currency are needed to make it convenient for people to compile exact amounts or make change; before the idea of a medium of exchange was invented, people had to rely on trading (barter); money eliminates several problems associated with trading and makes economic exchanges much easier; early forms of money (such as wampum or precious stones) were less convenient to store and use than more modern coins and paper money; American coins and bills include a representation of a past president or other significant American on one side and an American symbol on the other side, words and numbers indicating the value of the coin or bill, and other material such as slogans, information about the depicted person, and information about when and where the money was manufactured; money is made in factories (mints) run by the federal government; banks not only provide safekeeping for money but also pay interest on accounts and provide loans, checking accounts, credit card accounting, and other financial services; budgets are plans for managing finances (and in particular, keeping spending within one's means); writing checks and using credit cards allow people to transfer money without having to exchange bills and coins, but they need to keep track of these transactions because the money

1. Today we're going to talk about money. What is money?

2. Why are there so many kinds of money? There are twenty-dollar bills, ten-dollar bills, quarters, pennies, and so on. Why is that?

3. Long, long ago, there was no need for money. Why was that?

4. Long, long ago, people often traded for the things they needed or wanted. How did that work? . . . Trading is difficult. Why is that?

5. As more and more trading occurred, people began buying and selling things using money. Why was that?

6. Indians used money known as *wampum*. What did wampum look like? Why don't we use it as money today?

7. Tell me about our money. What does it look like? How do you know how much it is worth? Tell me about the pictures and writing on the money.

8. Who makes our money?

9. What are banks? What kinds of services do banks provide for people? How does your family use the bank? . . . Anything else?

10. What kinds of jobs do people who work in banks have?

11. What is a budget? Why is budgeting important?

12. Some people write checks to pay for things. How does that work? Why do people use checks? Other people pay by credit card. How do credit cards work? Why do people use credit cards?

13. Imagine you were going to start a business such as a restaurant. What things would you need to think about?

14. People have garage sales to get rid of things they don't need. How do people know how much to charge?

15. How do people get money? . . . Any other ways?

16. Is Mexican money good in our country? Can we use our money if we travel to Mexico? Why? Why not?

FIGURE 1 Starter Questions

is deducted from their accounts at their banks; when people want to start a business (or buy a home, etc.) and do not have all of the money needed to do so, they can get a loan from a bank (they will have to pay back the loan plus interest, but they are willing to do so because this allows them to start the business or purchase the home now, without having to wait until they accumulate the full amount); the value of an item ultimately comes down to what potential purchasers are willing to pay for it; most people earn most of their money by working at jobs; and ordinarily a country's money is good only in that country, but it can be exchanged for an equivalent amount of another country's money, which then can be spent in that country.

To find out what primary-grade students know (or think they know) about these topics, we interviewed twelve students, six in first grade and six in second grade, stratified by gender and achievement level. You may want to use some or all of our interview questions during pre-unit or pre-lesson assessments of your students' prior knowledge. For now, though, we recommend that you jot down your own answers before going on to read about the answers that we elicited in our interviews. This will sharpen your awareness of ways in which adults' knowledge about money differs from children's knowledge, as well as reduce the likelihood that you will assume that your students already know certain things that seem obvious to you but may need to be spelled out for them.

If you want to use some of these questions to assess your students' prior knowledge before beginning the unit, you can do this either by interviewing selected students individually or by asking the class as a whole to respond to the questions and recording their answers for future reference. If you take the latter approach, an option would be to embed it within the KWL technique by initially questioning students to determine what they <u>k</u>now (or think they know) and what they <u>w</u>ant to find out, then later revisiting their answers and recording what they <u>l</u>earned. An alternative to preassessing your students' knowledge about topics developed in the unit as a whole would be to conduct a separate preassessment prior to each lesson, using only the questions that apply to that lesson (and perhaps adding others of your own choosing).

Children's Responses to Our Money Interview

Previous research on developments in children's economic understanding has shown that young children tend to believe in a benevolent world in which people get whatever money they need from banks simply by asking for it and shopkeepers sell items for the same price at which they were bought (Byrnes, 1996). Even when children's economic understandings are valid, they often are limited: they may know that money is printed by the government but not realize that the amounts of money in circulation are carefully regulated; they may know that banks are places to keep money safely but not know anything about other banking operations; or they may think that the value of an item depends only on the resources that go into producing it. In addition, certain misconceptions are common: the price of an item depends on its size, property is owned by those who use it, or the value of money depends on its color, picture, size, or serial number (Schug & Hartoonian, 1996). Knowledge about shop profits and about banking operations (deposits, loans, interest, and their relationships) usually is not acquired until at least ages nine or ten, although it can be taught earlier (Berti & Monaci, 1998).

When asked, "What is money?" all twelve of the students whom we interviewed generated accurate responses. Eight said that money is used to buy things. In addition or instead, eight described paper money and/or coins. Additional comments were mostly descriptive elaboration: George Washington's face is on the dollar, coins are silver, and so on. Two students mentioned gold coins, possibly thinking of dollar coins, but perhaps thinking that pennies are made of gold.

For the next question, students were shown a twenty-dollar bill, a one-dollar bill, a fifty-cent piece, a nickel, and a penny and were asked why there are so many different kinds of money. Four students (all first graders) could not explain this. Another four expressed the idea that you need a sufficient variety of values to allow you to put together the exact cost of an item (e.g., "We need all different kinds of money so we can pay the right amount.").

Two students conveyed the idea that money would be less convenient if it only came in low denominations: you wouldn't want to have to carry around or count out large sums of money if you had only single dollar bills and pennies. Finally, two students articulated misconceptions. One thought that each U.S. state has its own money, and the other thought that a new bill (denomination) is introduced each time we elect a new president.

When asked why there was no need for money long, long ago, one student said that people didn't know how to make money then and had to use shells instead. The other eleven all said that people back then had to hunt for and gather food, make their own clothes, and so on, so there was no need or use for money. One second grader added that people traded things back then.

The next question informed the students that people traded long, long ago and asked how trading works. Four first graders could not define or give examples of trading. One second grader's example involved purchase (exchanging goods for money) rather than barter (exchanging goods for other goods). The remaining seven students adequately defined trading or gave examples of it (e.g., exchanging a teddy bear for a toy cash register or exchanging food for clothes).

When asked why trading was difficult, eleven students produced responses that were accurate as far as they went. Five first graders said that you might be unwilling to part with an item that the other person wanted (e.g., you wouldn't trade your bike for anything else because you want to keep and use your bike). These responses made no mention of the relative value of the items.

Another three students said that you might be unwilling to accept what you were offered for your item. One gave an example of a failed attempt to trade a bad Pokemon card for a good one, one said that the other person might not have what you need, and the third said that you might not want what the other person has to offer. The remaining three students, all second graders, articulated in child language the idea that it can be hard to evaluate the items under discussion (it's hard to tell if it's even, it's hard to decide what to do, it depends on how much the things are).

When asked why people started using money, only four students suggested explanations, including the three who answered the previous question by noting that it can be hard to determine the value of items offered for barter. Three said that people started using money simply because it was invented (referring to the invention of metal and the means to make coins), and the fourth said that they began to use money after the idea of money was invented. No student specifically stated that money was invented because it was easier to use or more convenient than trading.

We next asked what wampum looked like and why we don't use it today. These questions were intended to see if students understood that modern coins and paper currency are easier to carry and use than the more bulky forms of money used in the past. However, none of the students knew what wampum looked like. Nine of them could not respond, one described it as "little furry stuff," one as a triangle with a dot in the middle, and one as similar to modern coins.

When asked why we don't use wampum today, three students were unable to respond and six others said that wampum is money from the past and we have our own money today. The remaining three students thought that wampum still is used, at least sometimes, by Indians. Two of these meant contemporary Native Americans, but the third said that we don't use wampum because "we don't live in India and are not Indians." Once again, no student said anything about modern money being more convenient or easy to use.

The next question asked students to describe American money, with follow-up probes focusing attention on the pictures and the writing and asking how we know how much the money is worth. Most students' descriptions reflected the bills and coins they were shown: whitish/greenish paper, brown or silver coins. Once again, however, two students referred to gold coins. None spontaneously mentioned the numbers or writing on the money, but one said that George Washington is on the dollar bill (which he went on to say was carved out of wood and then painted). Another said that money is needed to pay for things in stores ("or else it's stealing") and to buy a job (young children commonly believe that jobs cost money).

All twelve students said that the individuals depicted were presidents, and some identified Washington or Lincoln. No other presidents were mentioned, although one first grader said that the depicted presidents included George Washington Carver, Abraham Lincoln, and George Carvington. Four second graders thought that the president depicted on a coin or bill was the president whose succession number corresponded to the value of the coin or bill—the first president is on the one-dollar bill, the twentieth president is on the twenty-dollar bill, and so on. Two expressed puzzlement that Washington is not on the penny because this is the one-cent coin and he was the first president.

Two students thought that the presidents make the money and put their own images on it. One added that this makes sense because the presidents want people to remember them after they die. Some thought that only presidents can be depicted on money (one added that the money wouldn't look right if someone less prestigious were depicted on it), but others included other special people such as "popular guys who lived back then" or "the guy who invented light."

Only four students talked about the tail sides of the coins, two noting the White House and two noting the eagle. When asked why the eagle was shown, one could not respond but the other said that it represents "the USA or freedom." Finally, one first grader said that coins have a head side and a tail side so you can flip them to start football games. Young children frequently display this kind of teleological thinking—noting that something can be used for a particular purpose and therefore assuming that it was specifically invented for that purpose.

Ten students were able to respond to the question about the writing. Four thought that it said something about the depicted people, explaining that they lived here or honoring their contributions to the country. Three noted that the writing explains how much the coin is worth ("It says quarter, nickel, or dime."). Other comments included "This says, 'Liberty, 1974, and In God We Trust,'" "When the first one came out it said, 'one cent,' so the others put the same thing on the coins they made," "Some is cursive and some is print. There is different writing because some of them don't live in the United States," and "If a coin says Los Angeles, then it means that it was made there."

In addition to these spontaneous comments, some students added elaborations in response to specific probes. When asked about the word "Liberty," one student said, "That's what it stands for," and another said, "Our pledge is about liberty—it ends with 'liberty and justice for all.'" When asked about "In God We Trust," one student could not respond but others said, "Because if you break the money, you break the rules, and you are not going to trust anybody or anything," "To show that we trust God and like him," and "Maybe the president believes in God."

Concerning how we know how much money is worth, four students could not explain but the other eight noted that the value is stated on the coin or bill. Most referred to the printed words, but three noted the numbers as well. In general, the students' descriptions of money were mostly accurate but indicated that they had not spent much time studying or thinking about the words or images on coins or bills.

When asked who makes money, five students could not respond, three said the presidents, and three said a company or factory (none used the term *mint*). The twelfth student said that money is made at the Liberty Coin Shop (a local coin business) and described watching a television show depicting how coins are manufactured. No student said anything to the effect that only the federal government can make money, that each bill has a unique serial number, that precautions are taken against counterfeiting, or that worn bills are taken out of circulation.

When asked about banks, six students described them as places to put extra money for safekeeping. In addition or instead, five described banks as places to go to get money (simply by asking for it). Other responses included banks manufacture money; banks have money because stores send it to them; you can pay bills there; and each person's money is kept in a separate box (i.e., a safe-deposit box), and money is put into or taken out of this box every time the person makes a transaction. All of these responses have been observed frequently in previous research on children's knowledge about banking. An exception was the response of a first grader who noted that you can get money just by using the ATM machine but if you use the drive-through window you can ask for lollipops.

Subsequent questions asked what services banks perform or how banks help people, and more specifically, how the student's own family uses its bank. Six students spoke of banks holding your money for you and giving it back whenever you come to ask for it. Another five (four of them first graders) spoke of banks as places where you can go to get money on request (without specifying that it is your own money). Finally, one first grader spoke of using banks to pay bills and cash checks but did not talk about savings accounts or getting money through means other than cashing checks. Elaborations included the following: if your bank ran out of money, you would have to go to another bank; the bank holds your money for you and will not steal it; anyone can get money from a bank but you have to show identification; and banks get their money from the money factory. No student said anything about checking accounts, loans, or financial services other than paying bills and cashing checks.

When asked how their families use banks, most students spoke of the mechanics of operating ATM machines or using drive-through windows (typically describing sending and receiving materials through vacuum tubes). Most students depicted families going to banks to get cash, but two spoke of making deposits and two spoke of getting lollipops or suckers. Some of them could not talk about the inside of the bank because they had not been inside (or if they had, not recently or not often enough to build up an image of what goes on there).

When asked about jobs held by people who work at banks, four students could not respond and the others mostly emphasized helping people by giving them money (none used the term *teller*). When probed for details, various students depicted bank workers talking on the phone, using computers, or writing on papers, but usually could not specify the content of these transactions. Other than giving people the money they asked for, the only specific elaborations included using computers to send money and helping people by "giving them bills that they need to pay." The only non-teller job mentioned was a person who "stands at the front and says 'Good morning,' 'Have a nice day!' and things like that." These responses replicated children's ideas documented in previous studies, especially their notion of the world as a benevolent place where people can get money just by going to banks and asking for it and their tendency to think about banks merely as storehouses for money without knowing much if anything about their other functions and services.

The students were unfamiliar with the term *budget*. Ten could not respond and the other two guessed "like a discount or something" and "a savings account."

When asked how checking works, one student could not respond but the others all gave responses (of varying accuracy and specificity) that focused on the ideas that you use checks to get money or to transmit money to someone else. Three mentioned only the first of these uses for checks, six mentioned only the second, and two mentioned both.

Among students who spoke of using checks to get money, most referred to writing your own check and cashing it, but one spoke of getting a check from someone else (e.g., as a birthday gift). Among students who spoke of writing checks as a way to transmit money, most mentioned paying for store purchases but some spoke of sending money to someone living elsewhere (e.g., as a birthday present to a relative).

Only four students, all second graders, noted that the money specified on checks that people write is debited from their bank accounts. Explanations of when or why people use checks included if you were sick at home and couldn't get out to pay personally; for big amounts like one hundred dollars; if you don't have enough money with you to pay in cash (two students); and because it is more convenient—you don't have to count out the money.

When asked about how credit cards work, most students initially spoke of the mechanics of using the cards (e.g., slide it through the slot, sign the slip, etc.) but then went on to describe credit cards as alternatives to cash that can be used when making purchases at stores, restaurants, gas stations, and so on. However, two first graders spoke only of using credit cards to get money from ATM machines.

Half of the students said that you would use credit cards if you didn't have enough money with you or didn't want to spend the cash, and three noted that amounts charged against your credit card are debited from your account at the bank. Other elaborations: using credit cards is like using checks except that you just get your card back, without money; credit cards are quicker than checks because you don't have to wait for the bank person to process the paper and count out the money; you could use it at a gas station if you didn't want to go inside to pay; a credit card is like a check except that you use it at a store rather than a bank; it's the same as with checks except that it works through computers; you can get change back if you want; and it enables you to buy things without having to carry around a lot of cash that might get stolen. In general, most of the students knew something of the mechanics involved in writing checks and using credit cards, but only a minority understood that the transferred money is debited from your bank account.

When asked about what they would need to think about if they were planning to open a restaurant, the students gave sensible answers emphasizing staff hires, food purchases, recipes, prices, and so on, but only two mentioned getting together the money needed to start the business. When asked about this, seven spoke of getting money from a bank, two said that you would have to accumulate savings from money earned in previous jobs, two couldn't respond, and two said that you would have to get it from other people (one couldn't say from whom and the other said from people already in business who had money available in their cash registers). Among students who spoke of getting money from the bank, the first graders thought that you could just go to the bank and ask for it (one spoke of going back many times because a lot of money would be needed), whereas the second graders clearly stated that the money would be from your own account.

No student mentioned getting a loan. One second grader did say that you might not need all of the money but would need a lot or most of it, but couldn't say more when asked how you would get the rest. These findings support findings from our shelter interview indicating that primary-grade students know little or nothing about financing major purchases (whether homes or businesses) by getting mortgage loans from banks.

Students had difficulty with the question about how people running garage sales know what to charge for their items. Several began by saying that you would charge what the item originally cost, but all but one of these changed their thinking when probed. One ended up saying only that bigger things would cost more than smaller things, and another that he might be able to charge as much as the store would charge because some people wouldn't know how much they should pay.

The remaining nine students eventually determined that items would (or at least should) cost less at a garage sale than at a store. Three said that this was because the garage sale items were used and the store versions were new. Two others said that things would be cheaper at a garage sale but could not explain. The remaining students gave the following rationales: a garage sale is a sale and the store might not be having a sale; you pay more at stores because they have more stuff there; stores charge a lot because they want to make a lot of money, but you could choose to charge less (i.e., be less greedy); and you could really charge whatever you want, but people tend to bargain at garage sales and expect to pay less than they would pay at the store. No student mentioned supply and demand or said that an item is worth whatever potential purchasers are willing to pay for it, although the student who talked about people bargaining at garage sales appeared to have partial understanding of the latter idea.

When asked how people get money, most students initially said from banks. Only four (all second graders) initially spoke of people earning money from their jobs, but the others understood that people get money this way when asked about it. Several made reference to payday in talking about money earned from jobs.

When probed about other ways of getting money, various students mentioned getting change in transactions at stores (two); other people might give you money or you might find it on the ground; garage sales; and alimony/child support (this student did not use these terms but talked about how her father gives her mother money every month that is used to buy necessities for her mother and herself).

Some students were asked about how they themselves might get money. Most mentioned doing chores at home and getting paid by parents. Other responses included getting an allowance, baby-sitting, setting up a lemonade stand, and doing good things for others and getting rewarded for it.

When asked if Mexican money is good in our country, all twelve students said no. Most could not explain beyond saying that it is different from our money, we only take our own money, and similar statements. Elaborations included if you tried to use Mexican money, people would think that you were Mexican and you don't dress like they do; Mexican money is good only in Mexico; Mexican money is money after all, so some people might be willing to take it if they were planning to go to Mexico; we don't read their language or know how to work their money, so we can't take it and use it.

Responses to the next question about whether we can use our money in Mexico were similar. One first grader said yes (but couldn't explain), but the other students all said no (because our money is different, they only take their own money, etc.). Elaborations included the following: If you tried to use American money, they would think you were American and take you back to the United States; American money is still money, so some Mexicans might take it; and Mexicans do not speak our language or know how to work our money, so they wouldn't know what it is worth.

When asked about how one might get Mexican money, most students could not respond. One said that you would have to go to Mexico and get a job there, another that maybe you could just find it, and a third that maybe a relative would visit Mexico and bring some back for you. No student showed any awareness of the possibility of exchanging money at banks or currency exchanges, or even of the idea that two currencies can be equated in value and exchanged for like amounts. The students seemed to think that money is of no value outside of its own country.

At the conclusion of the interview, students were asked what questions they would like to see answered in a unit on money. Most responses focused on the process of making money (who makes it, where, and how). Other questions included How much money can there be in a bank? Does the whole world have money, and if so, how many different kinds are there? How do you get money? and Why was money invented?

Overall, the students' responses indicated that the second graders knew more about money than the first graders, but none of the students knew very much about the big ideas that are emphasized in the unit.

Overview of Money Unit—Barbara Knighton

Everyone loves to talk about money, and young learners are no different. On the one hand, you will find that your students are highly motivated by the idea of talking about money. However, it can also be difficult to focus their thinking on big ideas other than spending money.

Another interesting aspect of this unit is the fact that children have had experiences with money and economics that they didn't clearly understand. As you teach, your lesson might trigger a memory of an event or comment they've heard. These are not necessarily misconceptions, but just information that needs to be clarified and connected to the right concepts. For this reason, I felt that students needed to have the opportunity to share stories, not just ask questions. I provided the story sharing time outside of my regular lessons to give that extra processing time.

During the course of the unit, several parents mentioned that their children were very aware of the family's economic transactions. Many children talked about bills, credit cards, and other topics introduced. Parents and children had the opportunity to engage in meaningful conversations that pertained directly and easily to their daily lives.

The idea of bartering—the idea of two people choosing to trade two different things—is a key component to this unit. Be sure to give yourself permission to take extra time if necessary to solidify the students' understanding of bartering. With my class, we actually had a bartering day when students brought something from home to trade. Walking away from that experience with something new that the other person didn't want was powerful. It also allowed me to refer back in later lessons to the idea of two people trading something valuable.

Each of the lessons contains several different big ideas to structure your teaching around. Be sure to review all the big ideas before teaching each lesson. Prioritize them to be sure you cover the most important ones. Also, as you teach later lessons, watch for chances to connect to the big ideas from previous lessons.

Lesson 1

Money Basics

Resources

- Bulletin board that depicts the range of U.S. money types, people using money, process of making money, and questions associated with the study of money
- Coins
- Shells
- Feathers
- Plastic cards (credit card, debit card)
- Personal check
- TWL chart (think we know, want to learn, learned)
- Book display/interest center

Children's Literature

Berger, M., & Berger, G. (1993). *Round and Round the Money Goes*. Nashville, TN: Ideals Children's Books.

Cribb, J. (1990). *Money*. New York: Dorling Kindersley.

Flanagan, A. (1998a). *Buying a Pet from Ms. Chavez*. New York: Children's Press.

Flanagan, A. (1998b). *Choosing Eyeglasses with Mrs. Koutris*. New York: Children's Press.

Flanagan, A. (1998c). *Mr. Santiago's Tasty Treats*. New York: Children's Press.

Flanagan, A. (1998d). *Mr. Yee Fixes Cars*. New York: Children's Press.

Gill, S., & Tabola, D. (2000). *The Big Buck Adventure*. Watertown, MA: Charlesbridge.

Godfrey, N. (1998). *Ultimate Kids' Money Book*. New York: Simon & Schuster.

Herman, H., & Herman, P. (1999). *Money Sense for Kids*. Hauppauge, NY: Barron's.

Lewin, T. (1996). *Market*. New York: Harper Trophy.

Maestro, B. (1993). *The Story of Money*. New York: Mulberry.

Spies, K. (1992). *Our Money*. Brookfield, CT: Millbrook.

General Comments

Prepare a bulletin board with visuals (pictures and money-related items such as a credit card, personal check, coins, etc.) that will stimulate questions about money during the next several weeks. Here are sample questions that could be included:

What is money?

Where does money come from?

Who makes it?

Why are there so many different kinds?

What is the difference between a check and a credit card?

What is the history of money?

What is bartering?

How did people long ago get the things they needed and wanted?

General Purposes or Goals

To: (1) pique the students' interest in the study of money; and (2) help students understand and appreciate the functions of money.

Main Ideas to Develop

- Money is anything that a group of people accept in exchange for real items or as pay for work.
- It takes a family's money as well as help from the government to buy all the goods and services we need to survive.
- Taxes are collected by the government from families and businesses to help pay for things that would be too expensive for individuals to buy (e.g., schools, roads, parks, teachers).

Teaching Tips from Barbara

As I began this unit, I found that most of my students' questions about money centered around the composition and creation of actual money instead of economic concepts. Be sure to use strategic questions to push past these very concrete ideas. The use of imagining was a good way to get fresh ideas and more conversations. The picture drawing activity was a great way to begin a discussion of goods and services. To make sure that I get a variety of pictures, I have students tell me what they will draw before I give them a piece of paper.

Starting the Lesson

Pose questions regarding money: What is it? Why do we need it? Where does it come from? Using the questions, pictures, and artifacts displayed on the bulletin board and available in the interest center, begin a class discussion. Elicit student responses/speculations. Write them on a TWL chart under the Think We Know and Want to Learn categories. Periodically during the unit, refer to the student speculations and check out their conceptions and/or misconceptions. Connect student questions to the specific lessons. Encourage students to expand the responses as understanding and application develop.

After the class has provided a substantial set of questions and the conversation begins to wane, ask students to imagine life without money. How would they pay for their clothes? Their food? Their family vehicle? How could they buy their video games? Their school supplies?

Suggested Lesson Discussion

Without money, it would probably be very difficult to survive, wouldn't it? People didn't always have access to money and you will learn about that; also, there still are things you can do for free (e.g., play in the snow, look up at the sky at night and enjoy the stars, enjoy the beautiful clouds in the sky, etc.). However, in today's world you need money to satisfy your needs and wants. Money is something a group of people accept in exchange for real items or work done to help people. Goods are the real items you need and want such as food, clothing, shelter, and so on. [As a class, list other items.] Services are the work done by other people to help you. For example, you need money to pay the dentist for cleaning your teeth or to pay the bus driver to take you to your destination. and so on. [As a class, make a list of other services available.]

It takes your family's money along with money provided by the government to buy all the goods and services we need to survive. The government collects tax money from families and uses it to pay for such things as teachers, parks, schools, and roads. The government pays for things that families couldn't afford to pay for on their own.

Today we need money for almost everything, yet long ago, people didn't have any. How could that be? What do you think happened? [List the students' speculations on the board.]

Activity

Ask students at each table to list or draw all the ways we need or use money. Then categorize each according to a good (G) or service (S). If responses include services provided by the government, separate them by giving them a code of GS. Share responses with the whole class.

Summarize

- Money is anything a group of people accept in exchange for real items or as pay for work.
- It takes a family's money along with money provided by the government to pay for all the goods and services we need to survive.
- Money is very much a part of our lives and we have a lot to learn about it, as evidenced by the questions we have posed.

Assessment

Have each student draw the most important thing she or he has learned about money. Then discuss the ideas as a class and prepare an individual or group journal entry using open-ended statements as prompts:

Money is _____.

People today need money because _____

_____.

Home Assignment

Have students review what they learned by sharing their drawings about money and by reading their class or individual journal entry to their families. Then as a family they should talk about all the ways they use and need money. Finally, have families look at all the different kinds of items they have in their household that represent money (e.g., money order, personal check, coins [U.S. and other], debit card, charge card, etc.). As a family, they should write down one idea associated with money that was discussed and send it to class for your upcoming session.

Dear Parents,

We are beginning a unit on money. Please spend a few minutes with your child discussing this topic. He or she has a drawing and a journal entry to read to you. As a family, discuss all the different ways you use and need money. If you have items representing different forms of money (bills, coins, checks, etc.), please examine them together. Finally, write down one idea you talked about and send it to school with your child for our upcoming discussion. Thank you.

Sincerely,

FIGURE 2   Model Letter to Parents

Lesson 2

History of Money

Resources
- Time line—Long, Long Ago; Long Ago; Today
- Pictures depicting life long, long ago; long ago; and today
- Props illustrating the story of money (include bag of grain, salt, shells, objects of approximately equal value for trading, coins, paper money, shell bracelet, fur, etc.)
- Globe
- U.S. map
- Sets of cards with pictures and captions that tell the story of money for a sequencing activity in which students determine what happened first, next, and so on (see Activity for listing of items to be included)
- Blank money time lines

Children's Literature
Cribb, J. (1990). *Money*. New York: Dorling Kindersley.
Maestro, B. (1993). *The Story of Money*. New York: Houghton Mifflin.

General Comments
This lesson is intended to create a sense of wonder and fascination about the story of money and how it has evolved from unnecessary for people long, long ago to an essential part of our lives today.

General Purposes or Goals
To help students understand and appreciate: (1) how and why long, long ago, there was no need for money; (2) how the need for money arose; and (3) why money is such an important part of our lives today.

Main Ideas to Develop
- Long, long ago there was no need for money because people lived very simply and they satisfied their needs themselves.
- As time passed, things changed. The numbers of people grew; more food was needed; climates began to change; people learned to do more things such as raise crops, bake, build; and people began to communicate with one another.
- Trading to get the things you need or want is known as bartering.
- Bartering worked only when each trader wanted something that the other had and both agreed it was a fair trade.

- As time passed, people began to use objects for money.
- Any object can be used as money as long as people agree on its value.

Teaching Tips from Barbara

Before beginning the history lesson, take time to make sure your students understand how time lines work. I usually spend a few minutes adding some basics to define long, long ago; long ago; and today. For example, in the Long, Long Ago section I added a cave, bow and arrow, and a person in animal skins. After establishing the three time areas, then I focused on long, long ago. I spent one day with long, long ago so that I could spend extra time on bartering. I wanted to be sure that that concept was firmly planted in my students' minds. Bartering (trading something that both people value) is an important idea that comes up frequently throughout the unit. The second day, spend the time talking about coins and bills and how they developed as you move through long ago to today. I found that the sequencing activity worked best with the whole group, because of the amount of reading involved.

Starting the Lesson

Discuss the responses to the home assignment. Explain that long, long ago, people lived very simply. They lived in caves or simple huts. To get food, they hunted animals and gathered plants. As you share the story of changes over time, use a time line and add pictures or drawings illustrating key points. You might don a hat or a simple costume to represent each of the time periods—long, long ago (cave people), long ago (Native Americans, pioneers), and today. An option is to make a time line on a white board and add words and sketches as you share the story.

Use Table 1 as a guideline. It compares the time periods and illustrates that long, long ago there was no need for money because people lived very simply and satisfied their needs themselves. Gradually the numbers of people grew; more food was needed; people learned to do more things; and people began to barter. As time passed people began to use objects for money. At the end of the story the class might fill in a similar chart and discuss how things have changed.

Suggested Lesson Discussion

[Read the beginning section of *The Story of Money*, show the illustrations, and reference the time line and pictures or drawings as the narrative unfolds.] Long, long ago there was no need for money because people lived very simply and they satisfied their needs themselves. As time passed, many things changed: the numbers of people grew; climates changed; people began to settle in places where soils and climate were conducive for growing crops; people began to learn how to do more things; people be-

Table 1   Time Period Comparison Chart

CAVE PEOPLE'S MONEY	NATIVE AMERICAN/ PIONEER MONEY	OUR MONEY TODAY
There was no need for money because people lived very simply. People satisfied their needs themselves.	People continued to live very simply and satisfy their needs themselves. As time passed, the numbers of people grew. People began to settle in places where soils and climate were conducive to growing crops. Gradually people began to do more things and to have a surplus in the things they grew or made. People began to travel and communicate and to trust each other. People began to exchange goods and services. This is known as bartering. Gradually people figured out that they needed to use objects as money. Still later, people learned that they needed to use lightweight objects as money. In 1790, the U.S. government created a money system.	Even today, some people barter for things sometimes. Coins, bills, credit cards, and checks are examples of the forms of money used today.

gan to have a surplus in the things they grew or made; people began to travel and communicate and trust other people, and as a result they began to exchange goods and services. This is known as *bartering*. Of course, this system worked well only when each trader wanted something that the other person had or could provide as a service—and when both agreed on what made a fair trade.

[Continue reading from *The Story of Money,* underscoring the difficulties that often arose when the items to be traded were very different.] It was difficult to determine how many eggs were needed to pay for a quilt—and even then, the individual who wanted to trade the quilt probably did not want that many eggs. Gradually, people figured out that they needed to use other objects as money. The items that people decided to use usually were scarce, not plentiful or easy to obtain. [Point out places on the globe where bartering was occurring.] Examples used long ago were salt and grains [show examples]. Later as people began traveling great distances to trade, they needed to find something that was easier to take with them. They needed something that was fairly lightweight, would not spoil or be damaged easily, and something that people everywhere would accept in trade. Silver was hard to find, highly prized, and something that everybody wanted. [Point out the general area of the former Sumeria on the globe, explaining that Sumerians traveled great distances to trade.] The Sumerian merchants began to use silver as money. They melted the precious metal, formed it into bars, and began stamping its exact weight and using it for exchanging goods and services. They were the first people to invent metal money. [Show pictures of early types of metal money, explaining that early governments adopted them as official.] Most were round; however, some of the earliest ones were shaped like shells or animals. They were made of many different metals. Even after coins were invented as money, the barter system did not disappear. Even today, there are places in the world where people trade item for item or use valuable objects as money. [Optional: See pp. 18–26 of *The Story of Money* for additional details describing the history of money.]

[Return to the globe. Point out France, England, Spain, and the New World. Point out Long Ago on the time line.] As people from Europe began to travel to America, they began trading. The settlers and pioneers in America traded fish, furs, lumber, and other items for goods made in Europe [show examples]. The pioneers also traded with the Native Americans. Objects used as money included grains such as corn, fish, and tobacco. The Native Americans used shells strung into belts and bracelets, known as *wampum* [show examples].

Obviously with the range of items, coins, and later paper being used as money, trading became very confusing. [Demonstrate using multiple objects such as feathers, silver bars, foreign coins, and a sack of salt how confusing the money situation and trading became.]

Finally, the U.S. government established an official currency, meaning that only certain coins would be recognized as having value. The first coin minted in America was the copper cent. [Point out 1787 on the time line, indicating this was the year when the first official U.S. coin was made.] In 1790 the money system became law. The dollar was established as the basic unit. A mint was opened to make coins. Today a mint in Philadelphia and another in Denver make coins. [Point out these cities on a map of the United States.} U.S. paper money is printed in Washington, D.C. {Point out this location on a U.S. map.}

Activity

Give each table a set of cards and ask the students as a group to put them in order to tell the story of money, beginning with the card that describes what happened first, then next, and so on. The set of cards should include the following:

- No need for money because people satisfied their needs.
- Numbers of people grew.
- People began to grow more crops and make more things, such as clothes, rugs and tools, than they needed.
- People began to exchange goods and services.
- People had difficulty bartering when things had different values.
- Objects such as grain or salt began being used as money.
- As people traveled greater distances, they figured out they needed to trade with things that were lightweight, not easily damaged, and things that other people wanted.
- Silver was the first metal to be used as money.
- Early governments adopted many different types of metal money.
- People from Europe traveled to early America and traded their goods for fish, furs, lumber, and so on.
- The Native Americans used wampum for trading.
- Trading became confusing because so many different items were used.
- The government in America established an official currency, giving a coin a certain value.
- The dollar was established by the U.S. government as the basic unit.

As a class, review the story of money across time. Return to the Time Period Comparison Chart.

CONDENSED VERSION OF THE TIME LINE

No need for money.
Numbers of people grew.
People began to have extras of the things they grew and made.
People began to exchange goods and services (bartering).
People used objects as money.
When they began traveling, they had to use lightweight objects.
The government created the money system—bills and coins.
Credit cards, personal checks, and debit cards were created for
use as money.

Review the appropriate sequence that describes the story of money. Refer to the time line as you talk, underscoring the fact that long, long ago there was no need for money because people satisfied their own needs.

Summarize

- Long, long ago, there was no need for money because people lived very simply and satisfied their needs themselves.
- As time passed, things changed. The numbers of people grew; more food was needed; people learned to do more things and began to trade.
- People gradually began having more wants and realized that they could satisfy these wants in more ways.
- People began by bartering, later used objects, and still later used money.

Assessment

Give each student a blank time line on which to draw pictures that represent the story of money over time.

Home Assignment

Have each student share his or her illustrated time line that tells the story of money with his or her family. Encourage families to discuss the changes over time, then talk about why money is such an important part of their lives today.

> Dear Parents,
>
> Your child is bringing home a time line (with his or her illustrations) that characterizes the story of money over time. As a family, talk about these changes. Then discuss why money is such an important part of your life today. Make sure your child has at least one idea to share during our upcoming discussion. Thank you.
>
> Sincerely,

FIGURE 3   Model Letter to Parents

Lesson 3

The Market

Resources
- Pictures of open-air markets—past and present
- Video footage depicting open-air markets
- Photos of a local market
- Globe
- Props for creating an "outdoor" market in the classroom
- $2 objects brought by class members for bartering
- Thirty small items (e.g., cookies, candy, popcorn balls, etc.) to sell
- Nickels—each student will be asked to bring thirty for the sale

Children's Literature
Lewin, T. (1996). *Market*. New York: Harper Trophy.

General Comments
This lesson is intended to create a sense of wonder and interest in market day, a phenomenon that began long ago when people couldn't use everything they made or grew so they began trading goods.

For a part of this lesson, students will reinvent market day in their classroom. Students will be expected to bring an item for $2 or less that they would like to trade or barter, and thirty cookies, candies, popcorn balls, or other small items that they would be willing to sell. Each student should also bring thirty nickels for buying purposes.

General Purposes or Goals
To help students understand and appreciate: (1) what markets are like; (2) why they exist; (3) how they operate; and (4) how they are similar to and different from those of the past.

Main Ideas to Develop
- A market is a public gathering place held at regular times for buying and selling goods.
- Long, long ago people came from miles around to buy and sell goods. No money was exchanged. Instead, all exchanges were in the form of barter.
- Gradually, certain objects were used as money.
- Today, in most parts of the world, people use money in exchange for goods and services.

- There are places—even sometimes where we live—where people still barter (exchange one good or service for another.)
- All over the world, even today, people come to the market to buy and sell.
- When people talk about going to markets, they usually mean going to an outdoor site to buy or sell goods.

Teaching Tips from Barbara

My students enjoyed the bartering part of this lesson the most. They were able to trade an item from home with another child. There were some interesting discussions after one student didn't find anything he wanted to trade for. The market is another powerful activity and is worth the extra time it takes. It can be modified to simplify things by having just a few families provide items to buy. Then assign students the role of either buyer or seller. Limit the amount of money (real coins are much more meaningful) each child can spend. Then have the two groups switch jobs. This is an easy and natural place to integrate math by having students record their purchases on a "receipt" as an addition or subtraction problem.

Starting the Lesson

Begin by sharing the results of the home assignment. Then ask students, "What comes to mind when you think of going to a market?" Write their responses on a white board. Some students might begin talking about supermarkets. Acknowledge that they are modern-day places where goods and services can be purchased indoors.

Suggested Lesson Discussion

Long ago as populations grew and people settled in one place, they began to trade what they could not use themselves. [Show pictures of early markets.] A sheep might be traded for tools, a sack of corn for woven cloth, or a dozen eggs for a loaf of bread. Sometimes individuals would provide a service, such as fix a roof in exchange for wood, or work on a farm in exchange for food and a place to sleep. Later, specific goods were used as money, and today money usually is used to buy goods and services.

There are markets even today in many parts of the world. They serve the same purposes—places to buy goods and services, usually with money, but sometimes with other goods. Markets are usually in a part of the town or city that is easy to get to (often in the center) and often near modern stores. Markets provide people with fresh products and homemade and unusual items.

[Visit a market via a video clip or virtual field trip as a means of providing context and sensitizing students to the unusualness of a market. Ask students who have visited a market to describe their experiences. If your town or city has one, a field trip might be a nice option. An alternative is to take photos of the local site and share them with the class.]

[Introduce the book *Market* by Ted Lewin. Select at least two of the four sites: Ecuador, Ireland, Uganda, and the United States (New York). Point these out on the globe. If you have been to others, be sure to bring photos and share their special features (e.g., fish market in Bergen, Norway, or antique market in London, England). Read the sections from the book underscoring the idea that people come to market to buy and sell. Ask students how they think markets would be different from indoor shopping.]

Activity

After spending time talking about markets and imagining how they are different from regular stores, quickly set up the center of your classroom (or another nearby site) as an outdoor market. Using cardboard as stalls and makeshift props, have students come to the market first to barter trade their $2 items) and then to sell their products for nickels. Invite parents and/or other community members to assist. Be sure you adequately explain the goals and main ideas you want students to develop. To add interest, ask parents, upper-grade mentors, and other teachers to bring small items to sell or trade.

Make sure you spend adequate time for the debriefing. Suggested questions: How did it feel to be a part of market day? How was your experience different from going to a regular mall or store? Which way would you prefer to shop? Why? Why do you think many people today still go to the outdoor markets?

Summarize

- A market is a gathering held at a regular time and place for buying and selling goods.
- Long, long ago all exchanges were in the form of barter.
- Gradually certain objects (that were highly valued because they were needed and wanted) were used for money.
- Markets can be found throughout the world. Most people who buy goods or services at markets exchange money, although even today some customers exchange other goods or services (barter).

Assessment

Conduct a thumbs up/thumbs down survey.

1. Thumbs up   Markets are public gathering places for buying and selling things.
2. Thumbs up   Long, long ago all exchanges were in the form of barter.
3. Thumbs down   Barter means giving dollar bills for something.

4. Thumbs down   Markets are usually found in very remote places—secretive spots.

5. Thumbs down   Markets today exist only in towns and cities where there are no stores or modern shopping malls.

6. Thumbs up   Markets usually sell fresh fruits, flowers, vegetables, and handmade or homemade things such as sweaters, rugs, and bread, although some markets also sell items that are found in regular stores.

At the conclusion of this exercise, ask each student to complete three "I learned" statements about markets. Encourage students to use the word wall to help with their ideas and with their spellings.

Revisit the TWL chart. Revise and add as appropriate.

Home Assignment

Encourage students to share their "I learned" statements about markets with their families. Then as a family they should talk about their experiences at open-air markets and why they do or do not frequent them.

Dear Parents,

Our class has been learning about markets, described as gathering places held at regular times for buying and selling goods. Encourage your child to share his or her responses about what was learned. Then as a family discuss your experiences in going to a market, either locally or somewhere else in the world. If you have photos or artifacts from a market experience, please send them to school for sharing. Thank you.

Sincerely,

FIGURE 4   Model Letter to Parents

Lesson 4

Coins and Bills

Resources
- Display of U.S. coins and bills
- Handful of pennies—one for each student in the class
- U.S. map
- Display of U.S. paper money, various denominations
- Display of coins and bills from other parts of the world
- Globe
- Magnifying glasses (optional)

Children's Literature

Berger, M., & Berger, G. (1993). *Round and Round the Money Goes*. Nashville, TN: Ideals Children's Books.

Godfrey, N. (1998). *Ultimate Kids' Money Book*. New York: Simon & Schuster.

Maestro, B. (1993). *The Story of Money*. New York: Houghton Mifflin.

Spies, K. (1992). *Our Money*. Brookfield, CT: The Millbrook Press.

General Comments

The intent of this lesson is to create a sense of wonder and curiosity about coins and bills, with an opportunity to examine them more closely and learn about how they are made. It will be important for students to examine them up close and become familiar with some of the special information about them. Look for natural integration opportunities with math.

General Purposes and Goals

To: (1) pique students' interest in examining coins and bills up close and learning more about them and how they are made; (2) develop an understanding and appreciation for the government's role in making money and controlling the amount that is in circulation; and (3) develop an understanding and appreciation for the range of currencies that exist in the world, all of which are made very carefully and are interchangeable.

Main Ideas to Develop

- The Treasury is the part of our government that makes money and controls the amount that is in circulation. Besides printing new bills, it destroys worn-out ones.
- Another name for money is *currency*. It refers to both coins and paper money.

- By law, U.S. money cannot show a living person. The law was passed so that no one could mint coins as a sign of power.
- The official unit of currency in the United States is the dollar. Almost every country in the world has its official unit of currency (e.g., pound, peso, yen), although the former currencies of many European countries have been replaced by the euro.

Teaching Tips from Barbara

Students were extremely motivated during this lesson. They had many questions and wanted to see the coins up close. It would be helpful to allow access to the coins before the lesson and allow them to begin comparing and contrasting them with each other. The students will have lots of questions, so it will be important to set up a routine for asking questions so that they don't interrupt the flow of the lesson. Also, be sure to keep the main ideas at the front of your mind as you teach this lesson so that you don't get derailed.

Starting the Lesson

Discuss the results of the home assignment. Share and discuss any photos and/or artifacts representing markets brought in by students. Then show students the display of United States currency and pose the question, "What kinds of questions come to mind when you see these coins and bills?" List them on the white board. A follow-up question might be, "How do you think these are made?" In two columns, list student responses, first about coins and then about bills.

After you have sufficiently piqued their interest and they realize this is new territory for them to explore, return to the display and explain that during this lesson many of their questions will be answered. They will be encouraged to use the books displayed as well as adults as resources to learn about this interesting topic—something that is very much a part of their daily lives but which they know little about.

Suggested Lesson Discussion

[Pick up a handful of pennies and locate Denver and Philadelphia on a U.S. map. Explain that if these pennies were made recently, they were probably made in one of these two places. (We used to have mints in San Francisco and New Orleans as well.) Pass out a penny to each student.] Look for the tiny letter next to the face on the penny. The face is Abraham Lincoln. [Elicit responses from the students regarding where their coins were made.] Turn the coin over. You will notice there is a picture of the Lincoln Memorial in Washington, D.C. [Ask for a show of hands of those who have visited this historic site. Use pp. 28–33 *Our Money* or p. 26 of *Round and Round the Money Goes* for illustrations and expanded explanations.]

Coins are made of metal that is poured into molds to make bars. Machines roll the bars into sheets. Blanks for each type of coin are punched from the sheets. The blanks are heated, bathed, and shined. The coins are then placed on an edge-rolling machine that produces a raised rim. Designs are stamped on both sides of coins. [Return to the pennies.] In addition to a face on one side (usually a former president), every coin has the word "Liberty" stamped on it to remind us we live in a country where people have lots of freedoms. [Write *Liberty* on the white board. Point out "E Pluribus Unum" on the penny. Write these words on the white board, explaining that they mean many people joined together to form the United States of America ("From many, one"). Explain that the phrase "In God We Trust" also appears on all coins minted since 1984.]

Optional [Depending on the level of student interest, you might decide to examine nickels, dimes, quarters, and other coins. Show a Kennedy half-dollar, indicating that it is the most recent coin with a U.S. president on it.] [End of optional section]

Once the finished coins are made at the mint (run by the U.S. government, Department of Treasury), they are counted by machine, put in bags that are sewn shut, weighed, and stored or shipped to banks to begin using as old coins are destroyed. The government regulates (keeps track of and controls) the number of coins that remain in circulation at a time.

[Show a dollar bill.] Paper money in the United States is called *dollar bills*. [Refer to the display and the list of student speculations about how bills are made.] All bills are the same size and color; however, they have different values. Dollar bills are made by the U.S. government at the Bureau of Engraving and Printing. [Use illustrations to assist in explaining the process. See pp. 21–22 of *Round and Round the Money Goes* and pp. 32–37 of *Our Money*.] First the designs are hand-tooled into steel plates. Many different engravers are involved. For example, one may do the face of the person (portrait), another the border, and another the numbers. Next the designs are transferred to printing plates. The bills are printed on very special paper. Green ink is used for the back and black for the faces. The paper is run through a press at a very high speed. After the printing they are cut apart and examined for mistakes. [Return to the display of bills. Pass out one-dollar bills and allow students to examine them (e.g., fine lines, dots, and dashes used to create the portrait of Washington).] The heavy and fine mixtures of lines are used to make counterfeiting difficult. The serial numbers and series ID are included so that the government knows which bills are in circulation. The treasury seal [see pp. 19–20 of *Our Money* and pp. 24–25 of *Ultimate Kids' Money Book* for illustrations] shows the bald eagle, our national bird. It stands for strength.

Optional [Depending on the level of student interest, you might decide to examine other U.S. bills. For example, you might show the twenty-dollar bill, which has pictures of Andrew Jackson and of the White House.] [End of optional section.]

The government keeps track of how much money is made and used. New money (currency) is provided and old money is taken out of circulation. The old money is shredded.

[Revisit the list of student questions and speculations that was recorded on the white board. Then review the fact that the official currency in our country is the U.S. dollar.]

[Show the display of foreign currencies.] Most countries have their own official currency (e.g., Mexican peso, Japanese yen, English pound, etc.). Most countries make their own currencies using special papers, inks, and processes. They create their own designs to represent their history and cultural values. Using different exchange rates (e.g., an English pound equals [at this time] more than a dollar), the governments agree on the relative values of different currencies. Therefore, people can still buy things when they visit other countries.

Activity

Table Talk—Encourage each group to talk about the most important things learned about money. Using upper-grade mentors or parent volunteers as recorders, have each table group create a paragraph that reflects its conversation. (An alternative is to create a whole-class summary paragraph.) Share and discuss the responses in class.

Summarize

- The government makes money and controls how much is in circulation.
- *Currency* is another name for our money.
- U.S. currency can only show people who have died (to avoid signs of power).
- Almost every country around the world has official units of currency.
- Governments around the world work together to assist people in buying and selling in different currencies.

Assessment

Use the artifacts (e.g., coins, bills, and globe) to conduct a true/false quiz. Have each student on a numbered sheet of paper write T if the statement is true and F if it is false. Allocate time for class discussion about ways of changing the false statements to make them true.

1. False   All U.S. coins are made in our home state.

2. True   *Currency* is another name for our coins and bills.

3. False   The bank controls the amounts of coins and bills that are circulated.

4. False   Anybody can have his or her face put on a coin or bill. It simply has to be voted on by the people.

5. False   All coins have two sayings on them: "E Pluribus Unum" and "In God We Trust."

6. False   The larger the coin, the more it is worth.

7. False   Coins are all made by hand.

8. True   Our dollars are made with special inks and paper.

9. True   Almost every country in the world has official currency.

10. False   We cannot buy things in other countries because we cannot figure out how much they cost.

Home Assignment

Duplicate the recorded table talk paragraphs that describe the main ideas associated with today's lesson about currency and encourage students to read the responses to their families. Then examine coins and bills and discuss the reason why money cannot show a living person and whether or not this decision was a good one.

Dear Parents,

Today we learned about currency and how it is made. Please encourage your child to read the responses that groups of students prepared. Then as a family examine coins and bills. Discuss the idea that by law, money cannot show a living person because the government didn't want people doing this as a sign of power. Do you think this is a good idea? Why or why not? Please be sure your child is ready to share your family response with the class during our next lesson.

Sincerely,

FIGURE 5   Model Letter to Parents

Lesson 5

A Trip to the Bank

Resources

- Permission slips for field trip to the bank
- Volunteer chaperones and transportation if bank isn't nearby
- City map
- Deposit and withdrawal slips
- Bank statements
- Personal check
- ATM card
- Debit card
- Photos of bank (interior and exterior)
- Copies of Figure 7: Student Activity Sheet: Bank Activity, clipboards, and pencils (include a second blank copy of the Student Activity Sheet with the home assignment)

General Comments

The intent of this lesson is to take the class on an actual field trip to a nearby bank and conduct some planned observations and interviews regarding what services banks provide and what kinds of jobs people have who work there. The trip will give students an opportunity to observe some of the kinds of workers connected to the banking industry. For this lesson, recruit parents to act as group leaders. In addition, you (and perhaps parent volunteers as well) should previsit the bank to work out the logistics of the trip, consult with the manager, and "walk through" the Student Activity Sheet (Figure 7).

General Purposes or Goals

To develop an understanding and appreciation of: (1) what kinds of services banks provide; and (2) what kinds of jobs people who work in banks have.

Main Ideas to Develop

- A bank is a business that keeps money for customers, makes loans, and provides other related services (e.g., safe-deposit boxes).
- It takes a lot of people to run a bank.
- A loan is a sum of money borrowed for a certain amount of time.
- Loans are for things like buying houses. These loans are called mortgages.
- Banks earn money by charging fees for the services to customers and by lending money to them.

- People decide whether or not they want to save some of their money, how much they want to save, and where to keep it.

Teaching Tips from Barbara

Our trip to the bank was very successful. I spent time before the field trip at the bank discussing our goals and lessons. My students were astonished by the fact that banks are in the business of making money. The people at the bank were very impressed by the amount of information that the students already knew. It was a terrific way to make connections and motivate learning in later lessons.

Starting the Lesson

Begin by discussing the responses to the home assignment. Introduce the lesson with a city map showing the route to the bank, a photo of its exterior, and several photos of its various departments. Talk about the roles, norms, and expectations of a bank customer and of a student on tour. Role-play guidelines to follow when on field trips.

If possible, organize each table as a group and assign a parent volunteer to conduct an overall "broad brush" tour of the bank to observe the layout and the types of work and services being done by the employees. Provide each small group of students and volunteer with a pencil and a Student Activity Sheet (Figure 7) attached to a clipboard. Decide in advance if all student groups will move together throughout the bank or rotate by sections.

At the conclusion of the field trip, hold a class debriefing and compile responses on a large sheet of chart paper. Use the ideas from this class data retrieval chart in a group reflective journal that the class will write. Emphasize the bank layout, what kinds of services banks provide, what kinds of work people do, how banks make money, and how banks are important to people in our community. Encourage students to read the group story to a family member.

Suggested Lesson Discussion

Banks are businesses. Like other businesses, banks need to have money left after they pay their expenses. This money is called *profit*. Banks make their profits by charging their customers for the services they provide.

Banks also make money by lending it. When you put your money in the bank, you are allowing the bank to use it. The bank puts your money and other people's money together to make loans. In return for using your money, the bank pays you interest. The person who borrowed the money pays the bank more money than the bank pays you, so the bank makes a profit.

As you look around your community, you have probably noticed that banks are in many different places—along main streets, in malls, and even in supermarkets.

It takes lots of people to run a bank. Each job requires certain types of knowledge and skills: a teller withdraws and deposits money for the bank's customers; a proof machine operator runs equipment at the bank and subtracts money from the bank accounts; a loan officer arranges for people to get loans; a security officer maintains safety at the bank; an accountant keeps financial records for the bank.

You probably wonder how banks keep track of everyone's money. [Show deposit and withdrawal slips.] Customers fill out slips of paper for every deposit or withdrawal. They get a receipt [show receipt] from the bank. Additionally, most banks provide their customers with monthly statements [show bank statement] that summarize transactions—times when money was added or subtracted from the account. The balance is the amount currently in the account.

When people need some of the money from their bank account, they can get it in a couple of ways. One way is to write a check. [Illustrate writing a check on your account to CASH, endorsing it (signing your name on the back), and stopping at the bank to get the check exchanged for cash.] The other way is to use an ATM card, which is available to individuals who have checking accounts. [Show ATM card.] Even if the bank is closed, people can get cash from an ATM machine when they insert the card into the machine and enter a personal identification number. If the machine does not recognize the number, the transaction cannot be completed. Your family also needs to be aware that some banks charge a fee every time it makes a transaction using the ATM card.

There is another card you might have observed your family using. It's called a *debit card.* Suppose your mother wants to buy you a new coat and she doesn't have enough cash in her purse and she doesn't have her checkbook with her, but she has a debit card. [Show a debit card.] When your mother uses the debit card to buy the coat, the salesperson slides the card through the card-reading machine. The machine contacts your family's account electronically to make sure there's enough money in the checking account to pay for the coat. If there is, the amount of the purchase is automatically subtracted from the account and sent to the store's account to pay for the coat.

When you put money in the bank, you can be sure that it is safe. The money is kept in steel fireproof vaults that can be opened only by certain people. The money is also insured by the government so in case the bank is robbed or goes out of business, the money is protected.

Besides your money, many banks have safe-deposit boxes that you can rent for keeping very important papers, jewelry, and other valuable items. These safe-deposit boxes are kept in a very large walk-in steel vault.

Banks are safe places to keep money and other valuable possessions. They are available to everyone. They are not allowed to discriminate against anyone on account of age, sex, religion, race, or culture.

Activity

At the conclusion of the field trip, hold a class debriefing and compile responses on a large sheet of chart paper. Use the ideas from this data retrieval chart in a group reflective journal that the class will write. Emphasize the bank layout, what kinds of services banks provide, what kinds of work people do, how banks make money, and how banks are important to people in our community.

Activity

Have each group give a mini-report focusing on a preassigned aspect of the bank (e.g., bank teller, mortgage department/loan officer, accounting, safe-deposit boxes, etc.).

Summarize

- A bank is a business that keeps money for customers, makes loans, and provides other related services (e.g., rents safe-deposit boxes to customers).
- Many people are needed to run a bank.
- People decide whether to use the services of a bank and where to do their banking.

Assessment

Ask each student to draw the most important thing he or she learned about banking during the trip to the bank and write a caption establishing the big idea.

Home Assignment

Encourage family members to serve as an audience for the student's reading of the group's journal entry and for discussing the student's drawing of the most important thing he or she learned about banking. Also, ask family members to budget a few minutes of their next trip to the bank to allow the student to point out some of the features of the bank, what banking services are available to the customers, and who provides them. (Include a blank copy of Figure 7 with the home assignment.)

Dear Parents,

We encourage at least one family member to act as an audience for your child's reading and to discuss the drawing related to our class trip to one of the banks in our community. We would also encourage you to budget a few minutes of your next trip to your bank to allow your child to point out some of the features he or she learned about. Then point out features that would be new to your child. A copy of the class activity sheet that we used on our class trip is enclosed.

Your child will undoubtedly have lots of questions as well as information he or she acquired on our class trip.

Sincerely,

FIGURE 6   Model Letter to Parents

1. What does the outside of the bank look like? _____

_____

_____

2. What does the inside of the bank look like? _____

_____

_____

3. What does the bank do for members of our community? _____

_____

_____

4. Do all the people in our community come to this bank? _____

Why or why not? _____

_____

_____

5. It takes a lot of people to run a bank. List all the workers you observed on your bank visit and explain what each does.

Example: Security Officer   makes sure customers and bank workers are kept safe

1.   _____

2.   _____

3.   _____

4.   _____

5.   _____

6.   _____

7.   _____

8.   _____

Continues

FIGURE 7   Student Activity Sheet: Blank Activity

6. Banks are businesses. How do they make money? _____

_____

_____

7. Why do lots of people keep their money in a savings account at a bank instead of simply stashing it in a piggy bank? _____

_____

_____

8. How does cashing a check or using your ATM card at the bank work?

_____

_____

9. Why do people choose to rent safe-deposit boxes at their bank? _____

_____

_____

10. Describe the room at the bank that holds the safe-deposit boxes. _____

_____

_____

FIGURE 7 (Continued)

Lesson 6

Earning Money: A Class Project

Resources

- Word cards: Consumers, Market Survey, Business Plan, Supply, Demand, Produce, Income, Profit, Collateral, Scarcity, Need, Want, Cost, Raw Materials, Product, etc. (one set for each table)
- Popcorn popper, bags, popcorn oil, salt
- Market survey
- Copies of Figure 9: Interview Schedule

Children's Literature

Zimelman, N. (1992). *How the Second Grade Got $8,205.50 to Visit the Statue of Liberty*. Morton Grove, IL: Albert Whitman & Co.

General Comments

The focus of this lesson is on earning money. While the jobs elementary school students can have are limited, learning about income is important because throughout life people need to earn the money that they spend.

General Purposes or Goals

To help students: (1) understand and appreciate the reasons for earning money—in order to spend it on the things that one needs and wants; (2) understand and appreciate the meaning and importance of supply and demand, scarcity, and profit, and apply these concepts to the goods that they produce and sell at school.

Main Ideas to Develop

- Income is money that a person gets from selling a product or service, salary or wages for doing a job, interest, investment, or money earned some other way.
- Most elementary-age children are limited in how they make money because their main job is going to school.
- Ways elementary-age children can earn money include watching pets, raking leaves, or having a small business such as running a lemonade stand or selling popcorn.
- Individuals who run small businesses need to consider supply, demand, scarcity, and profit if they are to be successful.
- As adults, your students will be able to make choices about the kinds of work they will do.

Teaching Tips from Barbara

To begin this lesson, we followed a modified problem-solving process. First, we identified several problems within our classroom. Next, we discussed possible solutions to those problems. Then we chose a problem where one of the solutions required money. We decided that the lack of indoor recess games was the problem to solve. One additional step that I added was working to solve the problem without money too. We had several students donate old, used games to our collection as well as earning money with a popcorn sale to buy games.

Starting the Lesson

Share homework responses from the previous lesson. Then pose the question, "Do any of you earn money? How?" List the responses on the white board. Watching pets, picking up toys, washing dishes, and dusting furniture will probably be included as responses. Underscore the idea that children in America are required to go to school, which limits the amount of time there is to make money. Also, many of today's jobs would be too difficult for children to do. Lots of jobs have changed over time or are no longer needed because of technology.

Suggested Lesson Discussion

Besides earning money as income, you can also earn money by keeping it in the bank and getting interest from it. Money you get for your birthday or on other special occasions is also income.

While most elementary students earn money as allowance by doing chores around the house, a few work for others and do things such as take care of somebody else's pet. Many children your age like being in business for themselves—with the supervision of family members. [Ask students if they have ever had a lemonade or fruit stand, for example. Explain that during this lesson the class will plan and implement a popcorn business, which will run for a short time.] The business will need to make a profit. *Profit* is the money you have after you have paid your expenses.

The first thing you need to do is to find out whether your business has a chance of succeeding. One way to figure this out is to conduct a market survey. A market survey is used to find out what people like and dislike, what they are willing to buy, and how much they are willing to pay. For example, if our class is going to sell popcorn, we need to conduct a market survey to determine if other students in the school like popcorn and if they would buy it from us. We also need to find out how much they would be willing to pay for it. Our market survey would look something like this. [Show typical survey questions on large chart paper.]

Do you like popcorn? Yes _____ No _____

Do you eat popcorn more than once a month? Yes _____ No _____

Would you buy popcorn at school if it became available?

Yes _____ No _____

Would you be willing to pay 25 cents a bag for it?

Yes _____ No _____

Once we have determined that students at our school will buy our product, we need to put together a business plan. The business plan will describe our product, which is popcorn, and explain how it will be sold. In our case, we can borrow the school's popcorn popper (we will not need to rent one). We will need to describe the materials we will need for producing and packaging the popcorn, how much money we are going to need to start our business, and how much profit we expect to make on each bag. We also need to describe our advertising strategy in our business plan.

If we have to borrow money from a bank to start our business and we've never borrowed from a bank before, we may need collateral. *Collateral* is something valuable like a car or jewelry. If we can't pay our loan, the bank has the right to sell our collateral. Therefore, it's very important that we develop an accurate business plan. [Review other economic terms that have been used during the unit (e.g., *consumer, producer, needs, wants*). Use word cards, pictures, illustrations, etc. to stimulate the discussion. Consider the existing background knowledge of the students and the time and resources available as you collect the materials you need for producing popcorn (popcorn poppers, bags, oil, salt, popcorn). Purchase the goods as a class.]

Supply is the amount of goods (popcorn) that will be available to the customers (students and others in the school). *Demand* is the desire of the customers for popcorn. We want to be in a situation where we have enough popcorn to sell and we have enough customers or students to buy all of our popcorn. If we have slightly more customers than popcorn, we can charge a higher price. *Scarcity* will result if many students want our popcorn but we have a limited amount of popcorn and bags—fewer than we have customers. In other words, not everybody who wants our popcorn will be able to purchase it. When the demand is greater than the supply, we can charge a slightly higher price. If there's a decreased demand for popcorn, the price will probably need to go down.

[Review the major understandings that you intend students to draw from this hands-on learning opportunity. Then conduct the sale with the help of volunteers. Make mental notes of individual conversations, questions, options, etc. Debrief the learning opportunity by posing questions such as Should we have advertised more? What happens when you don't have enough of your product to sell to everyone that wants it? What would have happened if we had charged more? What would have happened if we had had popcorn left over? What should we have done? Can we take all the money in our cash register and spend it on what we want? Why not? Demonstrate and figure out the amount that was profit. Explain that you will use this on a class project. See Lesson 12, "Children Can Make a Difference by Donating Some Money to Help Others."]

Optional   Take the money to a bank and open a class account.

Optional   Use the book *How the Second Grade Got $8,205.50 to Visit the Statue of Liberty* and compare what happened in the book with the popcorn project. How were the projects similar? Different?

Activity

Ask table groups to talk about what they learned about running a small business. Provide each table with a set of cards and ask the students to use as many of them as they can in their talk. Appoint a student leader to manage the cards. Elicit a volunteer parent to "listen in" on each conversation. Cards to include: Market Survey, Business Plan, Collateral, Consumers, Produce, Income, Supply, Demand, Profit, Scarcity, Need, Want, Cost, Raw Materials, Product.

Encourage each table to share what it discussed. Use the cards to enable a flow of ideas.

Summarize

- Income is the money received from selling a product.
- To figure out how much profit you have, you need to subtract your expenses from the money (income) you earned. The difference is the profit.
- Individuals who run small businesses need to consider supply, demand, scarcity, and profit if they are to be successful.

Assessment

Have each student write a story describing what he or she learned about selling popcorn (running a small business). Encourage students to sequence the things they needed to do to be successful with their business. Encourage the students to use the word wall for their writing.

Home Assignment

Encourage students to share their individual stories describing what they learned about running a small business with their families. Suggest that, if possible, each student interview and/or have a conversation with a small business owner that the family knows. (Send home a copy of Figure 9: Interview Schedule for students to use for this assignment.) They should discuss income, supply, demand, scarcity, and profit as it relates to the owner's specific business. The student should be prepared to share what he or she learned from the business owner during the next class session.

Optional   Invite small business owners to share their stories with the class.

Dear Parents,

We have been learning about running a small business. Our class had a popcorn sale and we learned firsthand about supply, demand, scarcity, income, and profit. Encourage your child to read the story he or she wrote.

We would like you and your child to talk with a friend or neighbor who owns a small business. We have provided an interview schedule for your child to fill out. Discuss supply, demand, scarcity, income, profit, wants, needs, and so on as they relate to the business and those who buy the goods or services (customers).

Your child will be asked to share what she or he learned with classmates. Thank you!

Sincerely,

FIGURE 8   Model Letter to Parents

Name _____

1. What small business do you own? _____

_____

_____

2. Did you do a market survey? Explain. _____

_____

_____

3. Explain your business plan. (Describe your product or service. How did you figure out how much money you would need to start your business? How did you decide how much to charge for your good or service? What is your plan for advertising? Etc.) _____

_____

_____

_____

_____

4. What do you need to know about supply and demand related to the product or service that you sell? _____

_____

_____

5. What do you need to know about needs and wants? _____

_____

_____

6. How and why is profit important in your business? _____

_____

_____

FIGURE 9 Interview Schedule

Lesson 7

Budgeting

Resources

- Graphic illustrating a child's budget (If you have students whose parents implement budgets with their children, be sure to call upon the families to serve as resources. Ask them to share examples of these budgets with the class.)
- Graphic depicting teacher's monthly budget (see Figure 11 for example)
- Family budget graphic and cards for group activity (one packet for each group) (sample cards: Mother's salary, Dad's salary, children's part-time jobs, interest on money earned from savings, money donated to charity, housing [rent or mortgage], groceries, telephone bill, electric bill, car payment, taxes, food, clothing, etc.)

Children's Literature

Godfrey, N. (1998). *Ultimate Kids' Money Book*. New York: Simon & Schuster.

General Comments

Keeping track of how much money comes in and how much money goes out can provide useful information. Introducing this at a young age and planting seeds regarding the importance of budgeting can help students plan their futures. Underscore the idea that all people can benefit from planning.

General Purposes or Goals

To help students: (1) develop an understanding of and appreciation for the importance of keeping track of where one's personal money goes; (2) underscore and appreciate the value of budgeting and how to create a budget; and (3) apply ideas about budgeting to their own lives.

Main Ideas to Develop

- A budget is a plan that shows how much money comes in and how much money goes out.
- People obtain money in different ways: earn wages by working, sell things, receive money as gifts, get an allowance, invest, and so forth.
- People spend money to buy things that they need or want. The choices people make about money are very personal.

- Needs are things you must have and wants are things you would like to have but don't necessarily need.
- Balancing a budget means trying to make sure that the money going out is equal to or less than the money coming in.

Teaching Tips from Barbara

I began this lesson with my budget first to introduce the idea of budgets and how they work. I used hypothetical situations like vacations and medical emergencies to show how a budget needs to adjust. Then I showed the simpler child's budget. It was most powerful when students analyzed budgets to decide if they were "good" or "bad." Students had to explain their answers with reasoning about budgets.

Starting the Lesson

Share homework responses from the previous lesson. Then pose the question, "Where does money go?" List the student responses. Explain that this is a very important question that their families need to answer—and they will need to answer when they have money of their own.

Suggested Lesson Discussion

Keeping track of how much money you have, thinking about what you are spending it on, and deciding whether or not you have enough to get the things you need and want are really important matters if you are going to have success with your money.

A *budget* is a plan that can help people manage their money. There are two parts to a budget: One part shows your income—money that comes in from your job, from gifts, or from interest on money you have saved and stored in the bank. The other part of a budget is the money that goes out. This part shows how you use your money. Usually families spend a lot each month to pay their bills. Families often put some of their money in the bank (savings) and donate a portion to their church or to a charity such as the American Cancer Society or the Food Bank.

[Show a child's budget.] A child's budget is much like a family budget, only it's on a smaller scale because students in the early grades don't earn much money as allowance. They don't do many jobs for pay and most of their time is spent going to school.

CARLISLE'S WEEKLY BUDGET

Money In

Income

Allowance	$ 8.00
Birthday gift	10.00
Total	$18.00

Money Out
   Spending
      Snacks at school $ 3.00
      School supplies   2.50

   Saving
      (For baseball
         glove, ball, and bat   1.50

   Sharing
      Food Bank   .50
      _____
      Total $ 7.50

Carlisle doesn't spend more than she has, so her budget would be considered a good one. This month Carlisle spends $7.50 out of her $8.00 allowance. She saves $.50 plus her birthday money. (Remember, Carlisle receives birthday money only once a year.)

One way to avoid running out of money is to have a spending plan. Some people plan by the week while others plan by the month. Whichever plan you have, it is important to stick to it. Your plan needs to include a list of all the money you have coming in. This is known as *income*. You next need to list all the things you spend money on regularly. Also list any extra expenses you expect to have, such as a gift for somebody. Then think about what you want to be saving for. Decide on an amount you need to put aside each week to make that happen. List any money you want to donate, or share with others. When you finish your plan, you need to subtract the money you spent from the money you brought in. If the money you spent is less than the amount you brought in, your budget is in good shape.

As you grow up, finish school, perhaps go to college, and get a job, you will have more money and of course you will be able to pay for more things. The choices you make about money are very personal.

[Show a graphic that you will develop as you role-play and explain your family budget. Use Figure 11 as a guideline.]

[Present a role-play situation with the setting being your family meeting to plan its budget for a month. Build the graphic using word cards and pictures. Use hypothetical or real figures according to your comfort level.]

[Discuss all the money coming in. Put each item on a word card. Post. List all the things your family regularly spends money on, plus extras (one of the children needs a new pair of shoes, etc.). Complete the graphic by posting all items that represent the money in and money out. Then subtract the money out from money in. Explain that the budget needs to show a surplus or at least balance.]

In balancing a budget, a family tries to make sure that the money going out is equal to or less than money coming in. [You may want to use Monopoly money to illustrate money allocations for each of the categories. Underscore the idea that wherever there is money, it has to be managed.] Organizations such as PTA, Boy Scouts, and even the government need to manage their money.

Optional   [Invite a resource person to talk to the class about the budget he or she manages. It could be a personal family budget or an organizational budget.]

Activity

Provide each table with a graphic depicting where money comes from and where money goes along with a packet of cards that describes places money comes from and places money goes. Have each table decide where to place each card on the graphic.

Summarize

- People obtain money in different ways: by working, investing, receiving gifts, or selling things.
- People spend money on the things they need (e.g., food, shelter, and clothing, cars and insurance, heat, water, electricity, etc.). They also spend money on things they want, such as recreation.
- A budget is a plan that shows how much money comes in and how much goes out every month for paying bills.

Reminder   Have you and your class been updating the TWL chart that you started in Lesson 1?

Assessment

Conduct a thumbs up/thumbs down survey. Have each student gesture thumbs up if the statement is true and thumbs down if it is not true.

1. Thumbs down   A budget only shows the money that goes out.
2. Thumbs down   People make all the same choices about money.
3. Thumbs up   People obtain money in many different ways.
4. Thumbs up   One way people get money is by working and earning wages.
5. Thumbs up   People can earn money by selling things.
6. Thumbs down   Some people spend more money than they make. The result is that their budget is balanced.
7. Thumbs up   One way money comes in is by receiving money as gifts.
8. Thumbs down   Only people who don't have much money need to budget.

| 9. | Thumbs up | Some people use some of their money to buy some-body a present or donate money to a worthy cause. |
| 10. | Thumbs up | A want is something you would like to have but don't necessarily need. |

Home Assignment

Have the students talk with family members about budgeting. They should discuss how family members earn money and things they spend money on to satisfy their needs and wants. What is their family saving for? Then encourage families to discuss some of the problems families have regarding money and budgeting. For example, sometimes unexpected things happen (e.g., invited to a party and want to take a gift; the family car breaks down; new tires are needed, etc.).

Dear Parents,

We have been learning about budgeting in school. We encourage you to talk with your child about how your family earns and spends its money. Discuss what things your family is saving for. Finally, talk about the problems families have with money and budgeting. For example, unplanned things occur such as being laid off from a job, the family car breaking down, and so on. We will encourage your child to share responses during our next class session.

Sincerely,

FIGURE 10   Model Letter to Parents

Money In

    <u>Income</u>

        Salary   _____

        Interest on savings   _____

Money Out

    <u>Spending</u>

        Housing (rent or mortgage, home insurance)   _____

        Household expenses (telephone, electricity, heat, water, cable)   _____

        Car payment and insurance   _____

        Taxes   _____

        Food   _____

        Clothing   _____

        Medical bills   _____

        Education expenses   _____

        Recreation   _____

        Extras (haircut, gifts, etc.)   _____

    <u>Savings</u>   _____

    <u>Sharing</u> (food bank)   _____

    TOTAL   _____

FIGURE 11   Teacher's Weekly Budget

Lesson 8

. . . .

Choice Making: Opportunity Costs and Methods of Payment

Resources

- Questions on word cards: How much should you save? How much should you spend? What should you spend your money on? What are you willing to give up to get what you want?
- Word card: Opportunity Cost
- Displays of items:
    1. Sweatshirt, CD, perfume or hair gel, book, running shoes, ticket to movie or concert
    2. CD, unique T-shirt, game, tickets to movie, computer game
- Display of cash, check, checkbook, credit card, debit card, credit card receipt, credit card monthly statement
- Figure 12, chart describing advantages and disadvantages of different types of payment
- Activity response sheet with purchasing scenarios

Children's Literature

Godfrey, N. (1998). *Ultimate Kids' Money Book*. New York: Simon & Schuster.

General Comments

The focus of this lesson is choice making. You have to choose what you do with your money. It really takes a lot of work to spend wisely and decide how to pay for the things we choose to buy.

General Purposes or Goals

To help students: (1) develop an understanding of and appreciation for what it means to make choices and the costs associated with these decisions; and (2) become acquainted with the several ways there are to pay for the things one buys.

Main Ideas to Develop

- There is a cost, called the opportunity cost, associated with every decision we make. The opportunity cost is what you give up when you choose to use your limited time or money to get something you want more.
- There are several ways to pay for the things you buy: cash, check, credit card, debit card.

- One very popular kind of cashless money is called a check. People write checks every day to pay bills and purchase goods. The company or store will be paid by the check writer's bank. (The bank takes the money out of his or her account.)

- People also use cashless money called credit cards. They allow people to buy now and pay later. If you do not pay the full amount when the credit card bill comes due, the item will cost a lot more because interest is added to the amount left unpaid.

Teaching Tips from Barbara

I found it very valuable to make connections to the budgeting lesson. Students very quickly grasped the idea that money choices are very critical. This lesson allows students to participate actively when discussing the opportunity costs for their decisions. In the activity, Scenario #2 worked the best for students to understand the choice-making process. This lesson worked best in two sessions, one for discussing opportunity costs and one for learning methods of payment. I found that methods of payment was a place with many misconceptions. Students often see their family using checks, credit cards, money machines, and other methods of payment without clearly understanding what's happening. The chart describing types of payment was very helpful for my students to go back to and compare after the lesson.

Starting the Lesson

Share homework responses from the previous lesson. Then pose the question, "Do you think it is easy or hard to spend money wisely? Why?" Elicit responses from the students, encouraging them to provide reasons for their answers.

Suggested Lesson Discussion

[Use a role-play scenario to examine choice making. Questions that might surface include How much should you save? How much should you spend? What should you spend it on? What are you willing to give up to get what you want? Display a series of items the students might be interested in buying (sweatshirt, CD, perfume or hair gel, book, running shoes, ticket to a movie or concert, etc.). You may want to include multiple options (at different prices) for some of the items.

[Conduct an interactive discussion with the class associated with the trade-offs and issues regarding each item.] If you spend the money on a sweatshirt, you might never have a chance to see the rock group, whereas if you buy the tickets now, you could save for the sweatshirt next month. However, if you don't have a warm shirt to wear to the concert and you're cold, you wouldn't enjoy the concert very much. [And so on.]

Each time you choose to do something or buy something, you are choosing not to do something or buy something else. That means there is a cost, called the *opportunity cost,* associated with each decision you make. The opportunity cost is what you give up when you use your limited time or money to get something you want more (for example, money you spend on a bike can't be used to buy something else you want, like a Game Boy, so using the money for the bike costs you the opportunity to use it for the Game Boy). [Post the words *opportunity cost* on the white board or word wall.]

[Display another series of items that your students would like to have, such as a CD, unique T-shirt, a game, tickets to a movie, and a computer game. Select a student to participate in the role-play. Again, you might want to price each item and encourage students to take price into account in their decision making (e.g., if you buy a cheaper alternative, you can save more of your money or use it to buy somthing else).]

[Conduct an interactive discussion with the actor explaining what she or he will buy and why and what she or he will be giving up (opportunity cost).]

[Repeat the role-play with another student and the set of items.] Money involves lots of personal choices. People need to think about what they need and want today as well as tomorrow.

[Show a display of items used to pay for the things we buy: credit card, debit card, cash, check.] When you buy something, you need to figure how you will pay for it.

There are several ways you can pay for the things you buy. Cash helps you figure out if you can afford it; however, it's unhandy to carry it around and many people fear losing it. One kind of cashless money is called a *check.* [Show your checkbook and a blank check.] People write checks every day to pay bills and purchase goods. The company or store will be paid by check writer's bank, which takes the money out of his or her account. [Demonstrate the store endorsing the check and depositing it in its account.]

Another kind of cashless money is the *credit card.* The credit card allows people to buy now and pay later. If you do not pay the full amount when the credit card bill is due, the item will cost a lot more because interest is added to the unpaid amount. [Show a credit card, credit card receipt, and monthly credit card statement.]

[Use a simple example illustrating that if your monthly bill were $20.00 and you paid only $10.00, next month, even if you did not use your credit card, your bill would be $11.80 because there is an 18 percent interest rate.] Credit card charges are not free money. You do have to pay them back. And the longer you take to pay them, the more you end up paying.

Optional [Explain that even Barbie encourages borrowing.] Among the items sold by Mattel is Cool Shoppin' Barbie. She comes with a toy credit card. In real life, however, credit cards are no game. You have to pay a bank for what you buy, plus extra fees, like interest. [End optional section]

A *debit card* [show debit card] is one used to transfer funds electronically. For example, you can call a store, place an order for something, give your card number, and the item will be sent to you. The bank will use its computer to automatically take the money from your account and put it into the seller's account.

[As a class, summarize the types of money you have discussed and their advantages and disadvantages.]

Activity

Using a series of scenarios, have students at each table identify the opportunity cost of each choice and the best way of paying for the item. Prepare a simple response sheet (see Figure 13, p. 180). When all groups have finished, discuss the responses and review the chart focusing on types of payment and the advantages and disadvantages of each.

Summarize

- Opportunity cost is what you give up when you use your limited time or money to get something you want more.
- People have many choices to make when budgeting or spending money.

Table 2   Advantages and Disadvantages of Different Types of Payments

TYPE OF PAYMENT	ADVANTAGES	DISADVANTAGES
Cash	You can easily determine if you have enough money to pay for the item.	It can be unhandy to carry. It can be easily stolen or lost.
Check	They are safe to send or carry. A check has value only if it is signed by the owner of the checking account.	If you forget to record the amount of your check, you may not have sufficient funds to pay for the item and the check will bounce. You will end up paying a fine for all the extra paperwork.
Credit Card	It is easy to use. You can have things before you have enough money to pay for them.	If you don't pay your monthly credit card bill in total, you have to pay interest.

- There are several ways to pay for the goods and services that we buy. There are trade-offs associated with each method of payment.

Assessment

Have each student write a paragraph explaining the choices that she or he and her or his family make about money. Encourage students to use the word wall for prompts and spellings. Responses you can expect include the following: spend or save, what you give up to get something you want more, how to purchase an item.

Home Assignment

Encourage the student to share his or her paragraph regarding choice making with family members. Then they should discuss the question, "Is it easy or hard to spend wisely? Why?" Tell students to be prepared to discuss the responses in an upcoming lesson.

Dear Parents,

Your child has been learning about choices associated with spending. We encourage you to ask your child to read the paragraph he or she wrote about this topic. Then as a family, discuss the question, "Is it easy or hard to spend wisely? Why?" Talk about specific examples, illustrating your response. Your child will be asked to share your ideas with the class. Sending written responses would be very helpful.

Sincerely,

FIGURE 12   Model Letter to Parents

Scenario #1

Barney has $1.00 to spend on snacks. Choices include a Coke, a bag of chips, a box of gummy bears, a box of popcorn, and a caramel apple. (Each costs $1.) What should he buy? <u>Coke</u>

What is the opportunity cost? <u>He takes the opportunity to satisfy his thirst but gives up the opportunity to buy something to eat.</u>

What is the best way to pay for the purchase? <u>He has four quarters to use to pay for the coke.</u>

Scenario #2

Beth wants to have a birthday party. Her mother has budgeted $20 for the occasion. Things she could buy for the guests include: party hats ($2), prizes for the games ($5), balloons for decorations ($5), pizzas ($15), Coke ($5), and invitations ($5). What should she buy? _____

_____

What is the opportunity cost? _____

_____

_____

What is the best way for her to pay for the items? _____

_____

_____

Scenario #3

John's mother has promised to buy him some new school clothes. She has budgeted $75 for shopping. Things John wants include new tennis shoes ($40), jeans ($25), sweatshirt ($10), windbreaker ($10), cap ($5), and gloves ($5). What should he buy? _____

_____

FIGURE 13   Identifying Opportunity Costs and Payment Choices

© 2003 by Janet Alleman and Jere Brophy from *Social Studies Excursions, K–3: Book Three.* Portsmouth, NH: Heinemann.

What is the opportunity cost? _____

_____

_____

What is the best way to pay for the purchase? _____

_____

_____

Scenario #4

Amy's family has decided to go on a vacation. Currently it has $100 in its budget for recreation. The family could rent a hotel (with swimming pool) locally for a night ($80), go to Chicago for a weekend and spend $500, or stay home and wait until there's more money in the budget. What should the family do? _____

_____

_____

What is the opportunity cost? _____

_____

_____

If the family decides to take a vacation now, how should it pay the bill? _____

_____

_____

FIGURE 13   (Continued)

Lesson 9

. . . .

Choosing a Job

Resources

- Photos and pictures of jobs that illustrate the factors that contribute to job choices (e.g., physical features such as lakes, mountains, climate/weather, population, resources such as people and natural economy)
- Resource people to share stories about their jobs in the local area
- Mounted pictures illustrating factors that contribute to job choices (three per table)
- Copies of Figure 15: Future Job Possibilities

Children's Literature

Flanagan, A. (1998a). *Buying a Pet from Ms. Chavez*. New York: Children's Press.

Flanagan, A. (1998b). *Choosing Eyeglasses with Mrs. Koutris*. New York: Children's Press.

Flanagan, A. (1998c). *Learning Is Fun with Mrs. Perez*. New York: Children's Press.

Flanagan, A. (1998d). *Mr. Santizo's Tasty Treats*. New York: Children's Press.

Flanagan, A. (1998e). *Mr. Yee Fixes Cars*. New York: Children's Press.

General Comments

The focus of this lesson will be on earning money locally—the jobs people can choose based on factors such as climate/weather, physical features, and natural and human resources. Engaging a panel of guests from the local area who have a range of jobs will bring this lesson to life for the students.

General Purposes and Goals

To help students understand and appreciate: (1) how jobs have changed over time; and (2) the factors that contribute to the availability of job choices.

Main Ideas to Develop

- For many, many years people have worked at different jobs. Jobs have changed over the years. Some have disappeared completely and new ones have been created.

- People's jobs have a lot to do with where they live. The climate/ weather, physical features (mountains, plains, lakes, etc.), and population density all contribute to the choices.
- Producers need natural, human, and capital resources to make goods and services.

Teaching Tips from Barbara

This lesson is a very natural way to connect to other units that you might have done in the cultural universals series. For example, if you have already done the food unit, you can have students remember the jobs related to making peanut butter. Then evaluate those jobs based on the factors that contribute to job choices. You can also use parents and family members as resources to begin your discussion about jobs.

Starting the Lesson

Begin by discussing the home assignment from the previous lesson. Then show a series of pictures and photographs that clearly illustrate the range of natural factors that contribute to job choices (e.g., mountains and skiing, lakes and boating/fishing, plains and farming, cities and mass transit). Ask students what they notice about the pictures and photos. Then ask how they think their parents decided on what jobs to take. List their ideas on the white board.

Suggested Lesson Discussion

[Use a time line and pictures from one of your previous units.] Long ago people had limited wants and needs and often their family satisfied them. Together, family members (human resources) provided for food, shelter, and clothing. Gradually people began specializing in making goods and services that were suited to the human, natural, and/or capital resources that were available. As more people moved into an area and individuals became more specialized [review bartering], people began to buy things that they did not produce themselves. Today money facilitates the exchange of goods and services.

[Share descriptions of the job choices your family members have made (e.g., self—teacher needed to be in a densely populated area where there were lots of schools, husband—design engineer for cars and trucks needed to be in an area where there are large factories that manufacture cars and trucks). Show photos of a mountainous region, an area surrounded by lakes, a gulf coast, a plains area, etc.] Physical features influence what people do (the kinds of jobs that are available).

[Invite to the class a resource person or panel of local workers whose jobs are dependent on climate/weather, physical features, availability of resources, etc. For example, a lawn care service worker could be brought in to talk about providing lawn care service in the spring, summer, and fall because during the growing season there's a lot of grass to be cut, fertilized, etc. During the winter, business shifts from lawn care service to snow removal service. Show pictures of a densely populated city (human resources) and ask what sort of jobs would be available for providing goods and services. Examples might include taxi drivers, bankers, salespeople in stores, school and church employees, etc.]

[After discussing with the panel or individual guests what they do and the factors that contribute to their job choices, introduce *Mr. Santizo's Tasty Treats*.] Several years ago, Mr. Santizo moved to the United States from Guatemala. He decided that to get a job in America he needed to move to an area where there were a lot of people—people who had a *need* for his work. He got a job in a bakery. The owner of the bakery provided the capital resources (store space, ovens, raw materials, etc.). Many people came daily to buy the *goods* that were produced there (doughnuts, cookies, breads, cakes, etc.). He worked hard to learn new techniques (decorating cakes, etc). He provided a *human resource*. He provided the goods that would satisfy his customers. A dense population was important to ensure that there would be enough customers to buy the goods. [Other books in the series that can be substituted are *Choosing Eyeglasses with Mr. Koutris, Buying a Pet from Ms. Chavez, Learning Is Fun with Mrs. Perez,* and *Mr. Yee Fixes Cars*. The emphasis should be on the connection between the job and the factors that influence it being available as a choice. Underscore the natural resources, if needed, such as climate, specific land forms, etc.; human resources (skilled workers); and capital resources (money needed to form the company).]

Did these job choices exist in the past? Why or why not? For example, long ago there were no bakeries and pioneer families produced everything themselves (e.g., they made their own bread and no one had time to decorate cakes). Decorating materials weren't even in existence yet.

Activity

Provide each table with three pictures mounted on three sheets of paper that illustrate factors that contribute to job choices. Have students list all the jobs that they think people could have that relate to that factor. For example, show a picture of a warm climate or a beach. Jobs could include life guards, hotel and restaurant workers, jobs related to tourist attractions, and jobs related to outdoor warm-weather recreational equipment (surfing, skateboarding, etc.). Upon completion, share and discuss the responses as a class. Discuss whether or not these jobs would have existed in the past (why or why not?). Using the pictures as a class, identify the natural, human, and capital resources illustrated and connect them to the jobs.

Choosing a Job

JOB YOU MIGHT LIKE TO HAVE AS AN ADULT	DRAW/LIST FACTORS THAT CONTRIBUTE TO THE CHOICE	RESOURCES
Firefighter	Lots of people, houses, businesses	Natural—water Human—people (firefighters, trainers of these men/women) Capital—money to pay the firefighters, buy equipment

Summarize

- People's jobs are often related to where they live.
- Natural, human, and capital resources are needed to produce goods and services.

Assessment

Ask each student to identify one job she or he thinks would be a good one to have as an adult, then draw or list the factors that contribute to that choice. Finally, they should list the natural, human, and capital resources that will be needed to produce the good or service.

Home Assignment

Encourage each student to share his or her assessment response. Then have families discuss jobs held by family members and the factors that contributed to their choices. Send home a copy of Figure 15 for families to record their responses.

Dear Parents,

We have been learning about job choices and the factors that contribute to those choices. Please encourage your child to share his or her response regarding a possible future job choice. Then discuss the jobs of the family members using the enclosed response sheet. Your child will be encouraged to share your family's response. Thank you!

Sincerely,

FIGURE 14   Model Letter to Parents

Job You Have as an Adult	Draw or List Factors That Contributed to Your Choice	Resources Needed to Produce the Goods or Service
_____ _____ _____		Natural _____ Human _____ Capital _____
_____ _____ _____		Natural _____ Human _____ Capital _____
_____ _____ _____		Natural _____ Human _____ Capital _____
_____ _____ _____		Natural _____ Human _____ Capital _____
_____ _____ _____		Natural _____ Human _____ Capital _____
_____ _____ _____		Natural _____ Human _____ Capital _____
_____ _____ _____		Natural _____ Human _____ Capital _____

FIGURE 15   Future Job Possibilities

Lesson 10

. . . .

Taxes

Resources

- Photographs and pictures of local community sites
- Photographs of local community workers
- Local and state tax statements
- Map of the local community
- Photographs of local community sites where services for the residents are provided
- Resource people who provide services to the community as a result of tax money paid by residents

Children's Literature

Flanagan, A. (1998). *Officer Brown Keeps Neighborhoods Safe*. New York: Children's Press.

Lewiston, W. (1998). *A Trip to the Firehouse*. New York: Grosset & Dunlap.

General Comments

To help students understand and appreciate that: (1) people depend on each other to provide the services they need; (2) every community provides certain kinds of services for the people who live there; and (3) families pay money to the community to pay for services that individuals could not afford to pay for by themselves (e.g., roads, schools, police and fire protection, etc.).

Main Ideas to Develop

- A community (township, town, suburb, city) is a place where people live. People have many needs and wants. Among them are community services that people could not afford to pay for by themselves (e.g., fire and police protection, roads, schools, etc.).
- Families pay money to the government. This money is called taxes. It pays for the community services.

Teaching Tips from Barbara

Students hear their families discuss, and often complain about, taxes, but they know very little about them. The key to making this lesson meaningful and personal is to focus on the things that taxes provide for us. If possible, take pictures of places in your community supported by taxes to help make this lesson more interesting. By the time we finished, my students were eager to remind their families of all the wonderful things that they receive from paying taxes.

Starting the Lesson

Review the results from the home assignment. Then start the lesson by role-playing a family scene in which one of the adult members is writing checks to pay bills. Included in those bills being paid are the local and state income taxes. Your child has several wants that you as a parent say he'll have to wait for because the taxes are a top priority. Show a tax statement. Your child questions you: "Why do you have to pay taxes anyway? What do they buy?"

Suggested Lesson Discussion

[Show pictures or photos that illustrate services provided by your local community.] Think about the services you and your family depend on every day. You need good streets to walk or ride to school on. You need a safe school building. You need buses to ride to school in. You need teachers at school to help you learn. You need police officers, firefighters, and ambulance drivers to help and protect you. The public library offers books and tapes that you can take home and read or listen to. You may get water from a source that is operated by your community. All of these services are paid for by part of the money that people earn while working at their jobs. This money is called *taxes*. People who work and/or own property pay taxes to the government. The government uses that money to pay for things that individuals on their own could not afford (e.g., fire protection, police protection, library services, good roads, public transportation such as school buses and public transport [city buses]).

[Using a map of the local community and photographs of the services provided, locate the sites of the local services. Select one or two of the local services and expand on them. If possible, invite one or two individuals who provide local community services to visit your class and explain what they do.] Community services make the community a cleaner, safer, and/or more pleasant place to live. These services are paid for by the taxes the residents pay. Tax money provides services that individuals could not afford to pay for on their own. [Use nonfiction literature sources to set the stage for the community service employee's visit to the class or for a class field trip to the community site.]

The taxes used to pay for community services are paid to the government. There are many kinds of taxes. In many communities, you pay a small tax every time you buy goods. People who own their own homes pay a tax on their property. People who rent pay taxes as part of their monthly fees. Some tax money is used to support local services and some is used to support services provided by the state and federal governments. [See also the unit on government.]

Activity

Provide students with a list of things families buy directly and things communities pay for with tax money because they are too expensive for individuals to pay for themselves. Ask students to write Family beside the item if the family usually pays for it directly and Tax if tax money is usually used.

1.	Tax	Fire protection	8.	Family	Personal computer
2.	Family	Groceries	9.	Family	Movies
3.	Family	Private transportation (e.g., personal car or truck)	10.	Family	School clothes
			11.	Tax	Library
			12.	Tax	Police protection
4.	Tax	School bus	13.	Family	Television set
5.	Tax	Parks	14.	Family	Family vacation
6.	Tax	Playgrounds			
7.	Tax	City streets			

Summarize

- Communities provide services for families and individuals that they cannot provide for themselves.
- Community services are paid for by the money that people pay to the government. This money is called taxes.

Assessment

Encourage each student to brainstorm with a peer about all the community services that are provided locally. Then ask each student to select three of these services and visually or in words describe what the services provide. Then have students write sentences explaining why it is important that the people who live in the community pay taxes to the government to support these services.

Home Assignment

Have each student share his or her story with a family member about local community services including why it's important to pay taxes to the government to support them. Then the family should talk about other community services that are very important to the community and write a paragraph explaining why.

Optional Ask families to visit the site where a local service is provided and get information about it that can be shared at an upcoming class session.

Dear Parents,

We have been learning about local community services that are paid for by tax money. We encourage you to discuss with your child what she or he has learned and reasons that paying money to the government as taxes is necessary. Talk about local community services that your family especially values and why (examples include library, parks, community recreation center, etc.). If possible, visit a local site where the service is provided. Any materials your child can bring to the class about the service would be greatly appreciated. Thank you!

Sincerely,

FIGURE 16   Model Letter to Parents

Lesson 11

....

Global Connections

Resources

- Globe
- Display of objects imported from other parts of the world (e.g., bananas from Central America and Africa, coffee from Brazil, shoes from Spain, silk blouse from Japan, gouda cheese from the Netherlands, soap from France, perfume from Bulgaria or France, etc.)
- Display of objects that represent services from other parts of the world (e.g., Japanese flower arranging, transportation [delivery of goods], communication [news from around the world, e-mails], etc.)
- Display of coins and bills used as currency around the world
- Large word cards for each table: Red = Imports; Green = Exports
- Copies of Figure 18: Interdependence Activity Sheet

General Comments

This lesson is intended to open children's eyes to the global connections that are very much a part of their lives. The hope is that students will get a flavor for what it means to be interdependent.

General Purposes or Goals

To help students develop an understanding of and appreciation for: (1) what it means to exchange or trade goods and services with others in the world; and (2) what it means to be interdependent.

Main Ideas to Develop

- Countries throughout the world trade with one another by exchanging goods and services.
- We are interdependent, which means that we count on people throughout the world to help supply the things we need and want.
- Interdependence occurs because we have to buy what we cannot produce ourselves.
- Goods that a country sells to other countries are called exports. Goods that are bought from other countries are called imports.
- Scarce resources are not available to all producers, so the producers usually specialize in producing the goods or providing the services most suited to their resources.
- Money facilitates the exchange of goods and services.

Teaching Tips from Barbara

To begin this lesson, firmly establish the terms *import* and *export* in your students' minds by using classroom examples. For instance, students will import their lunches and export library books from schools. By using a school example, you can then relate to states, countries, and continents. Two good resources to use when discussing these products are catalogs and sale fliers. When you review the home assignment, be sure to share ways to figure out where imported products are from. Also, be sure to let your students know that not everything is either imported or exported. Many products are used in the same country where they are produced.

Starting the Lesson

Review the responses to the home assignment. Locate approximately where your part of the United States is on the globe. Gradually spin it and ask, "Can you think of ways we are connected to other parts of the world?" Write students' responses on the white board.

Suggested Lesson Discussion

[Using the objects that represent goods and services, explain each one and why we in the United States buy these from other parts of the world.] We buy goods from all over the world. In some cases we don't produce them at all; in some cases we buy things from other countries to give people more choices; and in some cases the things can be produced more cheaply in other countries because of lower labor costs.

Goods and services that a country sells to other countries are called its *exports*. [Write the word on the white board, explaining that countries around the world send goods to our country and we send goods to their countries.] Exports are sent off by the countries that make them. They are exported to other countries.

We buy goods from other countries. These goods coming into our country are called our *imports*. We import them into our country. [Write the word on the white board. Use the globe to further solidify the idea.] When countries exchange goods and services, we say they are *interdependent*. [Write the word on the white board.] Each of us is interdependent with people around the world because our families purchase things in stores that were imported from other parts of the world, and people in those parts of the world buy things that were exported from here.

People and companies who make things are called *producers*. Scarce resources are not available to all producers, so producers usually specialize in producing the goods most suited to their resources. For example, America doesn't have the climate and soil conditions needed for growing bananas. Bananas are produced in places that have a warm, moist climate and year-round growing season. [Point out on the globe Central America and parts of Africa where bananas are grown.] The growing of bananas depends on natural and human resources. Another product that we regularly purchase from another country is coffee. [Locate Brazil on the globe.] Our supply is exported by Brazil and imported to America. Special climatic conditions are needed to produce it. We in the United States [point out your location on the globe], for example in the Midwest, have suitable climate, adequate rainfall, rich soils, and long enough growing seasons to grow grains such as wheat and corn. We export these grains to places in the world where they cannot be grown because the climate is too hot or too cold. [Use local resources and/or those of particular interest to the students in your locale to expand on imports and exports.] Money facilitates the exchange of imports and exports that provides us with the goods and services we need and want. [Show students coins and bills used as currency around the world.] Governments work together to make sure there is a fair exchange.

Activity

Provide short scenarios that illustrate imports and exports and further enhance the meaning of these as they satisfy people's needs and wants. Direct each table of students to decide as a group whether the response should be Export or Import and then signal the answer by raising the appropriate card.

RED = IMPORTS	GREEN = EXPORTS

POSSIBLE SCENARIOS

Scenario #1 The United States buys toys from Japan. Toys coming into our country are known as **IMPORTS**.

Scenario #2 The United States buys spices from Central America. Spices sold by Central America are called **EXPORTS**.

Scenario #3 The United States produces lots of wheat. It sells wheat and corn to parts of Asia. For the United States, these crops sold to other countries are known as **EXPORTS**.

Scenario #4 The United States does not produce any silk. It buys most of its supply from Japan. For the United States, bolts of silk fabric are known as **IMPORTS**.

Scenario #5 The U. S. clothing industry buys some of its design ideas from Europe. For the United States, these purchased designs are known as **IMPORTS**.

Scenario #6 The United States purchases some of its cheeses from the Netherlands and Switzerland. These varieties give more choices to the American consumers. When the United States brings them into our country, they are known as **IMPORTS**.

Scenario #7 The United States produces lots of vegetables and fruits. Many are processed (e.g., canned and frozen) and shipped to other parts of the world. For the United States, they are known as **EXPORTS**.

Scenario #8 France is one European country that grows flowers that are processed and made into perfumes and soaps that are then sent to other countries around the world. For France, these products are known as **EXPORTS**.

Use the globe to expand understanding of exports, imports, and interdependence.

Summarize

- Countries throughout the world trade with one another by exchanging goods and services and, therefore, they become interdependent.
- Goods that a country sells to other countries are called exports and those they buy from other countries are called imports.
- Money facilitates the exchange of goods and services.

Assessment

Have each student visually depict one way that she or he depends on other people around the world. Then the student should write two or more sentences explaining the visual illustration. For example, "I depend on Japan for my silk blouse or shirt. Mulberry leaves and silk worms are needed. We do not have the proper climate in the United States," or "I depend on reporters stationed around the world for news from those places."

Home Assignment

Encourage students to share with their families what they have learned about being interdependent with other people and places in the world. Then, with a family member, they should tour the house looking for products and services that are connected to other parts of the world. Send home copies of Figure 18 so that together, they can make a list of these global connections that reflect global interdependence.

Dear Parents,

We have been learning about global connections or interdependence, which we have come to understand as buying and selling goods and services around the world to satisfy our needs and wants. After having your child share his or her visual and written response explaining interdependence, please inventory your household and list examples of your family's connections to the world on the enclosed response sheet. Make sure your child brings the list to school for our upcoming class discussion.

Sincerely,

FIGURE 17   Model Letter to Parents

Products or Services	Imported From
Examples:	
Sony television	Japan
Silk shirt	Japan
Bananas	Central America
1.	
2.	
3.	
4.	
5.	
6.	
7.	
8.	
9.	
10.	

FIGURE 18   Independence Activity Chart

Lesson 12

Children Can Make a Difference by Donating Some Money to Help Others

Resources

- Photos of individuals who contribute money, a gift, or time to a worthy cause
- Local map
- Pictures and photos of local organizations where people can go to get temporary help for food, shelter, clothing, etc.
- Resource person from a local organization (e.g., Food Bank, Red Cross, etc.)
- Copies of Figure 20: Helping Others Assessment

General Comments

The focus of this lesson is on citizenship, underscoring the idea that even elementary students can assist in making the world a better place. One of the choices people make about their money is whether or not to spend some of it to help others. This lesson will address how a class might devote time and money to help others.

General Purposes or Goals

To help students: (1) develop an understanding of and appreciation for what it means to be a good citizen; and (2) learn about the what, why, and how of age-appropriate social actions that students can undertake in or out of school to help others by donating time and money.

Main Ideas to Develop

- Even children can practice good citizenship, which includes helping others by donating time and money.
- Some people use part of their money to buy someone something or donate to a worthy cause or charity.
- The choices people make about money are very personal. What is important to one person may not be nearly as important to another.
- Some people who are unable to pay all their bills receive help from the government. This kind of help is called welfare. The government collects this money from all members of the community who pay taxes.

Teaching Tips from Barbara

Our district requires students to participate in Service to Community projects. This was a great way to take care of that requirement as well as put some of these ideas to use.

Starting the Lesson

Share homework responses from the previous lesson. Then explain once again that the choices people make about money are very personal. Say, "What is important to one person may not be as important to another." Show photos of individuals who contribute money, a gift of food, or time to a worthy cause. Say, "Some people pay attention to their own wants while others are more concerned about the needs of others." Ask students to share examples of how people can help satisfy the needs of others. List student responses.

Suggested Class Discussion

[Revisit the main ideas from the lesson on budgeting.] Sometimes people have unfortunate things happen that require more money to go out than the amount that comes in, and as a result, they can't balance their budget. Sometimes they can't even pay for the things that they need, so they have to ask for help.

There are places in every community that provide temporary help for people in need. [Point out several on a local map. Use pictures and photos to illustrate. Invite someone from a local organization (e.g., food bank, Salvation Army, etc.) to serve as a resource person for the class.] People in the community can give money, items (food, clothing, furniture, cooking utensils, etc.), or time to help provide for people who because of a misfortune can't balance their budgets, can't buy the things they need.

[After the resource person has explained what the specified organization does and how the class can help, tell the students that they could give some of the money raised from the popcorn sale (profit) to the organization. Even children can practice good citizenship, which includes helping others by donating time and money. Recall that parent volunteers were asked to help with the sale, which is the normal procedure when students want to give time and money. That is part of promoting good citizenship in the community.]

[Review the content and practices learned during Lesson 6. It focused on producing a good that someone is willing to consume.] During the popcorn sale, members of the class and parent volunteers gave their time as well as money. The money we made after we paid our expenses was the *profit*. *Expenses* included the money we paid for the popcorn, butter, salt, and bags. We can give some of our profit to the selected local organization. [An alternative would be for a class member with his or her parent to deliver the gift.]

Besides the gifts that individuals provide to help others in need, people can get temporary help from the government. This kind of help is called *welfare*. The government collects taxes from adult members of the community and uses some of this tax money to pay for welfare programs.

Activity

Table Talk—Have each table discuss two questions: (1) Why is it important as members of the community to help others who can't balance their budget because of unusual circumstances? (2) How did you feel when you were able to give time and money to help others?

Summarize

- Even elementary school children with the help of adults can help others by donating time and money.
- Some people decide to use some of their money to help others meet their needs.
- There are local organizations that provide help to members of the community who can't balance their budgets.
- Some people who are unable to pay all their bills get help from the government.

Assessment

Have each student respond to the three open-ended statements in Figure 20.

Revisit the TWL chart. Use it as a focus for a class discussion and review.

Home Assignment

Have students share their open-ended statements with their family members. Then they can discuss ways that they have helped others in need or ways that organizations in the local community have assisted them.

Dear Parents,

We have been learning about the personal choices people make in how they spend their money. For example, some people use some of their money to help others. A visitor from _____ explained to our class how that organization helps people in the local community who have needs that they cannot meet. We have decided to donate some of the money we raised during a recent popcorn sale to that organization.

Please ask your child to share what she or he has learned by encouraging her or him to read her or his open-ended statements. Then as a family, discuss how you have contributed to a local organization or how you have been helped when you had a family crisis. Thank you!

Sincerely,

FIGURE 19   Model Letter to Parents

1. It is important to help others in need by _____

    _____

    _____

    _____

    _____

    _____.

2. When I help others by giving goods, time, and/or money, I _____

    _____

    _____

    _____

    _____

    _____.

3. Places people in our community can go to get help in satisfying their basic

    needs include _____

    _____

    _____

    _____

    _____

    _____.

FIGURE 20   Helping Others Assessment

Lesson 13

. . . .

Performance Assessment

Resources

- Photos of the class popcorn sale
- Drawing of a budget illustrating money that comes in, money that goes out to pay bills, money put into savings, and money donated
- Photos of a bank's exterior and interior, including safe-deposit box
- Local map and photos of a local organization that helps people in need
- Display of items appealing to an early elementary school student (e.g., sweatshirt, soccer ball, CD, football, hockey stick, school supplies)
- Display including cash, credit card, debit card, personal check
- Display of coins and bills
- Pictures of open-air markets
- Props or pictures illustrating the story of money (e.g., bag of grain, salt, shells, objects of approximately equal value for trading such as coins, paper money, shell bracelets, fur)
- Time line—Long, Long Ago; Long Ago; Today
- Display of pictures and words that illustrate goods and services people pay for with their own money and services provided by tax money
- Display of pictures and/or photos of jobs emphasizing variables such as climate, population density, and physical features that influence the types of work available
- Display of items exported from and imported to the United States
- Local community map with sites of local services marked
- Upper-grade mentors or parent volunteers, one at each station
- Questions printed on large cards (laminating is optional)
- Timer for the purpose of monitoring movement from station to station

General Comments

For performance assessment in social studies, the "laboratory" model can be useful. You probably experienced this model in your high school or college science classes. On "test" day, stations are located at desks, bulletin boards, white boards, murals, wall charts, computer screens, and other appropriate places. Each station displays materials such as a time line, collection of objects, a map, or pictures. Since the students in the early grades have limited writing competencies, an upper-grade mentor or parent volunteer should facilitate the questioning sequence and/or manipulation of the photos, objects, and so on. Recording individual student responses and level of correctness is optional. Misconceptions need to be noted and discussed during the debriefing.

When instructed to do so, students move to the next station. You might want to allow some time for returning to stations where questions have been left unanswered. When all the students have finished, check their answers. This model can work very successfully as a means of fostering authentic assessment in early elementary social studies.

If you are concerned about having a station for each student, divide the class in half. You can have half of the class participate in the performance assessment while the other half reads to their upper-grade mentors or parent volunteers, then switch roles. Students can later work in pairs to correct their responses. Another option is to have students participate in the assessment as pairs.

Plan a dry run of the model before you use it. Be open. There are no hard-and-fast rules except that the items must be based on your goals and matched to your instruction.

Main Ideas to Develop

- Money is anything that a group of people accept in exchange for real items or as pay for work.
- It takes a family's money as well as help from the government to buy all the goods and services we need to survive.
- Taxes are collected by the government from families and businesses to help pay for things that would be too expensive for individuals to buy (e.g., schools, roads, parks, teachers).
- Long, long ago there was no need for money because people lived very simply and they satisfied their needs themselves.
- As time passed, things changed. (The numbers of people grew; more food was needed; climates began to change; people learned to do more things such as raise crops, bake, and build; and people began to communicate with one another.)
- Trading to get the things you need or want is known as bartering.
- Bartering worked only when each trader wanted something that the other had and both agreed it was a fair trade.
- As time passed, people began to use objects for money.
- Any object can be used as money as long as people agree on its value.

- A market is a public gathering place held at regular times for buying and selling goods.

- Long, long ago people came from miles around to buy and sell goods. No money was exchanged. Instead, all exchanges were in the form of barter.

- Gradually, certain objects were used as money.

- Today, in most parts of the world, people use money in exchange for goods and services.

- There are places—even sometimes where we live—where people still barter (exchange one good or service for another).

- All over the world, even today, people come to the market to buy and sell.

- When people talk about going to markets, they usually mean going to an outdoor site to buy or sell goods.

- The Treasury is the part of our government that makes money and controls the amount that is in circulation. Besides printing new bills, it destroys worn-out ones.

- Another name for money is *currency.* It refers to both coins and paper money.

- By law, U.S. money cannot show a living person. The law was passed so that no one could mint coins as a sign of power.

- The official unit of currency in the United States is the dollar. Almost every country in the world has its official unit of currency (e.g., pound, peso, yen).

- A bank is a business that keeps money for customers, makes loans, and provides other related services (e.g., safe-deposit boxes).

- It takes a lot of people to run a bank.

- A loan is a sum of money borrowed for a certain amount of time.

- Loans are for things like buying houses. These loans are called mortgages.

- Banks earn money by charging fees for their services to customers and by lending money to them.

- People decide whether or not they want to save some of their money, and if so, how much they want to save, and where to keep it.

- Income is money that a person gets from selling a product or service, earning a salary or wages for doing a job, interest, investment, and so on.

- Most elementary-age children are limited in how they make money because their main job is going to school.

- Ways elementary-age children can earn money include watching pets, raking leaves, or having a small business such as running a lemonade stand or selling popcorn.

- Individuals who run small businesses need to consider supply, demand, scarcity, and profit if they are to be successful.
- As adults your students will be able to make choices about the kinds of work they will do.
- A budget is a plan that shows how much money comes in and how much goes out.
- People obtain money in different ways: earn wages by working, sell things, receive money as gifts, get an allowance, invest, and so forth.
- People spend money to buy things that they need or want. The choices people make about money are very personal.
- Needs are things you must have and wants are things you would like to have but don't really need.
- Balancing a budget means trying to make sure that the money going out is equal to or less than the money coming in.
- Opportunity cost is what you give up when you choose to use your limited time or money to get something you want more.
- There are several ways to pay for the things you buy: cash, check, credit card, debit card.
- One very popular kind of cashless money is called a check. People write checks every day to pay bills and purchase goods. The company or store will be paid by check writer's bank, which takes the money out of his or her account.
- People also use cashless money called credit cards. They allow people to buy now and pay later. If you do not pay the full amount when the credit card bill comes due, the item will cost a lot more because interest is added to the amount left unpaid.
- For many, many years people have worked at different jobs. Jobs have changed over the years. Some have disappeared completely and new ones have been created.
- People's jobs have a lot to do with where they live. The climate/weather, physical features (mountains, plains, lakes, etc.), and population density all contribute to the choices.
- Producers need natural, human, and capital resources to make goods and services.
- A community (township, town, suburb, city) is a place where people live. People have many needs and wants. Among them are community services that they could not afford to pay for by themselves (e.g., fire and police protection, roads, schools, etc.).
- Families pay taxes to the government. Tax money pays for the community services.
- Countries throughout the world trade with one another by exchanging goods and services.

- We are interdependent, which means that we count on people throughout the world to help supply the things we need and want.

- Interdependence occurs because we have to buy what we cannot produce ourselves.

- Goods that a country sells to other countries are called exports. Goods that are bought from other countries are called imports.

- Scarce resources are not available to all producers, so the producers usually specialize in producing the goods or providing the services most suited to their resources.

- Money facilitates the exchange of goods and services.

- Even children can practice good citizenship, which includes helping others by donating time and money.

- Some people use part of their money to buy someone something or donate to a worthy cause or charity.

- The choices people make about money are very personal. What is important to one person may not be nearly as important to another.

- Some people who are unable to pay all their bills receive help from the government. This kind of help is called welfare. The government collects this money from all members of the community who pay taxes.

Teaching Tips from Barbara

The key to having the performance assessment work well is saving artifacts and planning for this as you go along. It is possible to do this activity without parent volunteers or outside assistance. You can set up the stations and escort groups of four or five students through the stations yourself while other students are journaling, coloring illustrations, or rereading money books from the unit.

Starting the Lesson

Begin by discussing the results from the home assignment. Pair the students with upper-grade mentors or parent volunteers. (An alternative would be to do this performance assessment activity with students' parents. It would provide a fine opportunity for students to showcase for their parents what they have learned about money.)

Select Station #1 and, as a whole class, model and discuss how it works. [For example, suppose that you have decided to have students visit each station in pairs, where an upper-grade mentor or adult volunteer will read the questions, manipulate the artifacts (such as photos of the popcorn sale), listen to the students' responses, and record them. They will make note of misconceptions or incomplete responses. At the conclusion of the assessment a large-group discussion will be held, which will include any needed reteaching. Having the artifacts available should make this task easier and more meaningful.] Provide each mentor or parent volunteer with anticipated student responses. Underscore the importance of the facilitator probing and offering clues or cues where needed.

Examples of Stations

Station #1   Photos of popcorn sale

1. What good or service did our class popcorn business provide? **Popcorn = good, making the snack readily available = service**

2. Who were the customers? **Other students, community members, teachers, other adults in the building**

3. If we thought we would have more customers than bags of popcorn, would we be able to charge more or less? Why? **More. The demand is greater than the supply**

4. What resources were needed for your sale? **People and their time, popcorn and other ingredients, money (collateral) to pay for the ingredients**

Station #2   Graphic illustrating a budget: money that comes in, money that goes out to pay bills, money put into savings, and money donated

1. Study Kaitlen's money plan. What is the name given to an individual's plan? **Budget**

2. Does Kaitlen have a good plan or a bad plan? **Bad** Why? **She is spending more than her income**

3. What could she do? **Spend less on school snacks, buy fewer school supplies, or perhaps put less into savings**

Station #3   Photos of a bank and safe-deposit box

1. What is the name of a business that keeps money for customers? **Bank**

2. What is a loan? **Money borrowed from the bank for a certain amount of time to buy something big like a house or a car**

3. Why do people rent these boxes at the bank? (Show photo of a safe-deposit box.) **To store their important papers, store their precious jewelry, keep other valuables safe**

4. Who decides if you are going to put some of your money in a savings account? **Every customer decides for him or herself**

Station #4   Local map and display including photos showing how service organizations help people in need

1. Who goes to this local organization for help? **People who have experienced a disaster (flood, fire), people who have lost their jobs and cannot satisfy their basic needs, etc.**

2. What kind of help does this local organization provide? **Money, food, clothing, temporary shelter**

3. Locate this organization on the local map.

4. If you had a little extra money and wanted to give it to this organization, how do you suppose the organization would use it? **Help pay for the food, clothing, or shelter. The organization might give some of the money to the people who need it for paying rent, etc.**

Station #5   Display items or pictures of items that would be appealing to an early elementary child (e.g., sweatshirt, soccer ball, CD, football, hockey stick, school supplies)

1. If you buy _____, what do you give up?

2. What is the name given to this? **Opportunity cost**

3. Why do people need to think about what they will need and want tomorrow as well as today? **People can't have everything. You need to make sure your needs are taken care of**

Station #6   Display including cash, credit card, debit card, and personal check

When you buy something, you need to figure out how you will pay. Explain when each is used, how it works, and the trade-offs associated with each.

1. **Cash helps you figure out if you can afford it. It is unhandy to carry and many people worry about losing it.**

2. **Credit card allows people to buy now and pay later. If you do not pay the full amount when the credit card payment is due, the item will cost more because interest is added to the unpaid amount.**

3. **Debit card. It is used to electronically draw money out of your bank account. It is easy to use. One problem is people often forget to write down how much they have spent so they run out of money in their account.**

4. **Personal check. You have these if you have a checking account at a bank. When your check is deposited by the person you bought something from, that amount is taken out of your bank account. Checks are safe to send or carry. You need to remember to record the amount of your check to be sure you always have enough money in your account.**

Station #7   Display of coins and bills

1. Who makes our money? **Department of Treasury**

2. Can our money display anybody's picture? **No**

3. Whose pictures can be displayed? **Important people who are no longer alive**

4. Why can't people who are alive be pictured on our coins? **There's a law against it. No person could mint coins as a sign of power**

Station #8 Pictures of open markets

1. Describe a market. **It is a public gathering place held at regular times for buying and selling things**
2. Why do people who go to these markets usually use money to buy the things they need? **Objects for trading are often unhandy to bring to the market. Objects for trading are often worth more or less than the things you want to buy. Using money makes it easier to buy and sell things**
3. Where is the nearest market in your area? _____ .

Station #9 Props or pictures illustrating the story of money (e.g., bag of grain, salt, shells, objects of approximately equal value for trading, coins, paper money, shell bracelets, fur)

1. Why didn't people need money long ago? **They lived very simply and they satisfied their needs themselves**
2. When did bartering work? **When each trader wanted something that the other had and both agreed it was a fair trade**
3. Select one of the items, such as fur. When can fur be used as money? **When the buyer and seller agree how much the fur is worth and the seller agrees to take it in trade (in place of money)**

Station #10 Time line —Long, Long Ago; Long Ago; and Today

Ask students to place the following words and cutouts/line drawings on the time line in the appropriate places:

1. Credit cards
2. Salt and grains as money
3. No need for money because people lived very simply and satisfied their own needs
4. Silver used as money
5. Shell bracelets (wampum)
6. Dollar as the basic unit of exchange
   Correct order: 3, 2, 5, 4, 6, 1

Station #11 Display of pictures and words that illustrate goods and services people pay for with their own money, and services provided by tax money

Ask students to sort the items into two piles: personal purchases of goods and services, and services provided by the government.

1. Personal purchases of goods and services **Examples: French fries, basketball, hockey stick**
2. Services provided by the government **Examples: Roads, police protection, fire protection, etc.**

Station #12 Display of pictures and/or photos of jobs emphasizing the variables such as climate, population density, and physical features (mountains, lakes, etc.) that influence the types of work that will be available

Ask students to look over the pictures that illustrate various jobs and name one geographic variable that might affect its availability. Students should select three and explain what the job is and why that job is available. Examples:

1. Catching fish—**lakes and ocean**
2. Working in a ski resort—**mountains, hills, cold weather**
3. Taxi driving—**lots of people who need transportation**

Then ask which job might be one the student would consider in the future and have him or her explain why.

Station #13 Display of items exported from and imported to the United States and a globe (examples: spices, bananas, coffee, shoes, silk, grain such as corn or wheat)

1. Ask the student to explain how the United States and its people are connected to the world. **Countries and people throughout the world trade with one another by exchanging goods and services. For example, bananas do not grow in the United States, so they are imported from Central America. Some of our shoes are imported from places like Brazil and Spain. We grow more wheat and corn than we can use, so some of it is exported to parts of Asia**
2. Give two examples of imports to the United States. **Toys, shoes**
3. Give two examples of exports from the United States. **Wheat, corn**

Station #14 Local community map with sites of community services marked (e.g., fire station, police station, library, town hall, road commission, etc.)

1. What do all of these places have in common? **They all represent community services that people could not afford to pay for by themselves. Families pay taxes to the government. Tax money pays for community services**
2. Select two examples and describe what services they provide to the local residents and why these services are so important.

Large-Group Discussion and Activity

Have each student return to the station where he or she started. Discuss the correct responses and clear up any misconceptions. As a class, write a thank-you note to the volunteers who assisted in the performance assessment.

Unit 3: Government

Introduction

To help you think about government as a cultural universal and begin to plan your teaching, we have provided a list of questions that address some of the big ideas developed in our unit plans (see Figure 1). The questions focus on some of what we believe to be the most important ideas for children to learn about government: what government is, who is the head of our government and how he gained office, who can become president, differences between presidents and kings or queens, totalitarian governments and how their leaders gain office, who is allowed to vote, differences between the Democratic and Republican parties, desirable qualities in a president, where the president lives and works and what he does, activities of the American government, where the state governor lives and what he does, activities of the state government, activities of people who work in the state capitol building, where laws come from, whether laws can be changed, examples of laws that are being enacted or changed currently, what citizens can do if they oppose a law, why we need rules and laws, the difference between a rule and a law, the functions of judges, the activities of people who work for the government, what government does for people, how the government raises money to pay for its activities, what taxes are, who pays taxes, what is done with tax money, how police officers and firefighters are paid, who owns the school, who pays the teachers, differences between public schools and private schools, and whether the child would like to be president when he or she grows up (with explanation of why or why not).

To find out what primary-grade students know (or think they know) about these topics, we interviewed ninety-six K–3 students, stratified by grade level, gender, and achievement level. You may want to use some or

1. Today we're going to talk about government. What is government? [If necessary, define government as the people who are in charge of running our country.] . . . What does government do?

2. Who is the head of our government? [If student says president, ask for name.]

3. How did he get to be president?

4. Can anyone be president or only certain people? [Follow up by probing for explanations.]

5. Some countries have kings or queens instead of presidents. How are presidents different from kings or queens? [If necessary, ask "How does a person become president? . . . How does a person become king or queen?"]

6. Some countries are run by people who were not elected. How did these people get to be in charge of their governments? . . . Do you know any countries that are run by people like that?

7. In our country, the president and other government leaders are elected by voters. Who is allowed to vote? [If necessary, ask, "Can anybody vote, or just some people?"]

8. In American elections, the voters are usually choosing between Democrats and Republicans. How are Democrats and Republicans different? . . . Like in the last election, why did some people vote for George W. Bush and other people vote for Al Gore?*

9. In an election, why do people vote for one candidate [if necessary, "one person"] rather than another? . . . What would you look for in a candidate for president? If you could vote for a president, what qualities would you be wanting in a candidate?

10. Our president right now is George W. Bush. Where does he live and work? . . . What does he do? . . . What are some things that the United States government does?*

11. We live in the state of Michigan. The governor of Michigan was John Engler. Where does he live and work? . . . What does he do? . . . What are some things that the government of Michigan does?*

12. What do people who work in the capitol building do?

13. Where do laws come from? [If necessary, ask: "Who makes laws?"] . . . Do you know about any laws that our government is working on right now?

* Substitute the names of the appropriate candidates and office-holders for these questions.

FIGURE 1   Starter Questions

14. Can laws be changed? . . . How do they get changed? . . . Do you know of any laws that have been changed? . . . What could your parents do if they didn't like a law?

15. People are supposed to follow rules and laws. Why do we need rules and laws? . . . What is the difference between a rule and a law? . . . What happens to someone who breaks a law?

16. Judges are part of the government too. What do judges do?

17. A lot of people work for the government. What are some of the jobs that they do?

18. Besides making laws, the government also helps people. What are some of the things that the government does for people? . . . How does the government help your family?

19. It costs money to pay the people who work for the government. Where does this money come from?

20. What are taxes? . . . Who pays them? . . . Who gets that tax money? . . . What do they do with it?

21. Here in our city, we get services from the township police and firefighters. . . . Who pays the police and firefighters? [If appropriate, probe to clarify where the money comes from.]

22. The kids in this city go to schools like this one. Who owns this school? . . . Who pays the teachers? [If appropriate, probe to establish where the money comes from.]

23. This school is a public school. What other kinds of schools are there, besides public schools? [Probe for whatever differences the child can mention, but especially information about who pays for the schools.]

24. Would you like to be president when you grow up? [Why or why not?]

FIGURE 1   (Continued)   213 all of our interview questions during pre-unit or pre-lesson assessments of your students' prior knowledge. For now, though, we recommend that you jot down your own answers before going on to read about the answers that we elicited in our interviews. This will sharpen your awareness of ways in which adults' knowledge about government differs from children's knowledge, as well as reduce the likelihood that you will assume that your students already know certain things that seem obvious to you but may need to be spelled out for them.

If you want to use some of these questions to assess your students' prior knowledge before beginning the unit, you can do this either by interviewing selected students individually or by asking the class as a whole to respond to the questions and recording their answers for future reference. If you take the latter approach, an option would be to embed it within the KWL technique by initially questioning students to determine what they know (or think they know) and what they want to find out, then later revisiting their answers and recording what they learned. An alternative to preassessing your students' knowledge about topics developed in the unit as a whole would be to conduct separate preassessments prior to each lesson, using only the questions that apply to that lesson (and perhaps adding others of your own choosing).

Children's Ideas About Government

More is known about children's knowledge and thinking about government than about any of the other cultural universals addressed in our series of studies (Greenstein, 1969; Hess & Torney, 1967; Moore, Lare, & Wagner, 1985). Young children tend to depict a benevolent world run by dedicated leaders who are concerned about the welfare of all. Their ideas tend to focus on the president, whom they view as personally running the country by making laws and executive decisions and providing individualized assistance to people who contact him. Only a minority of young children are aware of the Supreme Court, and an even smaller minority are aware of Congress. Most children imagine the president as running the country with the assistance of various "helpers." Similarly, ideas about state government focus on the governor and ideas about local government focus on the mayor.

When asked about what governments do, children tend to mention parks, snow removal, and other local government services, and also providing people with homes and jobs. They tend to know first about local government, then the state, and then the nation at the level of governmental activities, but first about the president, then the governor, and then the mayor in terms of individual leaders.

Primary-grade children tend to be pre-political, with images of political leadership limited to symbol recognition (the president "signs papers," "makes speeches," or "has meetings"). Later they acquire accurate but varied ideas about general governmental processes or functions (the president "makes laws," "runs the country," or "solves problems"). There is little or no awareness of specific functions, of the division of labor between the president and other officeholders, or of the roles of political parties or lobbies.

Children also tend to be vague about the role of taxes in funding governments. Most are familiar with taxes because of the sales tax, but vague about the purposes for which taxes are used and likely to confuse utility bills with tax bills. They also tend to be vague about distinctions between the public and private sectors, recognizing certain visible public figures such as police officers and judges as government employees (perhaps because of their uniforms), but being less sure about teachers, and sometimes including television news reporters as part of a belief that televised news is presented by the government. They tend to know more about the functions of the police, judges, and the courts than about other aspects of government, presumably from watching television.

Responses to Our Government Interviews

The K–3 students' responses to our government interviews replicated and elaborated these trends. The students in general and the younger ones in particular were unable to say much when asked to define *government,* and those who did respond often confused the term *government* with the term *governor* or otherwise identified the government with an individual person. Concerning what government does, they emphasized making and enforcing laws, running the country and solving problems, or helping people in need. Relatively neutral responses emphasizing making laws and running the country were more frequent than either very positive responses depicting government as benevolent or very negative responses depicting government as oppressive.

Most second and third graders knew that the president is the head of the government, could name the current president (then Bill Clinton), and knew that he was president because he won an election. The younger students tended to be vague or incorrect about who headed the government (often confusing the president with the governor of the state), and they were more likely to talk about virtues (honest, hardworking, good speaker, etc.) than about elections when explaining how one gets to be the president. Although more than half of the students did not realize that presidents are elected, none thought that the title was hereditary. Instead, they assumed that the new president would be chosen by the old president or governmental leaders, typically on the basis of competence or other evidence of deservingness displayed in prior government service. Thus, even young children who do not understand much about our form of government already have learned that our country is neither a monarchy nor a totalitarian state, and have been conditioned to view it as a meritocracy.

Almost half of the students understood that there is an age qualification for running for president. Otherwise, only third graders were likely to suggest factors that might disqualify a person from the office. Some of these ideas were accurate (criminality, prior terms in office). Others were technically inaccurate but understandable given base rates (no women or poor people).

When asked to compare presidents with kings or queens, most students focused on what they knew about kings or queens rather than on comparisons with presidents. Their responses reflected images of kings and queens drawn from children's literature and videos (live in castles or palaces, wear crowns and royal robes, live lives of luxury, etc.). A few responses reflected exposure to disputes over taxes between King George III and the American colonists, and a few others expressed beliefs that queens must be beautiful or that kings and queens existed only in the past.

Ideas about how people become kings or queens focused on inheriting the throne, qualifying by being very rich or owning a castle, or capturing the throne through force or guile. Those who talked about kings or queens exercising power or leadership did not describe them as benevolent in the ways that they typically described presidents. The minority of students who drew direct comparisons typically depicted kings and queens as basking in the trappings of inherited luxury while depicting presidents as working long hours for the good of the country during their limited time in office.

Questions 6–9 addressed issues relating to candidates, political parties, and elections. When asked what they knew about countries ruled by people who were not elected, most students could not respond and those who did said nothing about monarchies, dictatorships, totalitarian forms of government, or other alternatives to representative democracy (about which they had only limited knowledge as well). This fits well with earlier findings indicating that primary-grade children do not yet have clear concepts of nation-states and the political structures and offices involved in governing them (Berti & Benesso, 1998); instead, their images of political leadership focus on benevolent parental figures assisted by "helpers."

When asked about who is allowed to vote in American elections, almost half of the students mentioned an age qualification and smaller numbers mentioned other qualifications (must be a citizen, must be registered) or exceptions (criminals not allowed to vote). Most of these responses were accurate as far as they went, although some students thought that only the president or other governmental leaders could vote and others thought that people in government were not allowed to vote.

Only about 10 percent of the students were able to say anything substantive about the Democratic and Republican parties beyond versions of "they think differently." Most of these few substantive responses were based either on the image of Republicans as rich people or on knowledge that the Democrats (Clinton administration) were currently in power. Two responses depicted Democrats as criminals—bad people prone to "steal and kill" or "shoot somebody and lie about it." Although infrequent, such responses are worrisome because they suggest that the polarized political dialogue of recent decades has filtered down to children in highly emotional and counterproductive forms. Evidence of this phenomenon could be seen in responses to some of the other questions as well.

When asked what they would look for in a presidential candidate, most students emphasized generic virtues (nice, kind, helpful, not greedy, not bossy, etc.) or the specific traits of honesty and competence. About 20 percent (mostly older and more sophisticated students) mentioned the candidate's vision or policies.

Question 10 asked where the president lives and works and what he and the federal government do. About half of the younger students were unable to respond or guessed incorrectly, but most of the older ones were able to say that Bill Clinton lived in the White House and that the White House was located in Washington, D.C.

Responses to questions about what the president/government does mostly referred to the president individually rather than the government generally. Younger students' responses tended to focus on general virtuous behavior (doing good, helping people, etc.), without specific examples. When younger students did give examples, they often were unrealistic, depicting the president as personally stopping riots, cleaning the environment, or engaging in the activities of police officers, doctors, or judges (send people to jail, set broken bones, catch people who don't pay their taxes, etc.). Older students were more likely to describe the president's activities as office work or solving problems, and their examples tended to be more realistic (making executive decisions, appointing judges, etc.). Some imagined the president as mostly signing papers and doing office work, others as mostly carrying out daunting responsibilities requiring decisions about important problems, and still others as mostly traveling around the country providing speeches, photo opportunities, and autographs. These themes reappeared later when the students were asked about positive and negative aspects of being the president.

The next questions asked about the location and activities of the governor and people who work for the state government of Michigan. The students' responses paralleled in many ways their answers to previous questions about the president and the federal government. They also replicated earlier findings that children tend to have more information about the identities and activities of the president relative to the governor or mayor, but at the same time to have more information about governmental activities at the local or state level than at the federal level. Only fourteen students said that the governor worked at the capitol and only twenty said that the capitol was located in Lansing.

More than a third of the students were unable to respond when asked what the governor/government does. The rest gave answers similar to those given previously about the president, emphasizing generic virtuous behavior or speaking of solving problems without giving specific examples. Only an eighth of the students gave realistic examples (recommending or enforcing laws, making policy speeches, seeing that we have streetlights, etc.), and almost as many gave unrealistic examples (stopping riots, cleaning up things, acting as a judge, police officer, or physician, etc.).

Many of the examples conflated the activities of local government with those of state government, and some depicted the governor as a helper to the president. The students had more realistic ideas about state government than the federal government, but even so, most of their images of government activities were limited to vague notions of office work or problem solving, and there were frequent confusions concerning the respective functions of the federal, state, and local levels.

Fewer than half of the students were able to describe the activities of employees who work in the capitol building. Their responses included generic good deeds (helping people, etc.), generic office work (work on computers, write letters, stamp papers, etc.), specific examples of governmental activities (respond to questions that people send in, develop laws, act as aides to the governor, etc.), and other activities such as cleaning the building so that it will look good for visitors. Most examples of governmental activities were generated by older students, and most of these did in fact refer to governmental (as opposed to private sector) functions.

Questions 13–15 addressed students' knowledge about distinctions between rules and laws, the making and changing of laws, and current lawmaking in the news. Only about half of the students were able to draw clear distinctions between rules and laws, typically depicting rules as made by parents or teachers and applying only in the home or school but laws as made by governments and applying everywhere, or rules as breakable with only minor consequences but laws as requiring obedience under penalty of fines or imprisonment.

Most of the students didn't know much about laws or the lawmaking process. Lacking specific knowledge about the legislative branches of governments, the majority assumed that laws are proclaimed by the president, the governor, judges, or the police. More than two-thirds understood that laws could be changed, but again, most of these thought that the change would involve decisions made in the executive or judicial branches of government. Only eleven students described a revote by the people who made the laws in the first place. Similarly, when asked what their parents might be able to do if they were unhappy with a law, most students emphasized contacting governmental officials in the executive or judicial branches rather than the legislative branch.

Only about a fourth of the students were able to identify one or more laws that have been changed or might be changed or introduced. Most of these responses were accurate, focusing on bicycle safety, seat belts, or regulations concerning smoking, alcohol, drugs, or weapons. It was not surprising that students this young were aware of laws regulating the behavior of individuals but not laws regulating commerce, corporations, or governmental processes.

Responses to questions about possibilities for introducing or changing laws indicated that very few students had realistic knowledge about political organization or lobbying. However, a few third graders spoke of organizing to create political pressure, a few spoke about their parents seeking redress in the courts, and one mentioned the possibility of voting against the incumbent president in the next election.

The students' attitudes toward rules and laws were generally positive, reflecting beliefs that they make for a safe, well-ordered society and provide guidance about desired behavior. Several students drew apocalyptic visions of the chaos that would result if rules and laws were not in place (people would be shooting one another, there would be fires everywhere, etc.).

Question 16 asked what judges do. More than a third of the students were unable to respond or produced only vague generalities (help the government, talk to people, etc.). The majority, however, were able to draw on what they had seen on television to identify one or more specific things that judges do in courtrooms (decide criminal cases by determining if people are guilty or innocent, preside over the courtroom, bang their gavels to keep order, make rulings in civil lawsuits or divorces, lecture defendants about their misconduct, or ask questions of witnesses or defendants to elicit facts or motives). These responses were generally accurate for courtrooms in which the judge (rather than a jury) is in fact the arbiter who decides which side wins the case and what subsequent actions will be taken. The few students who mentioned juries depicted them as advisors to the judge. Most examples depicted criminal cases, but ten students depicted civil cases (including several who had been to court for divorce hearings).

Questions 17 and 18 asked about what government workers do for people, including the student's own family. Responses to these questions were surprisingly poor, given how much the students had said about government in response to previous questions. A majority were either unable to respond or could speak only in vague generalities when talking about government workers (they work, help the president, etc.) or functions of government (keep us safe, pass good laws, etc.). Sixteen identified safety net services (assistance to poor people or victims of fires, storms, etc.), ten identified basic community services (police, fire, paramedics, etc.), and eight described the government as an all-purpose provider (of homes, factories, grocery stores, etc., to supply whatever people need). Individual responses included certifying the safety of consumer products, providing insurance, providing schools, maintaining roads, and renewing run-down neighborhoods.

It was surprising that so few students mentioned local community services, roads, schools, parks, or other government institutions or services. We know that children are aware of these aspects of their lives and surroundings; apparently they do not yet connect them with images of government. What little students learn about government in the early grades focuses on leaders and the symbols associated with them (e.g., the White House), with little attention given to the specifics of government functions, especially government services. We believe that instruction ought to build on the basic idea that governments provide needed infrastructure and services that are too big in scope, expense, and so forth for individual families to provide for themselves. This would delineate a richer picture of public sector activities than most children possess and likely be of more interest and use to them than some of the more abstract notions often emphasized in lessons on government (e.g., how a bill becomes a law).

Questions 19–21 addressed students' knowledge about taxes as the main source of government income and about community services as local government functions paid for with tax money. Responses to these questions replicated developmental trends reported in previous research. Some students were unable to generate any response at all. Others expressed misconceptions, such as that governmental leaders pay government employees with money from their own personal funds or money obtained from banks (simply by asking for it). Still others knew that the government prints bills and mints coins, so they reasoned that it could manufacture whatever money it needs to pay its employees. Finally, the most mature students understood that governments collect taxes to fund their activities, including construction of police and fire stations and payment of police officers and firefighters.

Most of the students who used the word *taxes* understood taxes as bills to be paid. However, some of them confused taxes with utility bills, house or car payments, or other bills rather than defining *taxes* as money paid to the government. Students who did understand that taxes are paid to the government usually also understood that most of the money used to fund government activities comes from these taxes.

When asked who owns the police and fire stations, thirty-one students were unable to respond and thirty-six correctly said the government/governor/township or a similar response. However, nineteen said the boss (chief, deputy, etc.), and fourteen said the people who work in the building. Similarly, when asked who pays the police officers and firefighters, twenty-eight students were unable to respond and twenty-three correctly said tax money or the people who pay taxes, but the rest named the president or another executive (presumably using personal funds) or the people who use the services (including people who pay fines for speeding or calling in false alarms).

The next two questions addressed students' knowledge about public and private schools, probing in particular their understanding of a difference in the basis for their funding. Most students could not identify alternatives to public schools (Catholic schools, reading schools, tutorial schools, etc.) and most of those who could were not clear about how these alternative schools are funded. Only a small minority understood that their own public school was owned by the local government and that its teachers were paid using tax money. Many more could not respond to these questions or thought that the school was owned by the principal or the people who worked in the building and that the teachers were paid by the principal, the president or governor, or their own parents.

Students who were able to name alternatives to public schools typically described these schools as more exclusive, having higher academic standards, or offering more curricular alternatives or extracurricular attractions than their school did. However, only six students distinguished between public and private schools by stating that the public schools are paid for with tax money. The students' knowledge about public ownership and funding of schools was noticeably less developed than their parallel knowledge about police and fire stations.

The final question asked students whether they would like to be president when they grew up. Reflecting the findings of surveys conducted in recent years, a majority (fifty-six) of the students said that they would not want to be president when they grew up, eighteen were undecided, and only twenty-two said yes. Follow-up questions about positive aspects of being the president yielded responses that emphasized perquisites that come with the office (live in the White House, have a bowling alley or swimming pool in the house, get free cars, etc.) and the power to issue orders and make things happen (mostly orders for personal services, such as sending an aide to get coffee). Only twelve students mentioned opportunities to do good for the country by making things more fair, helping the needy, and the like. Follow-up questions about negative aspects of being the president yielded responses that emphasized having to work long and hard with little time for recreation or your family (thirty-one), daunting responsibilities (eleven), and being required to do a lot of work that is not enjoyable because it involves going to meetings and writing a lot (ten). Individual responses included the ideas that you need a lot of lawyers, you might be sent to jail for not following the rules, someone might try to kill you, you have to have guards that follow you around and watch you all the time, and you have to get into "all that political stuff."

We find it disturbing that less than a fourth of the students said that they wanted to be president when they grew up, and that many of these were more focused on perquisites than on opportunities to use the power of the office for the good of the country. Furthermore, even though most of these students attributed near-omnipotent power to the presidency, more of them associated the office with long hours, daunting responsibilities, and boring work than with exciting opportunities to serve the nation and make things happen. We think that the nation in general, the schools in particular, and the social studies curriculum most especially need to do a better job of emphasizing the common good, helping students to appreciate the many functions and services that governments perform, and socializing students to aspire to public service careers.

Overview of Government Unit— Barbara Knighton

The idea of teaching about government to early elementary students can seem intimidating. However, this unit becomes very manageable if you focus on the big ideas. I found this to be especially successful when I helped my students make connections between each of the different levels of government. As we discussed each lesson, we found similar threads that tied them to one another. Also, focusing on the functions of the government helped to make the information much more concrete.

It was important to help students begin to see the ways that governments affect their lives on a daily basis. To help accomplish this, I began to make casual references during our day (outside of the social studies lessons) about laws, regulations, and taxes. For example, as we got ready for the bus, I would talk about the requirements to become a bus driver. This lent authenticity to the information that I related during the lessons.

This unit required giving students time to verbally process the information as we were learning, so plan extra time for students to pair together or talk in small groups. Many of my students' conversations focused on the functions of government (e.g., what would happen, and why, if government laws, services, or other functions were or were not operating in a particular sector of society).

By the end of the government unit, I found that my students were very excited about becoming responsible citizens as adults. They discussed the importance of paying taxes and even wanted to include that information in their year-end program. Many of them talked about wanting to hold an elected government office some day and were enthusiastic about becoming old enough to vote.

Each of the lessons contains several different big ideas to structure your teaching around. Look to see which big ideas are covered in several lessons and use these as guiding ideas for the whole unit. You will find that the big ideas in the lessons of this unit frequently connect to each other, and you can use this to help your students organize the information.

Lesson 1

What Is a Community? What Is Citizenship?

Resources

- Photographs of your students illustrating how they live, work, and play with the family, school, and local community
- Word cards: Community, Rights, Responsibilities, Citizens
- Map of local community
- Photographs of a local park, a block party, a local school playground
- Photographs of a class meeting, depicting the classroom as a community
- Photographs that capture citizenship in action (child helping an elderly person across the street or carrying a bag of groceries)
- Photographs that illustrate conflict (two children who want to play different games)
- Photographs that illustrate protection of property, keeping people safe, etc.
- Sets of word cards for Table Talk activity: Community, Citizen, Rights, Responsibilities, Rules, Protection, Keep Us Safe, etc.
- Copies of Figure 3: Good Citizenship Worksheet

Children's Literature

Adams, P. (Illus.). (1991). *Who Cares About Law and Order?* Singapore: Children's Play International.

Coster, P. (1997). *Towns and Cities*. New York: Children's Press.

Kalman, B., & Hughes, S. (1986). *I Live in a City*. New York: Crabtree.

General Comments

To launch this unit, collect instructional resources and visual prompts as a means of generating interest in the topic. Pay particular attention to the students' position within the context of community and how government and citizenship are parts of their lives in ways that they may not have realized.

Prior to the first day, post questions around the room or on the bulletin board. For example:

What are members of a community called?

Who are some of our leaders?

What are some of the problems our community leaders and its members have solved?

How does our government help us?

What are some of the services our community provides?

How are these services paid for?

General Purposes or Goals

To help students understand and appreciate what it means to be a member of a community and to practice citizenship.

Main Ideas to Develop

- A community is a place where people live, work, play, and share special times.
- People in a community work together, accomplish tasks, and achieve goals through cooperation.
- Members of communities are called citizens.
- Good citizens tend to be respectful, to be responsible, to think and act for the good of the community, and to be open to ideas of others that may be different from their own.
- Rules and laws are designed to remind people of their rights and responsibilities. They help people get along, keep things fair, protect individual and public property, and keep people safe.

Teaching Tips from Barbara

Begin collecting pictures for this lesson several weeks before you begin teaching. If you have access to a digital camera, it would enable you to show many different places in your community. I found it valuable to spend time establishing the relationship between neighborhood, city, state, country, and world. Several students struggled to clarify these entities and their connections to one another. I would recommend that you have your students spend some time processing and actually creating maps of each level. I also began talking about the students being *citizens* of several different *communities* and continued using those terms frequently during and after the unit.

Starting the Lesson

Begin the first lesson by establishing a context for the students. Ask students to describe what *community* means to them. List their responses. Use photographs of the students, their families, and other members of the community to add human interest and to underscore some important ideas that are rarely expressed in a systematic way. Use an interactive narrative laced with photos to revisit multiple contexts of community (family, school, classroom, local neighborhood/community) and what it means to be citizens within these contexts.

Suggested Lesson Discussion

[Tailor the narrative according to your local community.]

We live in the _____ community, a suburb of _____ [or a city, rural area, etc.]. [Show your local community on a map.] It is a place where people live, work, play, and share special times. [Show photos of the park, school playground, block party.] Families in the community often take their children to the park for a picnic or to go sledding. They may organize a softball game or plan a celebration of a special holiday such as the Fourth of July. For example, every year the _____ Township Fire Department has a community fireworks display at the local park. Sometimes families organize a special event to raise money for someone who needs help. For example, community members in _____ Township might have a fund-raiser (e.g., a dinner and dance) for someone who has been sick for a long time and has lots of hospital bills, or collect canned goods and clothing to help a family that has had an emergency (e.g., fire or job loss).

The community of _____ School District and _____ Township [refer to local map] is a place where people live, work, and share special times. People in the area work together, accomplish tasks, and achieve goals through cooperation.

On the weekends and in the summer, you spend time with your families and friends. On weekdays, you spent a lot of time in our school community. Our school is a community, too—one that you share with your teachers and friends in the classroom. [Show photos illustrating how your class has worked together on tasks to achieve certain goals by cooperating.] Let's recall times the class has worked together to solve a special problem to complete a specific task. For example, recently groups cooperated in order to make tie-dyed shirts for their class teams. Also, we held a class meeting to figure out how to get ready to welcome a new student who would be joining us soon. [Show photos illustrating your class as a community, for example, pictures of the class meeting and a photograph of the new student.] As members of communities, we are called *citizens*. Citizens have rights and responsibilities. [Show photos illustrating citizenship in action on the playground (e.g., right to swing and responsibility to take turns on the swings, right to have lunch and responsibility to pick up trash before you leave.)]

[Use photos of the classroom to capture citizenship in action.] Good citizens tend to be respectful, to be responsible, to think and act for the good of the community, and to be open to ideas of others that may be different from their own.

Rules are designed to remind people of their rights and responsibilities, as well as to help people get along, keep things fair, protect individual and public property, and keep people safe. [Using a classroom photograph that illustrates conflict (e.g., one child wanting to play I spy and the other wanting to play indoor baseball), explain that in this case baseball was selected because there is a classroom rule that says if you are Student of the Week you are the one who selects the indoor activity for recess on a rainy day.] There are many other rules in our classroom established to keep things fair, to protect individual and public property, and to keep us safe. [Optional: Have students generate a list of these rules and record them on a flip chart.] [Show other photographs that illustrate protection of property and keeping people safe (e.g., sign "Park Closes at 10 P.M.," stop sign, etc.). Elicit other visual examples of rules or laws that students have observed in the community. Record their responses on the white board.]

Activity

Table Talk—Give each table a set of word cards that focus on the main points of the lesson: Community, Citizen, Rights, Responsibilities, Rules, Protection, Keep Us Safe, and so on. The expectation is for each table to talk about the lesson using these key words in their conversation. Teacher modeling will be important.

Summarize

- Communities are places where people live, work, play, and share special times.
- People in communities need to work together and be respectful, responsible, and thoughtful of one another in order to accomplish tasks and achieve goals.
- When people exhibit these behaviors, they are viewed as being good citizens.
- Rules and laws are designed to remind people of their rights and responsibilities.

Assessment

Encourage each student to brainstorm with a peer about all the ways he or she can practice good citizenship in the classroom, at school, and in the local community. Then ask each student to draw a picture illustrating one way he or she has recently practiced being a good citizen. If upper-grade mentors are available, have them write captions below the drawings. For example, "I have practiced being a good citizen in the lunchroom by waiting my turn in line," or "I practiced being a good citizen in the park by making sure that our family picked up all of our garbage after our picnic."

Home Assignment

Using their drawings as stimuli, have students share what they have learned about citizenship with their parents. Then have them use the Good Citizenship Worksheet (Figure 3, p. 229) to discuss with their families what citizenship means to them, how they practice it in their community, and the rules that remind family members of their responsibilities as citizens of the community.

Dear Parents,

Your child has been learning about what it means to be a good citizen as a member of the class, a student at the school, and a citizen in the local community. Please take time to learn about your child's view of citizenship and how he or she has recently practiced it as expressed in his or her picture. Next, as a family, discuss what citizenship in your community means to you and how you practice citizenship. Finally, as a family, list rules (unwritten and written, including signs) on the enclosed Good Citizenship Worksheet that remind family members of their responsibilities as citizens of the community. Be sure to send your family response back to school so that our class conversation can be expanded.

Sincerely,

Figure 2   Model Letter to Parents

WAYS THAT MEMBERS OF OUR FAMILY PRACTICE
BEING A GOOD CITIZEN IN OUR COMMUNITY

Examples:

Pick up litter around our building.

Donate food to the area food bank.

1.

2.

3.

4.

5.

6.

Rules in Our Family and Community (Written and Unwritten, Including Signs)
That Remind Us of Our Responsibilities

1.

2.

3.

4.

5.

6.

FIGURE 3   Good Citizenship Worksheet

© 2003 by Janet Alleman and Jere Brophy from *Social Studies Excursions, K–3: Book Three*. Portsmouth, NH: Heinemann.

Lesson 2

Community Services Provided by the Local Government

Resources

- Map of local community
- Photographs and pictures of local community service sites
- Photographs of local community workers
- Photographs and pictures of other communities illustrating size and location as reasons for different/more or fewer community services
- Resource people who work for a local community service (optional)
- Community service data retrieval chart

Children's Literature

Duvall, J. (1997). *Who Keeps the Water Clean? Ms. Schindler!* New York: Children's Press.

Flanagan, A. (1998). *Officer Brown Keeps Neighborhoods Safe*. New York: Children's Press.

Kalman, B. (1998). *Community Helpers from A to Z*. New York: Crabtree.

Lewiston, W. (1998). *A Trip to the Firehouse*. New York: Grosset and Dunlap.

General Comments

Using a series of pictures and photographs, begin developing a context of community with an emphasis on community services. Underscore the idea that families want to live in a community that provides the services they need.

General Purposes or Goals

To help students understand and appreciate that: (1) people depend on one another to provide the services that they need; (2) every community provides certain kinds of services for the people who live there; (3) families pay money to the community for community services.

Main Ideas to Develop

- A community (township, town, suburb, city) is a place where people live and usually have many common needs and wants. Among them are community services.
- Many people work for the community.
- Community workers help make the community a better place to live.

- Different communities have different needs based on their location and size.
- Families pay money to the community. This money is called taxes. Tax money pays for the community services.

Teaching Tips from Barbara

I found it best to start with services directly related to the school and the students' personal lives. We talked about the school itself, the library, parks, and our local zoo. I then moved to community services that students are most familiar with, such as firefighters and police. Lastly, we talked about jobs and services that are usually less apparent to students. For example, most students have had few experiences with the water works or road commission. I was able to locate a good community map in our phone book and had it enlarged to use with this lesson and throughout the unit.

Starting the Lesson

Have the students share their responses from the home assignment. Then share photographs from your local community that illustrate services provided by the local government.

Suggested Lesson Discussion

A *community* is a collection of people that depend on a lot of others to help them meet their needs and wants. Every community elects leaders who help make the plans and laws. Plans include the services that people need that they cannot provide for themselves.

Think about the services you and your family depend on every day. You need good streets to walk or ride on to get to school. You need teachers at school to help you learn. You need police officers, firefighters, and ambulance drivers to protect and help you. The public library has books that you may take home to read. You may get your water from a source that is operated by your community. You might live in a community that needs snow removal services.

[Using a map of the local community and photographs of the services provided, locate the sites of local services. Select one or two local community services and expand on them. If possible, invite one or two individuals who provide local community services to visit your class and explain what they do and how they make the community a cleaner, safer, and/or more pleasant place to live. An alternative is to share one or two nonfiction literature sources that focus on specific community helpers. Possible sources include sections of *Community Helpers from A to Z, Officer Brown Keeps Neighborhoods Safe, Who Keeps the Water Clean? Ms. Schindler!* and *A Trip to the Firehouse.*]

Communities need different services depending on their location and size. Clearing the streets after a snowstorm, for example, is an important service for communities located in Michigan or New England. But is removing snow a needed service in Florida or Hawaii? . . . Why not?

The size of the community also makes a difference in the services that a community provides. Mass transit [show photographs] is a very important service in Chicago or New York, but less important in our local area (township) and not important at all in a farming community [show photograph]. Large communities need more services than smaller ones.

One way that communities get the money they need to pay for the services and service workers is by charging *taxes* to the people who live in them. This tax money is paid to the government. There are many different kinds of taxes. In many communities, you pay a small tax every time you buy certain goods. People who own homes or other buildings pay taxes on property. Some of this tax money is used to support local services and some is used to support services provided by the state and federal governments.

Activity

As a large-group, interactive activity, have the students complete a chart focusing on community services. Have the group list services they think would be found in a suburban community, a small rural community, and a large city. Encourage students to give reasons for their responses. Provide pictures and photos representing the three types of communities.

Summarize

- Communities provide services for families and individuals that they cannot provide for themselves.
- These services help make the community a better place to live.
- Different communities have different needs based on their location and size.
- Community services are paid for by the money that the people pay to the government. The money is called taxes.

Community Services

What services are found in the following communities?

A SMALL RURAL COMMUNITY	A SUBURBAN AREA	A LARGE CITY
School libraries only	A township public library	Many public libraries
Fewer teachers	Teachers	Many teachers
Volunteer firefighters	A few firefighters	Many firefighters
		Mass transit

Assessment

Encourage each student to brainstorm with a peer about all of the community services that are provided locally. Then ask each student to draw a picture illustrating one community service and describe in words what the service provides. A word wall can be provided to help students with their spelling.

Home Assignment

Have each student share his or her drawing with an adult or older sibling as a springboard for discussing community services. Then, encourage the family to select the community service it thinks is most important and write a paragraph explaining why. The paragraphs will be shared in an upcoming class session. Save the student drawings and family responses for subsequent lessons.

Optional   Encourage the family to take the opportunity to interview a service worker in the community in order to learn more about his or her job and how it helps the local residents. The responses would be a welcome addition to an upcoming class session.

Dear Parents,

We have been learning about community services that are provided locally. Please spend a few minutes with your child using his/her drawing as a springboard for discussion. Then talk about a community service that your family thinks is particularly important, and why. We would appreciate it if you would write out your comments so that your child can share them with our class.

Sincerely,

FIGURE 4   Model Letter to Parents

Lesson 3

The Local Government Makes Plans and Laws

Resources

- Pictures depicting a community (e.g., houses, stores, post office, library, fire station, etc.)
- Local leader as presenter or videotaped interview with a local government official
- Photographs of local government officials
- Local newspaper articles about the leaders
- Ballot—local candidates
- Photographs of local laws depicted in signs (e.g., Stop Sign, One-Way Street, No Dumping, Handicapped Parking Only, etc.)

Children's Literature

Burby, L. (1999). *A Day in the Life of a Mayor*. New York: Power Kids Press.

Coster, P. (1997). *Towns and Cities*. New York: Children's Press.

Kalman, B., & Hughes, S. (1986). *I Live in a City*. New York: Crabtree.

General Comments

Using another series of photographs and pictures, continue to develop the context for community. Review the fact that a community consists of many families who live close to one another and share common needs and wants (e.g., transportation system[s], fire department, hospital, police department, etc.), and underscore the idea that within every community there is a need for rules and laws. Usually the leaders of the community make the laws.

General Purposes or Goals

To help students understand and appreciate: (1) how a community works; (2) why a community (town, suburb, city) needs rules and laws; (3) who makes the laws; and (4) how the lawmakers are chosen.

Main Ideas to Develop

- A community (town, suburb, city) is a place where people live and usually have many common needs and wants. Among them is the need for rules and laws.
- Every township, town, or city makes plans and laws for itself.
- Usually the leaders of the community make the laws. Laws are rules made by the government that everyone in the community must follow.

234

- Leaders are elected by the people (of voting age) to make and enforce the laws.
- In some communities, the mayor is the chief leader. In other communities there are township boards. Other leaders help the mayor, manager, or board watch over the community.

Teaching Tips from Barbara

Continue to focus on the functions or jobs of the community and how they affect your students' lives. I used the familiar structure of our school and its rules as a way to make connections to the known for my students. I used the book about the mayor of New York (*A Day in the Life of a Mayor*) as a way to summarize information at the end of the lesson. Be sure to continue to use those "What if . . . " questions to support analyses of the effects of not having governmental support. For example, the question, "What if there were no speed limit in front of our school?" created a very realistic conversation about how this aspect of government protects and helps our students.

Starting the Lesson

Begin the lesson by discussing responses to the home assignment. Then show photographs of your local community. Explain that a community—which might be a suburb, town, or city—is a collection of people who live near one another and share governmental leadership and services. Community members have similar needs and wants, including the need for rules and laws to protect them, keep them safe, and so on. Communities share a common leader such as a mayor, manager, or township board. Explain your local government structure. Use photographs and local newspaper articles to add human interest to the story and to introduce the elected leaders. If possible, invite the elected leader to your classroom. Ask her or him to tell what she or he does, how she or he got the job, why it is important to the community, and how every citizen can help. (An alternative is to conduct a video interview of the leader and share it with the class.) Explain that this leader was elected by the voters (eighteen years old or older) who live in the community. If possible, show a ballot with the names of the local candidates.

Suggested Lesson Discussion

Three jobs of community leaders include helping to make plans and laws; solving problems; and making the community a pleasant place to live. These leaders make the rules that become laws, which need to be followed by everyone. Laws help to protect the rights of the people. Some laws help to protect property (e.g., zoning). Other laws are about health (e.g., antipollution ordinances) or safety (e.g., speed limits). Often there are signs in our communities to remind us of what we should and should not do. [Show photographs of signs seen in the local community.

Examples might include No Littering, $100 Fine, Speed Limit, 30 mph, No Trespassing, Handicapped Parking Only, Park Closes at 10 P.M., One-Way Street, No Dumping.]

Laws help guide our lives and remind us of our responsibility toward other people in our community. The police and judges who enforce the laws are also part of the local government. Once a law is made, there is a penalty for breaking it. For example, people in your community can get ticketed and have to pay fines for speeding, littering, or parking illegally.

Laws are intended to make the community a better place, not merely to constrict people. [Select one law and discuss why it exists and what would happen if it didn't or if people were frequently breaking it. For example, what would happen if people frequently parked in spaces reserved for handicapped people? What would happen if people drove at any speed they wanted?]

Local leaders are paid (as their job) to make sure that life in the community allows people to carry out their daily activities in a safe and orderly environment. They are paid with tax money collected by the local government.

Optional   Read the children's literature selection titled *A Day in the Life of a Mayor*. It provides a very human look at New York City's former mayor and what his days were like as a leader of the largest city in the United States. The book points out that he attended many meetings, met with the press, worked with the people, worked in his office, and tried to make a difference in people's lives.

Activity

Divide the class into groups, and ask each one to pictorially and in writing develop one entry for a class booklet titled *Local Government*. Starters for the entries are as follows:

Our community can be described as _____

_____.

Our leaders do the following jobs for our community _____

_____.

Our community needs rules and laws because _____

_____.

Note: If possible, seek volunteers who could duplicate the entries and compile them into booklets.

Summarize

- Communities have many needs, including the need for rules and laws.
- Every township, town, or city makes plans and laws for itself.
- Usually the leaders of the community make the laws.
- The leaders are elected by the people.

Assessment

Have student groups share their section of the *Local Government* booklet with the whole class and then participate in a "thumbs up/thumbs down" exercise. (Students show thumbs up if they agree with statement, thumbs down if they disagree.)

If they show thumbs down, each student should be prepared to make the statement true.

1. Thumbs down — Everybody votes for our mayor, council, and other elected leaders. (You must be eighteen years or older to vote.)

2. Thumbs down — Only some communities need rules and laws. (All communities need rules and laws to remind people of their responsibilities.)

3. Thumbs up — Usually the leaders of the community make the laws.

4. Thumbs up — There are consequences for people who break the laws.

5. Thumbs down — Our communities could get along just fine without people to enforce the laws. (Sometimes people need to be reminded of their responsibilities toward others.)

6. Thumbs up — The local government leaders have as their jobs to keep the community a safe and pleasant place to live.

Home Assignment

Have volunteers compile copies of the *Local Government* booklets for the students (or make them yourself). Encourage each student to take a copy home and share it with family members. Because of the time involved in copying, this assignment may not be enacted for a couple of days. Send a note home indicating that the booklets are forthcoming. Ask families to discuss why the local government is important to the family. Students should be prepared to share their responses during the next class session.

Dear Parents,

We have been learning about our local government. We encourage you and your child to talk about why and how local government is important to your family (e.g., some of the services it provides). Your child will be asked to share your ideas during our next social studies lesson. In a few days, your child will be bringing home a booklet about local government that we made in class. Please read it together and discuss its important ideas.

Sincerely,

FIGURE 5   Model Letter to Parents

Lesson 4

....

State Government Handles Matters That Affect Everyone in the State

Resources

- Maps depicting the community and the state
- Photographs of the state capitol, governor, governor's family, etc.
- Samples of state laws (e.g., motorcycle helmet, seat belt, teacher certificate)
- Sales slip illustrating sales tax, if applicable
- Driver's license
- Auto license plate
- Photo of roads in a developing country
- Visual depicting the branches of state government and simple illustrations to show how our state government helps us
- Resource person who works for the state government

Children's Literature

Flanagan, A. (1997). *A Day in Court with Mrs. Trinh*. New York: Children's Press.

Marsh, C. (1998). *Michigan Government for Kids*. Peach Tree City, GA: Gallopade Publishing Company. [Note: Select similar books written about your state.]

General Comments

The purpose of this lesson is to help students begin to position themselves as residents of a community within a state. The state government handles matters that affect people throughout the state. The citizens (of voting age) have the opportunity to elect leaders for the state.

General Purposes or Goals

To help students: (1) understand and appreciate their membership in a local community as well as in a state; (2) understand and appreciate how a state's government helps its citizens; and (3) become knowledgeable about state leaders—how they are selected and what they do.

Main Ideas to Develop

- A state is made up of many communities.
- Citizens of voting age have the opportunity to elect leaders for the state.
- Our state government is divided into three categories or branches: legislative, executive, and judicial.

- Our state government focuses on the services such as higher education, recreation, state highways, a system of justice, licensing regulations, and more. The state government handles matters that affect people throughout the state.

Teaching Tips from Barbara

As I shared information about our state government, I made as many connections and parallels as I could between the local and state levels. There are parallels in both functions and jobs. I found that using the actual names of the job holders at each level helped to bring a measure of realism to our discussion. Sharing the story of our governor and his life increased student interest and children began to talk about their possible future roles in government.

Starting the Lesson

Begin the lesson by discussing the results of the home assignment. Then review the meaning of community: it is a place where people live, work, and play. People live in communities so they can help one another and get things done—build a park, collect the garbage, install a new streetlight, and so on.

Suggested Lesson Discussion

A state is made up of many communities and, as citizens, we are members of a school community, a town/city community, and a state. [Use a local map and a state map as other means of developing a relationship between the community and the state. Note nearby communities on a local map. Also note major cities and features (lakes, state borders) on a state map.]

Every state government handles matters that affect people throughout that state. Our state government is divided into three categories or branches: legislative, executive, and judicial. [Use a graphic and pictures to explain functions and features.] The state government provides money for schools, builds and maintains state roads, and provides a system of justice. It also protects the health and safety of its citizens.

[Show a photograph of the state capitol.] The state capitol is the place where regular government business for our state is conducted. That is where the governor and the state leaders work. The citizens (of voting age) have the opportunity to elect leaders for our state every four years, including the governor, who heads the executive branch. His or her job is to enforce laws passed by the state legislators and oversee the work of the state to make sure that people are safe and that their rights and responsibilities are realized. [Share the story of your state governor. For example, the governor of Michigan is John Engler.] Our state governor was John Engler [show photograph of governor]. He was born on a farm near Mt. Pleasant. He joined 4-H at age 10 and won many ribbons showing cattle at the county fair. He read the newspaper every day before he went to school. He played football in high school. He graduated from Michigan State University and he knew then that he wanted to have a career in government service. While a student at MSU, he worked in the beef barn to make money to pay for his college expenses. As a junior at MSU, he was elected president of his dorm. He was first elected as a state representative at age 22. He later became a senator. He then went to law school and since 1991, he has been our governor.

The governor has a lot of power. After the legislators (people who work in the legislative branch—also elected by the citizens) approve a bill, it is sent to the governor. If she or he thinks it is a good one, she or he will sign it and it will then become a law. If she or he doesn't think it will be good for the people of our state, the govenor will veto it and it will not become a law.

[Show students examples of the results of state laws.] State laws are intended to protect the people of the state (e.g., seat belt restriction, teacher certificate/license, driver's license).

The state government also performs important services for the people in the state. To pay for these services, the government collects taxes. One form is the income tax (people who earn money pay a part of their earnings to the government). [Illustrate with graph showing income tax as a percentage of dollars earned.] Businesses also pay taxes. Another kind of tax is a sales tax. This is collected when someone buys an item. The amount of the sales tax is added to the price. [Illustrate by using a payroll check stub and a receipt from a purchase.]

The government also collects fees from drivers' licenses and license plates. [Show these items.] The government uses this money for roads and road safety as well as government workers' salaries, building new highways, assisting schools, and so on.

The services provided by the government are important for the citizens of the state—and are much too big for individual citizens or families to manage. In places throughout the world where people have less money to help pay for these services, the people have fewer benefits (e.g., poor roads, crowded classrooms, less police protection, less-qualified teachers, etc.). [Show a photo of a place that obviously has poor roads, etc.]

[Use visuals to depict the three branches of government and to explain what each does.] In Michigan, our government, which is similar to most state governments, has three major categories. The legislative branch makes the laws for Michigan. These individuals are elected by people in our state who are eighteen or older and who choose to vote. The legislators are known as senators and representatives. The executive branch is the second category, with the governor being the chief executive officer. It is his or her job to enforce the laws and maintain order in the state. The third branch is the judicial branch. [Optional: Read *A Day in Court with Mrs. Trinh*.] The judges preside over courtroom trials and decide on the punishments for people who are found guilty of breaking the laws. All three branches of government are very important to make sure our state is safe and orderly and that people get help with problems and issues too big for individuals and families to solve on their own. [Cite current issues that the state government is addressing that students can relate to (e.g., schools for blind students, double tanker trucks, potholes.)]

[If possible, invite a local community member who works in state government to come to the classroom to explain the role of his or her branch of government, briefly describe his or her work, and underscore through examples how state government helps the residents of the state.] In general, the fifty states provide similar help to their citizens (e.g., education, state parks, etc.).

Activity

Role-play (with the teacher as facilitator-player) what a student new to your state could learn from the students in your class who have just studied about your state's government. List the responses on the white board.

Summary

- A state is made up of many communities.
- Our state government is divided into three branches: legislative, executive, and judicial.
- State government focuses on the services it provides its residents.
- Citizens of voting age have the opportunity to select the leaders of our state.
- Most states are similar to ours in how they govern and in the services they provide.

Assessment

Have the class write a letter or e-mail to a pen pal class in another state describing your state government and why it is important. Identify and describe features of your state government that are unique (e.g., John Engler is only Michigan's governor; only the voters of Michigan could elect him). (Students who need help might refer to the list of responses generated as a part of the role-playing activity.)

Home Assignment

Encourage a family member to read the letter or e-mail from the class explaining the unique features of your state's government. Then, as a family, have them add to the list of features of your state government. These responses should be returned as soon as possible so that they can be shared in a subsequent class discussion.

Dear Parents,

We have been learning about our state's government. We encourage you to have your child read the letter that the class wrote describing the unique features of our state government. Then, as a family, add to the list of features. Please send your responses back to school so that they can be shared during our next class session.

Sincerely,

FIGURE 6   Model Letter to Parents

Lesson 5

....

National Government Handles Matters That Affect Everyone in the United States

Resources

- Map of community, state, and United States
- Aerial view of Washington, D.C.
- Street map of Washington, D.C.
- Three dioramas/learning centers with a range of photographs, pictures, and books describing aspects of the three branches of the U.S. government, emphasizing the three major sites: White House, U.S. Capitol building, and the Department of Justice
- Assortment of word cards describing the three branches of the U.S. government (Optional: Prepare a set for each student and use for a home assignment.)
- Replica of the U.S. Constitution

Children's Literature

Aria, B. (1994). *The Supreme Court*. New York: Franklin Watts.

Greene, C. (1985). *A New True Book, The Supreme Court*. Chicago: Children's Press.

McElroy, L. (1999). *Meet My Grandmother: She's a Supreme Court Justice*. Brookfield, CT: Millbrook Press.

Patrick, D. (1994). *The Executive Branch*. New York: Franklin Watts.

Sobel, S. (1999). *How the U.S. Government Works*. Hauppauge, NY: Barron's Educational Series, Inc.

Stein, R. (1995). *Powers of the Supreme Court*. Chicago: Children's Press.

Waters, K. (1991). *The Story of the White House*. New York: Scholastic.

Photos

President's house (see p. 6, *The Executive Branch* by D. Patrick)

Oval Office (see p. 17, *The Executive Branch* by D. Patrick)

Executive Branch Cabinet (see p. 33, *The Executive Branch* by D. Patrick)

Supreme Court (see p. 2, *Powers of the Supreme Court* by R. Stein)

General Comments

This lesson is intended to whet the students' appetites regarding our national government: where the work is done, how it is organized, and how it affects all of the people who live in the United States of America.

General Purposes or Goals

To help students: (1) understand and appreciate their connection to the federal (U.S.) government and how it is set up to deal with matters affecting the whole country; (2) acquire an interest in, understanding of, and appreciation for leaders in the U.S. government, how they are selected, and what they do for the citizens of our country.

Main Ideas to Develop

- *Government* is defined as people running the country.
- The lawmaking branch of our federal government is made up of men and women called senators and representatives. They are also called legislators. Together they are known as the U.S. Congress. These men and women are elected by the people from the state that they represent.
- The leader of our government is elected by the people of our country who are of voting age. The leader is known as the president.
- Our president is George W. Bush. He lives and works in the White House. The president is elected by the voters in the United States to serve as the leader of our country. The president's position is voted on by the people every four years and the same person cannot serve more than eight years.
- The power of the presidency goes with the office. When George W. Bush leaves the office, the new president will have the power and Mr. Bush will be an ordinary citizen.
- In the United States, we have two major political parties: Democrats, who tend to want more services and more taxes to pay for them, and Republicans, who tend to want fewer services and fewer taxes.
- A person who runs for a government office (asks to be elected to a leadership position) is called a candidate.
- The candidate has a platform—a list of ideas that he or she supports. In speeches and printed campaign materials, the candidate explains what he or she wants government to do and why. On election day, voters decide whom they want to represent them and why. Candidates who receive the most votes win.
- The U.S. government makes the rules and laws that affect everyone in the United States.
- The U.S. government does many useful things that keep our country running smoothly.
- A lot of people work for the United States in an effort to make life better for its citizens.

Teaching Tips from Barbara

This lesson works best if taught in two parts. On the first day, we began our "trip" to Washington, D.C., and our discussion of the national government and the presidency. I found that my students knew the names of several presidents but didn't know much about the actual job. On the second day, we covered the Supreme Court and Congress. At the end of the second lesson, my students really enjoyed talking about which of the three branches of government they would most want to participate in in the future. They were much more successful in writing about their choice when they had time to talk in pairs and rehearse their answers before trying to put their ideas on paper.

Starting the Lesson

Begin the lesson by discussing the responses to home assignment. Then set the stage for the lesson by telling the students that today the class will take an imaginary trip via plane from the nearest airport to Washington, D.C. To help students begin to feel a sense of time and distance, announce the trip a few hours before it is to begin. Use local and U.S. maps to identify the locations. Begin the lesson about the time the plane would arrive in Washington, D.C. Tell students, "Washington, D.C. is the capital of the United States. Most of the work of our national government goes on in Washington, D.C."

Begin with an aerial view of the city. Then use a street map of Washington, D.C. Point out the three major places that the class will visit. Then simulate a walking trip of Washington, emphasizing the three major sites: White House, U.S. Capitol building, and Department of Justice.

At this point in the lesson, have the students get out of their seats and walk to a diorama/learning center that has been set up to display photos, pictures, books, and other artifacts that focus on the White House—the home of the president.

Suggested Lesson Discussion

Have any of you visited the White House? [Show photos and pictures.] [Emphasize that this home is the place where every president of our country lives and works.]

Our nation's chief executive is the president of the United States. Our current president is George W. Bush. He was born in New Haven, Connecticut, during the time his father was studying at Yale University. He is the son of a former vice president and president of the United States.

George W. Bush, the oldest of six children, grew up in Midland, Texas. As a child, he was known for his love of mischief and his joking remarks. George attended Sam Houston Elementary School in Midland and then went on to San Jacinto Junior High School. He attended private high schools. While his grades were average, he was known for his lively personality and love of athletics. He played football, basketball, and baseball. George graduated from Yale, the college his father had attended. He was elected president of his fraternity. He was a member of the Texas Air National Guard and completed active duty, where he received the rank of lieutenant. In 1975, he graduated from Harvard Business School and began working in the oil business.

George's love of sports was ever present, and at one point he was part owner of the Texas Rangers baseball team. However, he was intrigued with politics, so he ran for governor of Texas. He won the election and later was reelected for another term. He became known for achieving success with a combination of personal charm and a willingness to compromise with leaders who had different ideas.

In 2000, George W. Bush ran for president of the United States. In one of the closest elections ever, he narrowly defeated Al Gore, the Democratic candidate and former vice president.

The main job of the executive branch is to carry out or enforce the laws. For example, the president is responsible for the agencies of the executive branch (e.g., Food and Drug Administration, FBI). He represents our country to other nations. He serves as the commander in chief of our armed forces. The president appoints many officials to help him run the executive branch (secretary of state, secretary of treasury, secretary of education, etc.). [See *The Executive Branch* by D. Patrick, pp. 35–59.]

The president is elected by the people of voting age in the United States who practice good citizenship by registering to vote and casting a ballot on election day. There is a presidential election every four years and the same person cannot serve as president for more than eight years.

The next stop on the walking tour is the United States Capitol. [At this learning center there should be a display of photos, pictures, books, and other artifacts that portray what the building looks like and explain what goes on inside.] It is in this building where the legislature or lawmaking branch, called Congress, makes the laws for the government. [Show pictures and photos of this facility and of the activities carried out by the legislative branch.]

Congress has two parts, known as *houses*—the Senate and the House of Representatives. Every state elects two senators and one or more representatives based on the population of the state. Our state has two senators and _____ representatives in Congress.

Besides making rules and laws that affect everyone in the United States, the U.S. government provides important services that are too big to be handled by individuals, families, communities, or even states. Among these are regulations that protect us and keep us safe (e.g., the

USDA conducts food/meat/crop inspections; the Department of Transportation regulates the size/weight of vehicles, speed limits on federal highways, etc.).

[Continue the "walking tour" by stopping at the diorama/learning center depicting the U.S. Supreme Court. At this center, there should be a display that describes what the building looks like and what goes on inside. Show photos (see pp. 4, 10, 17, 45 in *A New True Book, The Supreme Court;* pp. 6, 38 in *The Supreme Court;* and pp. 2, 4 in *Powers of the Supreme Court*) and pictures of the facility and the activities carried out by this branch of the government.]

The role of the judicial branch is to interpret the laws expressed by the Constitution by applying them to individual cases. For example, in 1966, *Miranda v. Arizona*, the Supreme Court ruled that suspected criminals must be informed of their rights when they are arrested. The police cannot force suspects to answer questions if they do not have a lawyer present. The U.S. Supreme Court is the highest court in the nation. It meets in Washington, D.C. The Supreme Court has made decisions on the questions of slavery, free speech, women's rights, children's rights, racial discrimination, and many other important issues. The place where judges work is called a *court*.

All laws must conform to the Constitution [show replica and explain purpose of this document]. It is the job of the Supreme Court to make sure that the laws agree with the Constitution. [At the conclusion of the tour, have the students return to their seats.]

A lot of people work for the government. Some help make the laws; some make sure people follow the laws; some make judgments about people who break the laws and decide on how these people should be punished. Other government workers provide services to our people. In some ways, the governments of towns, states, and our country all work together to make life better for people. For example, the U.S. Department of Transportation, the state highway commission, and the town transportation department work together to improve our roads. The U.S. Department of Education, the state department of education, and local school districts work together to educate our students. The FBI, the state police, and local police cooperate to arrest criminals.

Activity

Have students imagine that they are going to a quiet area on the tour to spread out a blanket, have a snack, and review what they have observed and learned about three branches of government. Using a stack of cards that give clues associated with a specific branch of government, ask the class to mentally match the card to the branch and correct site. Select volunteers to match the branch of government to the descriptor and take the cards to the appropriate sites.

Sample card descriptions:

White House

President Bush

Judges decide on punishments

House and Senate chambers

Laws that affect all U.S. citizens are made

Commander of the military

Laws related to federal income tax are made

A new leader is elected every four years

The number of people who are elected and work at this site are determined in part by each state's population

Summarize

- A lot of people work for the government.
- Some government workers make the laws; some make sure that people follow the laws; some decide what to do to people who break the laws; and some provide government services.
- The headquarters of our national government is in Washington, D.C.

Assessment

Have students write a paragraph about which of the three branches of government they might want to work in when they grow up and why. Students should include in the paragraph a brief description of the job they would like to do and how they could help U.S. citizens by doing it. (Note: Here is a place where upper-grade mentors could be helpful.) Word cards for this activity should be available for students who need visual cues as "thought starters" or who need assistance with their spelling.

Home Assignment

Option 1 Encourage students to share their paragraphs with family members and, if relevant, talk to individuals they know who work for the U.S. government. Have a member of the family list the tasks these people do and explain how their work helps U.S. citizens. The list and explanation should be sent back to school for a subsequent class discussion.

Option 2 Prepare duplicate sets of the cards used in the activity and send a set home with each student. As a home assignment, have the family participate in a matching game. This activity can serve as a stimulus for discussing the functions and features of the three branches of our national government.

Dear Parents,

We have been learning about the three branches of the United States government. Please encourage your child to read his or her essay describing which of the three branches that he or she might like to work in when he or she grows up and why. If possible, have your child talk to some people you know who work for the U.S. government. Then, together, list tasks these people do and discuss how this work helps United States citizens. Please send your response to school with your child so that it can be shared with our class.

Sincerely,

FIGURE 7 Model Letter to Parents

Lesson 6

. . . .

Voting

Resources

- Word Cards: Vote, Candidate, Ballot, Platform, Register, Citizen
- Scenario role cards and props (including a ballot)
- Photos and graphics to explain elected and appointed officials
- Voter registry
- Voter registration card
- Picture of voters registering
- Campaign paraphernalia (e.g., posters, pins, signs, ads)
- Graphics depicting state and federal branches of government and elected leaders
- Photos of a voting booth and voting machine
- Computerized ballot
- Flash cards that provide visual cues about voting for Table Talk activity
- Mini flash card packets for the home assignment (optional)

Children's Literature

Duvall, J. (1997). *Who Keeps the Water Clean? Ms. Schindler.* New York: Scholastic Library Publishing.

Flanagan, A. (1998). *Officer Brown Keeps Neighborhoods Safe.* New York: Scholastic Library Publishing.

Fradin, D. (1985). *Voting and Elections.* Chicago: Children's Press.

Maestro, B., & Maestro, G. (1996). *The Voice of the People.* New York: Lothrop, Lee, & Shepard.

Pascoe, E. (1997). *The Right to Vote.* Brookfield, CT: Millbrook.

Roop, P., & Roop, C. (1998). *Susan B. Anthony.* Des Plaines, IL: Reed Educational and Professional Publishing, Ltd.

General Comments

Many of your students probably have heard family members talk about voting and/or elections. There is usually a heightened awareness about these governmental matters when someone they know is campaigning for an office (e.g., school board member, township trustee, etc.) and/or during presidential election years. This lesson is intended to raise students' interest in these matters as well as encourage them to become informed about the process so that when they reach voting age, they will participate in the governmental (democratic) process as part of responsible citizenship.

General Purposes and Goals

To help students: (1) understand voting and how the process works in the United States; and (2) appreciate the importance of voting as a part of practicing responsible citizenship.

Main Ideas to Develop

- Voting is a method by which people choose among several alternatives.
- A democracy is a form of government in which people take an active role in the decision making.
- A ballot is the list of names and offices (and sometimes ideas about certain issues) on which voters make their decisions.

Teaching Tips from Barbara

The key to making this lesson successful is focusing on the function of voting instead of just the activity of voting. Be sure to talk about the cause-and-effect relationship between the importance of thinking about the way you want to vote and what will happen after the election. I used a situation close to their hearts by asking my students to vote about recess: "If you picked indoors because your friends picked that and you'd rather be outside. . . ."

Starting the Lesson

Share the results from the home assignment. Then introduce the concept of voting by setting up the scenario that students have differing views regarding what story the teacher should read next. We recommend using two selections that relate to government, although any two popular children's books can be used. The question to the class is, "How should we decide?" Indicate that one way the class could decide is for each side to pick a number from one to ten. The teacher would have placed slips of paper numbered from one to ten in a hat. The teacher would draw a number from the hat and the side with the number closest to the one drawn would get to select the story. Another way would be to have a coin toss. A third way would be to take a vote. Elicit responses from the students regarding the trade-offs associated with each method. Then say, "In this class, we are going to take a vote." Show a word card with the word *Vote*. Remind students that before one votes one should have all of the important information. One should always be an informed voter.

Suggested Lesson Discussion

[At this point, show the two books and provide key information about each. We suggest two books that focus on community services provided by tax money. One is entitled *Officer Brown Keeps Neighborhoods Safe* (Flanagan, 1998) and the other is entitled *Who Keeps the Water Clean? Ms. Schindler* (Duvall 1997).]

[Then show the students a ballot and explain that it lists the two books. The students will have a choice of which book they want the teacher to share. The book with the most votes will win and be shared with the class.]

In many situations (personal as well as governmental) all over the world there are elections. Long ago in the United States, only white male landowners were allowed to vote in national elections—no women, poor people, African Americans, or Native Americans. [*Option:* Share the story *Susan B. Anthony.* It is written for young children.] Now, everyone age 18 or over is eligible to vote. In about ten years, each of you will have an opportunity to vote in local, state, and national elections. Elections are held to choose our leaders. You will have a choice of candidates and you will be allowed to vote in secret.

The people in the community choose from among the candidates and vote for the ones they want to be their leaders. The people who get the most votes are elected. The leaders listen to the people in the community and try to solve community problems. In our local community, we elect township board members. In larger communities, the mayor is the chief leader of the community. He or she works with other leaders to help the community make and keep its laws. At the state level, people vote for the governor and the lawmakers known as state senators and representatives. At the federal level, the voters (registered citizens) elect a president and lawmakers known as U.S. senators and representatives.

The individuals who provide the services to the people are usually appointed by the leaders. For example, the local township board appoints the local fire chief. The governor at the state level appoints the director of parks and recreation, and the president of the United States appoints the secretary of the treasury. [Use pictures and graphics to explain elected and appointed officials.]

SOME COMMUNITY LEADERS

MAYOR
(*elected*)

CITY COUNCIL MEMBERS
(*elected*)

| Fire Department Chief (*appointed*) | Police Department Chief (*appointed*) | Sanitation Director (*appointed*) | Parks and Recreation Director (*appointed*) |

Before people (your family members who are eighteen or older) can vote, they must register. Their names are placed on the list of people who can vote. [Show the class a voting registry and a voter registration card.] People register at places such as the city or county clerk's office. In most states, people register just once—before voting the first time—unless they move. [Show a picture illustrating voters registering.]

Most voters want to learn about the men and women running for office. These people are called *candidates*. They give speeches and meet with voters before elections. They may pass out pins, banners, signs, and other materials. [Show campaign paraphernalia.] In local elections, candidates frequently post signs in the community urging people to vote for them. In major elections such as for state governor or president of the United States, candidates may debate on TV. They may also have radio and television commercials. [Show graphics that illustrate the three branches of state and federal government. Point out the leadership positions that are voted on by the electorate (registered voters).]

In the United States, most candidates for public office usually belong to one of the two main political parties. These are the Democratic and Republican parties. The Democrats tend to want more public services and more taxes to pay for them while Republicans tend to want fewer services and fewer taxes.

On election day (every four years for the president of the United States), people go to a neighborhood voting place, referred to as a *polling place*. They give their names to the election officials, who make sure that each person is eighteen and registered to vote. Then the person enters a private voting booth. Some private booths have voting machines. [Show photo.] If so, the voter pulls a lever to show choices. Other places have computerized ballots. [Show an example.] To use these, voters punch holes next to the name of their choices. In still other voting places, voters use a pencil to mark Xs next to their choices.

When you reach eighteen, you should register and then vote in each election. When people vote, they help to decide who their leaders will be; they also vote on issues such as how much taxes they should pay and how the tax money will be spent. This is part of living in a democracy. When you help make choices and live according to the results, you are practicing good citizenship.

Activity

Table Talk—Give each table a set of flash cards that provides visual cues about voting. Have the table plan a mini story using the cards. Each table should have some unique cards as well as some that might be the same. If possible, have older students provide guidance during the planning and individual table talk time. Then have each table share its story with the entire class. For example:

> People in a <u>democracy</u> can decide who they want to be their <u>leaders</u>. If they are <u>eighteen years old</u>, they can <u>register</u> to vote. On <u>election day</u>, they <u>vote</u> by turning in a <u>ballot</u>. The <u>candidate</u> with the most <u>votes</u> wins.

Optional   Use cloze sentences for students to complete.

Summarize

- A democracy is a form of government in which people take an active role in decision making.
- Voting is one method that we use to express our choices.
- People in the United States can begin voting when they become eighteen.
- People need to register before they can vote.
- Voting is part of our responsibility as citizens.
- Voting gives us an opportunity to make decisions that affect our country.

Assessment

Have each student draw a picture about the most important thing she or he has learned about voting and write a paragraph about it. Upper-grade mentors could be very helpful during this written assignment.

Home Assignment

Encourage each student to share his or her picture and story about voting with family members.

Optional   Send home a mini packet of word cards about voting—with possible story examples provided—so that students can share and discuss them with family members.

Optional   Ask families to have a conversation about recent or upcoming elections and their voting experiences.

Dear Parents,

Encourage your child to share his or her picture and accompanying paragraph about voting. Then, as a family, discuss the importance of being registered voters and voting. Your child will be asked to share your response during our next social studies class.

Sincerely,

FIGURE 8   Model Letter to Parents

Lesson 7

. . . .

History of Government

Resources

- Map of colonial United States
- Time line—Long, Long Ago; Long Ago; Today
- Pictures illustrating types of government that have existed over time
- Newspaper clippings including photos that illustrate fighting for freedom
- Pictures of kings, queens, palaces, etc.
- Pictures of tribal meeting
- Pictures of pioneer times—people arriving in America
- Pictures of colonists
- Pictures of Revolutionary War
- Pictures or replicas of governmental documents (e.g., Declaration of Independence, U.S. Constitution)
- Photos of people voting in an election in America
- Magazines
- Cutouts and words representing government long, long ago; long ago; and today (a set along with a blank time line should be available for each table)
- Individual blank time lines

Children's Literature

Dalgliesh, A. (1956). *The Fourth of July Story*. New York: Aladdin.

Levy, E. (1987). *If You Were There When They Signed the Constitution*. New York: Scholastic.

Maestro, B., & Maestro, G. (1996). *The Voice of the People*. New York: Lothrop, Lee, & Shephard.

Pollard, M. (1992). *Absolute Rulers*. Ada, OK: Garrett Educational Corporation.

Sobel, S. (1999). *How the U.S. Government Works*. Hauppauge, NY: Barron's Educational Series, Inc.

General Comments

The purpose of this lesson is to establish a sense of wonder about government and how it has evolved over time and in various parts of the world. Students at this age have limited capacity to understand and appreciate the complete story of our government, but they will be intrigued with the changes that have occurred and the explanations associated with kings, queens, pharaohs, and other types of leaders. We want students to begin to see the value of our participative government, which guarantees rights and freedoms for all.

General Purposes or Goals

To help students understand and appreciate: (1) how the story of government has unfolded; and (2) how our form of government (called *democracy*) benefits all of us.

Main Ideas to Develop

- It would be difficult and confusing for people to try to live and work together with no rules or laws, no government.
- The earliest societies were small ones ruled by tribal leaders. Later, societies grew to become nations ruled by kings or queens.
- People came to America long ago because they were unhappy with their home countries. They came seeking liberties and happiness.
- At first, settlers lived in colonies that were controlled by the King of England. But they wanted to govern themselves, so they declared their independence and fought a war against England to gain their freedom. They won the war and became a new country called the United States.
- The Declaration of Independence and the U.S. Constitution are important governmental documents that guarantee rights and freedoms to the people.

Teaching Tips from Barbara

As you begin the history lesson, establish the time periods of Long, long ago; long ago; and today by discussing food, clothing, and shelter during those times. After you distinguish the three time periods, begin your discussion of government. Use pictures copied from books to show the various forms of government over time. I found that focusing on changes over time and showing differences and new ideas worked the best.

Starting the Lesson

Begin the lesson by discussing responses to the home assignment. Today the students are going to have an opportunity to think about government and how it has grown and changed over time and in various parts of the world. Ask the students to use their imaginations as they learn about this story across time.

Suggested Lesson Discussion

Imagine many people living and working together with no rules or laws and no government. There would be lots of confusion. People would have many different ideas about doing things and lots of arguments would result. People would argue over speed limits, where to put stop signs and

stoplights, where to locate buildings, and what to do if people didn't follow rules. They wouldn't have money, so they'd have to trade. People in
need might not be able to find help. In fact, life would be mass confusion.
Governments help us avoid these problems by providing us with services
that do things for us that we can't easily do for ourselves. Governments
also provide regulations that enable us to live our lives and get along with
one another without constant negotiation and decision making. Government is needed in communities of all sizes (the classroom, the school, the
township, the city, the state, and the nation). Our national (U.S.) government controls the national laws, finances, trade relations with foreign governments, and other matters that affect the entire nation.

Long, long ago, there were no written rules or laws. Probably the
cave people quarreled about who should do what. [Place a picture on the
time line.] As more and more people lived close together, tribes were
formed. Tribes would often gather together and select a chief. The chief
and the tribal council served as the governing body (made laws and decisions). [Place a picture of a tribal council on the time line under the head-
ing Long, Long Ago.]

Later, as areas became more heavily populated and civilized, people
began to claim lands and resources (e.g., water holes). Often, wars broke
out as people began fighting over property. During this period, kings,
queens, emperors, pharaohs, and czars ruled over the lands. They were selected by lords, dukes, and other powerful landowners. Usually when a
ruler died, a son or daughter or another member of the family took his or
her place. They lived in beautiful places called castles, usually were very
wealthy, and controlled all the rest of the people by using an army [place
pictures on time line between Long, Long Ago and Long Ago.] In some
parts of the world today, a few very rich people still control the wealth and
own most of the land while the many peasants and workers are poor.

Long ago, people started coming to America from Europe. [Return
to time line and point out this move from Europe. Then show map of colonial America.] But, they were still ruled by the king and government of
England. They were unhappy with the way their home country was ruling
them. They thought differently and wanted to live differently. They
wanted to practice their own religion instead of being told what to believe; they wanted to decide what kind of work they would do; they
wanted to decide what taxes they should pay; and so on. They finally became so frustrated that they declared independence and went to war,
fighting with England until the king no longer tried to control them.
Thomas Jefferson put the people's ideas and wishes together in a document called the Declaration of Independence (beliefs about rule by the
people). [Show a picture or replica.] The people had to decide if the words

that Thomas Jefferson had written were true, good, and fair. After a long discussion, the men representing the thirteen colonies agreed and signed their names. John Hancock was the first to sign. The date was July 4, 1776. [Place on time line under Long Ago.] It was the birthday of the United States. Every Fourth of July we celebrate this very special occasion. [Optional: Share the children's book *The Fourth of July Story*.]

By winning the Revolutionary War, the colonies became independent from England. They joined together and called themselves the United States. They had to figure out how they wanted to be governed. They elected leaders to write the Constitution, which was finished in 1787. It was written very carefully because the people knew that a government with too much power could be dangerous. The Constitution was designed to ensure that power was shared—that no government decision could be made by just one person. Most of the power was given not to the U.S. government but to the states and to the people who lived in them. [Optional: Share sections of *If You Were There When They Signed the Constitution*.]

Today, every country has some kind of government—a system for running the country. Most governments are based on a written set of rules and laws and have a group of people in charge with the power to run the country. In our system, all of the people participate in government by voting for our leaders. This is called *democracy*. The Constitution [refer back to Long Ago on the time line] was created more than two hundred years ago. It contains rules and laws for setting up the government and running our country [show a picture of the Constitution]. The Constitution says that the government has three jobs: to make laws for the United States, to run the country (make sure the people follow the laws, work with other countries and their leaders, take care of the land the government owns, help keep our food, water, and air clean and safe, etc.), and to settle arguments when people disagree.

The people take an active role in voting. [Show picture of people voting.] Your parents and others of voting age elect a president, a vice president, and congressional representatives to speak for them in positions of leadership. These people work together to solve the problems of our country.

Activity

Provide each table with a blank time line and cutouts of pictures and words representing the changes in government over time. Have the students place the manipulatives on the time line and explain if they existed long, long ago; long ago; or today and give reasons why. (If possible, invite upper-grade mentors to serve as assistants.) After the time line placements have been discussed, the students at each table can paste the cutouts and words on the time lines.

Summarize

- The earliest societies had no leaders, but as time passed, they were ruled by tribal leaders.
- As populations grew, some civilizations had rulers who owned the land and controlled the wealth.
- Long ago, people began coming to America to seek liberty and happiness.
- The colonists fought and won the war against England, and as a result, the king no longer had control over them.
- The Declaration of Independence and the United States Constitution are important governmental documents that guarantee our freedoms.
- Americans live in a democracy that gives the people a strong voice in the government.

Assessment

Using words and simple drawings or cutout pictures from magazines, have students create their own individual time lines illustrating the history of government. Encourage students to use the word wall to assist in spelling.

Home Assignment

Encourage each student to share with family members his or her time line explaining the history of government. Ask families to have a discussion focusing on how government has changed over time and how important it is to live in a free country.

Dear Parents,

We have been learning about the history of government. Encourage your child to share his or her time line with you and to explain what he or she has learned. Together, talk about how government has changed over time and how important it is to live in a free country. Talk about what you see as the most significant recent change in our government and what it means to your family. Your child will have an opportunity to share your response with his or her classmates.

Sincerely,

FIGURE 9   Model Letter to Parents

Lesson 8

....

Governments Around the World

Resources

- Time line that focuses on today
- Globe
- World map
- Pictures illustrating types of government that exist in other parts of the world
- Photos of children and their families in Great Britain, Sweden, Japan, Cuba, and so on
- *The New Book of Knowledge* (1995 edition, Danbury, CT: Grolier Inc.), pp. 272–275
- Photos of individuals living under a dictatorship (see pictures in *Absolute Rulers*)
- Photo of Fidel Castro

Children's Literature

Kindersley, B., & Kindersley, A. (1995). *Children Just Like Me*. New York: Dorling Kindersley.

Pollard, M. (1992). *Absolute Rulers*. Ada, OK: Garrett Educational Corporation.

General Comments

The purpose of this lesson is to establish a sense of wonder about government as it exists in various parts of the world today. We want students to begin to realize that government exists across the globe, but not always in a form that looks like ours. Some countries even today have dictatorships, which means their people have few freedoms.

General Purposes or Goals

To help students: (1) understand and appreciate some of the forms of government that exist today in other parts of the world; and (2) recognize that several countries have basic freedoms similar to ours, although for traditional reasons, they may have kings, queens, or emperors.

Main Ideas to Develop

- Governments can be classified as democracies or dictatorships.
- Customs and beliefs (part of culture) are reflected in governments around the world.

- Several countries have basic freedoms similar to ours, although for traditional reasons, they still have kings, queens, or emperors. Elected leaders run the country and have the real power.

Teaching Tips from Barbara

Use the time line from Lesson 7 as a tool to help you discuss different types of government around the world. Once again, using specific names and pictures of people in government helped to make the information come alive for my class. Again too, some of the names I used were familiar to the students, but they didn't have any information about these people other than their names.

Starting the Lesson

Discuss the responses from the home assignment. Then begin the lesson by using the globe, world map, and pictures of children and families in other parts of the world (e.g., Great Britain, Japan, and Sweden). Explain that these countries also are representative democracies.

Suggested Lesson Discussion

These representative democracies have laws, elections, and basic freedoms. Elected men and women meet together in legislative assemblies similar to Congress. For traditional reasons (the way things have been done for a very long time), these countries still have kings, queens, or emperors who live in palaces and conduct public ceremonies. [Show photos and pictures of these figureheads.] However, they have no real power—they don't make the laws or run the country. The elected leaders do that.

[As you describe examples of countries that are representative democracies, complete a chart like the one on p. 263.] The governments of these representative democracies are much like ours even though they have figureheads whose titles make them seem powerful. The figureheads were powerful in the past, but today they just conduct public ceremonies, attend important events as representatives of their countries, and participate in national celebrations (e.g., parades, speeches, parties, etc.).

Sweden is a constitutional monarchy with a prime minister, a cabinet, and a parliament. The prime minister is the country's chief executive. This individual performs duties similar to our president's. Members of the Parliament are chosen by the voters. They make the laws for the country (similar to our Congress). Sweden also has a judicial branch similar to ours.

England is a part of the United Kingdom (England, Wales, and Scotland) and is also described as a constitutional monarchy. The prime minister is the head of the government and the Parliament is the chief lawmaking body, similar to our Congress. England also has a judicial system similar to ours.

Japan is also a constitutional monarchy or representative democracy. Japan has a prime minister who leads the government. The lawmaking body of Japan is referred to as the Diet (pronounced same as in English). Just as our lawmakers (Congress) are elected by the people, so are those in the Diet. Japan has a court system similar to ours in the United States, as well as the systems in Sweden and England.

In democracies, the people's consent is asked through elections. Their economic and social needs as well as their customs, traditions, and religions are taken into account by those who hold government offices. The elected officials (lawmakers, prime ministers, presidents) are charged with running the countries and carrying out the wishes of the people. The power is in the office. If an official loses an election, she or he no longer has any power. While in office, the leader's behavior must reflect the laws that have been set up to guarantee fairness, equity, and other basic rights. Usually when the laws of the country grow out of the needs of the people, the people believe in these laws and are willing to live by them and cooperate with them.

In all of these countries, cooperation among the three branches of government is necessary. The executive branch is headed by the president in the United States and prime ministers in Sweden, England, and Japan. This individual is the manager or director of the nation's government. These people make sure that the government runs smoothly and that the laws of the country are enforced and obeyed. They must promise to preserve, protect, and defend the constitution of their country. The leaders rely on many people to help them manage the business of running the country.

Governments of Representative Democracies

COUNTRY	EXECUTIVE	LEGISLATIVE	JUDICIAL
United States	President	Congress	Judges
Sweden	Prime minister (king or queen is figurehead)	Congress	Judges
England	Prime minister (king or queen is figurehead)	Parliament	Judges
Japan	Prime minister (emperor is figurehead)	Diet	Judges

The president of the United States and the prime ministers of Sweden, England, and Japan must concern themselves with the problems of the world as well as those of their own countries. Our president acts as the ceremonial head of our government. Ceremonial heads of countries perform enjoyable duties in which they represent their countries (e.g., lead parades, entertain distinguished visitors at their residences, open ceremonies by lighting torches, etc.). In Sweden, England, and Japan, the prime ministers have figureheads (a king, queen, or emperor) to help them with these duties.

Leaders of democratic countries must get the approval of the lawmakers (referred to as Congress, Parliament, or Diet) for their actions. When they cooperate, the government can move along smoothly.

The judicial branches of government in all of these countries are similar. Their job is to interpret the law and make sure equal justice is provided.

In all of these democracies, the citizens choose the people who will serve in the government. This was not always true. Long ago, some countries had absolute rulers. You may remember learning about the Pilgrims coming to America on the Mayflower in order to escape the rule of the king of England. They left their country in hopes of going to a place where they could enjoy freedoms (press, speech, worship, etc.).

As more and more people in the world learned about the freedoms that Americans enjoyed, they began to demand similar treatment. They did not want absolute rulers to control their lives and make decisions for them. Today, places such as Sweden, England, and Japan have taken away the powers that kings and emperors used to inherit. Now they are simply figureheads. They serve as ceremonial heads and represent their countries at official gatherings around the world.

However, there still are places in the world where absolute rulers exist. These leaders are called *dictators*. Their people have no say in the government. Instead, the dictators run the country by force, using their army to force people to do as they are told (e.g., tell them about where they can or cannot live, where they will work, what jobs they will have, and how much they will get paid). People who live in countries ruled by dictators have almost no rights. [Show photos of families from Cuba, North Korea, etc. Locate these countries on the globe and world map. Show picture from *Absolute Rulers*.]

Cuba and North Korea have totalitarian governments, so their people have no rights. Power is imposed on them. If they complain, they are often jailed. If they were to publish their complaints in the newspaper, the company or organization they work for would be shut down and the newspaper publishers would be punished. Often living conditions get so bad that the people fight or try to escape. In some places, people who do not agree with the dictator's rules or laws are killed.

For example, in Cuba in 1959 Fidel Castro [show photograph] formed an army, overthrew the government, and made himself dictator of Cuba. He promised the people lots of changes but controlled all aspects of Cuban life and permitted no political opposition. The land was placed under state ownership and the economy was regulated by the government. This meant that you could not own your own place to live, choose where you wanted to work, or own your own business. Cuba became a communist country. Life in Cuba has improved in certain ways (e.g., free education, modern health care), but the people must endure major problems such as rationing of food and other goods. Sometimes food products are not even available. Imagine standing in line for an hour to purchase a loaf of bread or a pound of meat and then finding that the supply was gone when you got to the head of the line.

Many Cubans have tried to escape to other countries where they can enjoy more freedoms. Some have come to the United States (especially to Miami), continuing a long tradition going back to the Pilgrims (immigration for freedom).

People all over the world want to have their rights and liberties guaranteed. [Show pictures from *Children Just Like Me*.] In a democracy, the citizens choose the people who will serve in the government. The *U.S. Constitution* describes the U.S. form of government and the process for electing the people who serve in its major offices. People everywhere want to enjoy the freedoms that we have as citizens in a democracy.

We practice representative democracy in our city councils, in our states, and at the national level of government. We hope that in the future more and more places around the world will enjoy the same freedoms that we have.

Activity

Table Talk—Have each table or small group of students focus on one of the countries described during the lesson. How is its government similar to or different from ours? After several minutes of table talk, elicit ideas from the groups. Then, as a total class, write a group journal entry.

Summarize

- Every country has its own form of government.
- Governments can be classified as democracies or dictatorships.
- Usually when the laws of the country grow out of the needs of the people, the people believe in the laws and are willing to live by them and cooperate with them.

- Some of the democratic countries still have figureheads who carry out ceremonial duties. There are also some countries who still have dictatorships. In those countries, the people are controlled by force and their lives are regulated by the military.

Assessment

Have students participate in a "thumbs up/thumbs down" quiz.

1. Thumbs down   All families around the world experience the same type of government that we have in the United States.

2. Thumbs up   A democracy allows for more rights than a dictatorship.

3. Thumbs up   In some places, people who do not agree with the rules or laws of the dictator are put in prison or killed.

4. Thumbs up   England and Sweden have queens that conduct ceremonies but do not have much power. Elected officials run the daily operations of these countries.

5. Thumbs up   It would be very uncomfortable to live in a country ruled by a dictator.

6. Thumbs up   A child and his family from North Korea would probably be very happy living in America because we have so many more freedoms here.

Home Assignment

Encourage each student to share with his or her family a copy of the group journal entry describing governments around the world today. Then have the family discuss life in a democracy compared with life in a dictatorship. Encourage family members to write down their ideas so that they can be shared during an upcoming class session.

Dear Parents,

We have been learning about governments around the world. Your child is prepared to share our class journal entry. Afterward, please discuss life in a democracy compared with life in a dictatorship. It would be helpful if you would write down your ideas so that they can be shared during an upcoming class discussion.

Sincerely,

FIGURE 10   Model Letter to Parents

Lesson 9

. . . .

Functions and Services of Government: Paying for Services

Resources

- Role cards
- Graphic illustrating kinds of taxes and where the money goes
- Paper, crayons, paste, cutout pictures/photos depicting services provided by the government, descriptions of communities (rural, large city in winter, Midwest suburb in the summer, etc.)
- Copies of Government Workers Sheet (Figure 12)
- Data retrieval chart: Comparing Local, State, and United States (Federal) Government: Sources of Money and Functions and Services (see Figure 13 for an example)

Children's Literature

Killoran, J., Zimmer, J., & Jarrett, M. (1997). *Michigan and Its People*. Ronkonkoma, NY: Jarrett Publishing Co. {Note: Look for similar sources focusing on your state.}

Marsh, C. (1998). *Michigan Government for Kids*. Peach Tree City, GA: Gallopade Publishing. {Note: Look for similar sources focusing on your state.}

Sobel, S. (1999). *How the U.S. Government Works*. Hauppauge, NY: Barron's Educational Series, Inc.

General Comments

The focus for this lesson is on functions and services provided by the government to local communities, individual states, and all citizens of the United States. The government is needed to do things that people cannot do by themselves.

General Purposes and Goals

To help students understand and appreciate: (1) the value of government services; and (2) how the funding of these services is supported (taxes).

Main Ideas to Develop

- Government services are needed to do the things that the people cannot do by themselves.
- All governments in the United States (e.g., community, township, city, state, and federal) provide some services for people.
- To pay for the services, the government collects money from the people. The money is referred to as taxes.

Teaching Tips from Barbara

The main function of this lesson for my class was to gather, review, and connect information from previous lessons. Be sure to use the artifacts, charts, and pictures from those lessons. I encouraged my students to talk with their families about governmental functions and services. Several parents reported having interesting, meaningful conversations about taxes with their children.

Starting the Lesson

Review the responses to the home assignment. Then introduce the new lesson with a role-play or skit depicting Mom or Dad paying taxes to the government. The student can ask questions such as Who gets the money? Why do you have to pay the money? How is the money used? Why can't the family simply keep the money?

Then, using a graphic, role cards, and role-players, show where the money goes (e.g., school, community college, public library, road commission, police protection, fire protection, etc.). Students could assume these roles if you assign role cards, or the role-play episode could be developed with upper-grade mentors as actors and actresses. Create a data retrieval chart to organize the information gleaned about taxes and services (see example in Figure 14).

Suggested Lesson Discussion

Every community provides certain kinds of services. Think about some of the services you and your family depend on every day. You need good streets to walk or ride on to get to school. You need police officers and firefighters to protect you and help you in times of emergency. You need teachers to help you learn in school. You need the garbage collector to pick up your rubbish so that your community will be clean. You may get your water from a water company run by your community. You want water that is safe to drink. Your community has traffic lights and traffic signs to help people travel safely. These are all services provided by the community.

Remember, you learned that different communities have different needs, so the services they provide might be different too. Location may make a difference in the services that a community provides. For example, clearing the streets after a snowstorm is an important service in northern communities, but snow removal is not needed in Orlando, Florida. The size of the community also makes a difference in the services that a community provides. Large communities need more services than small communities. For example, most communities don't have a subway system like New York and Chicago do because they don't have enough people to support it. Instead, most people drive to work. Some services are common to all communities (e.g., teachers, police officers, firefighters). Larger communities need more workers to provide more services.

Communities need money to provide the services that people need. The people who work for the community must be paid. Schools need money to pay for the teachers, building repairs, heating and electricity, buses and drivers. Firefighters and police officers need to be paid and their vehicles need to be repaired. Parks have to be taken care of and roads need to be repaired. Everyone in the community helps pay for these services.

Every level of government in the United States provides some services. The state government handles matters that affect people throughout the state, and the federal government handles matters that affect all of the people who live in the United States. To pay for these services, people pay taxes. We all pay because we all are helped by these services.

Activity

Provide each table with cutout pictures and/or photographs depicting community services, crayons, paste, large sheets of white paper, and a description of a community (rural, large city in winter, suburb in summer, etc.). Have students create murals illustrating the services that the government provides based on the needs of a particular kind of community. Share the results. Discuss how the government pays for the services.

Summary

- Families pay money to the government for the services that are provided.
- The money people pay to the government is called taxes.
- The tax money pays for the services provided by the local community, the state, and the nation.
- Different communities have different needs, so the services that they provide may be different too.

Assessment

Ask each student to complete an open-ended statement and illustrate it with a picture. For example:

It is important that our families pay taxes to our government because _____

_____

_____

_____

_____.

If upper-grade mentors are available, they could assist in this writing assignment. Compile the responses into a class booklet and title it *Why Our Families Pay Taxes to the Government*. Duplicate. Have each student take a copy home to share with family members.

Home Assignment

Encourage each student to read the class booklet titled *Why Our Families Pay Taxes to the Government* to family members. Have families discuss work roles of people who work for the government, noting especially family members and friends. Have them discuss what these workers do to help members of the community and take note on the Government Workers Sheet (Figure 13). Interviewing people who work for the government would be very beneficial.

Dear Parents,

We have been learning about the functions and services provided by the government. We encourage you to ask your child to share the class booklet titled *Why Our Families Pay Taxes to the Government*. Then, identify people you know who work for the government. If possible, interview them. Discuss the kinds of services they provide to the community and jot down notes on the enclosed form. Please send your response back to school so that we can include it in our next class discussion.

Sincerely,

FIGURE 11   Model Letter to Parents

Who do we know who works for the government to provide services to the community? State? Nation?

_____

_____

_____

_____

What does she or he do and how does she or he help members of our community?

_____

_____

_____

_____

FIGURE 12   Government Workers Sheet

Level of Government	Sources of Money	Functions and services
Local	Property tax: The amount of tax depends on how much the property is worth. Properties include land, houses, and other buildings.	Build and repair schools, local roads. Build and maintain libraries. Provide police protection and fire and rescue services. Provide a safe water supply.
State (Adjust the income and sales tax percentages to match the tax rates levied in your state. Omit if these taxes do not apply.)	State income tax: Every time a family member gets a paycheck, 4 percent of the money is held back by the employer and sent to the government. Sales tax: You pay an extra 6 percent every time you buy certain items (the more it costs, the more tax you pay). Gasoline tax: Drivers pay a tax for every gallon of gasoline they buy; the gasoline tax pays for building state highways.	Maintain local parks. Maintain state libraries and museums. Provide police protection on our state highways. Maintain state parks. Maintain state colleges and universities. Maintain state prisons. Welfare (provide services and safety nets for people needing special help).

Continues

FIGURE 13   Comparing Local, State, and United States (Federal) Government: Sources of Money and Functions and Services

Level of Government	Sources of Money	Functions and services
	Cigarette tax: All tobacco items include a tax that the store keeps and then sends to the state government.	Licensing (regulate goods and services provided; driver's licenses; licenses for vehicles). Licenses guarantee that people are qualified to do the jobs they say they can do.
Federal	Federal income tax	Provide extra money to schools through grants.

Build and maintain relationships with other countries (e.g., peace treaties, trade agreements).

Operate the U.S. Postal Service.

Maintain national parks.

Oversee food and medicine operations so they are safe for us.

Issue money.

Oversee people leaving and/or returning to our country and decide who can live in America permanently.

Provide protection (e.g., armed forces—army, navy, air force, marines, |

FIGURE 13   (Continued)

Lesson 10

Functions of Government Regulations

Resources

- Photographs of a second grader using regulations (rules and laws) throughout a typical day
- Copies of a Means and Functions of Government data retrieval chart (one for each table) (Make duplicates of completed charts for the home assignment.) (See Table 1 for an example.)
- Figure 15, Household Rules and Laws

Children's Literature

Coster, P. (1997). *Towns and Cities*. New York: Children's Press.

Kalman, B., & Hughes, S. (1986). *I Live in a City*. New York: Crabtree.

General Comments

This lesson will emphasize the importance of regulations (rules and laws) and provide students with ideas that move beyond the notion that rules and laws are merely a collection of "don'ts." Rules and laws are designed to help people get along, keep things fair, protect individual and public property, and keep people safe.

General Purposes and Goals

To help students: (1) understand and appreciate the value and importance of government regulations in their lives; and (2) become more aware of the written and unwritten rules and laws (regulations) that are part of their environment.

Main Idea to Develop

- Regulations (rules and laws) are designed to help people get along, keep things fair, protect individual and public property, and keep people safe.

Teaching Tips from Barbara

This was one of the most powerful lessons in our government unit. Students really connected with the information that we had already learned and used that information to discuss the pictures we had taken of one of their classmates (showing how governments affect her life each day from the time she gets up until the time she goes to bed). If you are able, recruit a parent to take similar pictures for you to use. After the lesson, I posted the pictures on a bulletin board so that students were able to relook and rethink at their leisure. Also, as you discuss and share information, again focus on the functionality of government.

Starting the Lesson

Begin by asking students to share the results of their home assignments. Then ask students why they think we have rules and laws in our community. As they share their responses, organize them into the following categories: Help People Get Along; Keep Things Fair; Protect Individual and Public Property; Keep People Safe.

Suggested Lesson Discussion

Rules and laws remind us of our rights and responsibilities. They and other aspects of government are very much a part of our daily lives. [Use a photo essay to "walk through" the life of a first or second grader on a typical day. Using an interactive discussion format, discuss the influences of rules, laws, and government. This should be a real eye-opener in making the value of government obvious to the students.]

[The daily activities of a first or second grader illustrated in the photos could include the following points.]

1. The child wakes up in the morning in a house or apartment that has passed inspection by the government, indicating that it is safe to live in (i.e., it is a solid structure, the roof doesn't leak, the electrical wiring is safe, etc.). The government sometimes helps families get loans and provides funds for helping to rebuild some neighborhoods.

2. The child gets out of bed wearing pajamas that are nonflammable. Special fire-resistant materials are required for the manufacture of bedclothes, and government inspectors test the cloth to make sure it follows regulations.

3. The child goes to the bathroom to brush his teeth. The water is supplied by the local community and tested by a government inspector to make sure it is safe to drink and use for tooth brushing. The toothpaste and toothbrush have government labels indicating that they are made from nonhazardous materials and are safe to use.

4. The child sits down to breakfast (fruit, cereal, and milk). All of the products display a seal indicating that they have been inspected and are safe to consume. The Departments of Commerce and Agriculture oversee the inspections.

5. The child gets dressed for school. In checking the labels of the clothing, the family will find that the items have been inspected for safety and are of a certain standard (imposed by the government) that is acceptable for purchase.

6. The child remembers that he needs lunch money for the week. The U.S. government manufactures the coins and currency we use.

7. The child goes to the bus stop and waits for the school bus. A police car drives by. The government is responsible for making sure that the school bus is safe for passengers, that the driver has passed a special test and earned a license to drive a bus (not just a car), that the

roads are safe, and that the rules and laws regarding driving are enforced. Police officers patrol the area to make sure that the rules and laws are followed and that children feel safe (stoplights and traffic signs help everyone drive safely and efficiently).

8. The child enters the classroom and once again encounters influence of the government. The United States and the child's state have departments of education that make sure that teachers have the proper education, that suitable instructional materials are available, that there are a certain number of school days every year, and that students have access to certain curriculum materials (e.g., approved textbook series).

9. The child is asked to take a note to the school secretary. Government regulations also influence her work life. The government makes sure that she and all other school employees have safe and healthful working conditions. The laws also ensure a minimum hourly wage, overtime pay, and freedom from employment discrimination. They provide unemployment insurance benefits to workers who lose their jobs and workers' compensation payments when workers are ill and cannot work.

10. The child goes to lunch, again surrounded by protection of the rules and laws created by the government. All of the foods have been tested or inspected by government officials who are a part of the Food and Drug Administration, which is connected to the U.S. Department of Agriculture, and government regulations ensure that the meals are nutritionally balanced.

11. When the child returns to the classroom for the afternoon session, he participates in a computer class that has computers that have been inspected by the government, making sure they are of high quality and in good working condition. The school received a grant from a government agency so that the costs were more affordable.

12. Later in the day, the class receives a visit from a police officer as part of the social studies unit. This community helper is a representative of the part of our government that protects people and enforces the laws.

13. At 3:30 the bell rings. The government even influences this by having established time zones. The electric bell itself has been inspected for quality and safety (e.g., its electrical wiring). The government's Department of Energy oversees all energy sources, prices, and uses.

14. The child rides the school bus home. [Review the government involvement of this activity.]

15. After school, the child watches television, which has government (Federal Communications Commission) regulations regarding what type of programs can be seen.

16. Later in the evening, the family goes to a restaurant for dinner. Again, government influences are ever present. All of the foods have

been inspected; the restaurant itself has been inspected by the health department as well as the housing department. All of the restaurant workers must have attained a certain age and are guaranteed by the government to experience certain working conditions. The heating and lighting in the restaurant has been influenced by the U.S. Department of Energy and the money exchanged was made by the U.S. Treasury Department.

17. On the trip home from the restaurant, the child recalls the Department of Transportation influences that are responsible for safe roads, a driver with a license, and helpful signage.

18. The child is pictured preparing a list of all the ways that the government helps him. [Have the class generate a list by way of a review.]

Regulations (rules and laws) and the government provide means of helping us and keeping us safe. Government provides certain guarantees for us. It also helps solve problems that individuals alone could not solve.

Table 1   Means and Functions of Government

MEANS OF GOVERNING US	WHAT DOES IT DO FOR US? (HOW DOES IT HELP US?)
1. Juice can label 2. Traffic light 3. USDA sticker on meat wrapper 4. Carton of milk 5. Teacher certification seal 6. Clothing labels 7. Computer certification label 8. USDA label on cereal box 9. Money 10. Stop sign 11. Driver's license 12. Television set 13. Police officer badge 14. Tube of toothpaste 15. Electric bill 16. House inspection document 17. Sick pay request form 18. Chauffeur's license 19. Photo of a classmate from another country 20. Clock 21. State curriculum standards	The government has created the Departments of Commerce and Agriculture to inspect all of the food items that we consume to make sure that they are safe. All food products display a seal or other marking indicating that they have been inspected.

Activity

As you identify a means of governing people, have table groups identify and discuss the functions. For example, what does the traffic light do for us and/or how does it help us? Have students give a thumbs up when ready to share their responses with the class. Give each table a copy of a chart like Table 1 to complete during the discussion. Then duplicate the charts so each child can share one with his or her family.

Summarize

- Government regulations (rules and laws) are important to all of us. They are very much a part of our daily lives.
- Regulations are designed to help people get along, keep things fair, protect individual and public property, and keep people safe.

Assessment

Have each student write a journal entry that focuses on how regulations (rules and laws) help us. Encourage students to select functions that they have learned about for the first time in today's lesson. Encourage students to use word prompts that you have posted around the room. Encourage students to read their entries to adults or older siblings as part of their home assignment.

Optional   This assessment could be done verbally if parent volunteers are available.

Home Assignment

Have each student read his or her journal entry to an adult or older sibling. Then, using a copy of the Means and Functions of Government chart as a guide, families should create a list of rules and laws that are a part of the household (Figure 15). Have families use the list to foster a family discussion, then pick two or three rules to write about. Encourage the student to return the list to school for sharing with his or her peers.

> Dear Parents,
>
> We have been learning about the functions of government regulations. Encourage your child to read his or her journal entry and share his or her Means and Functions of Government chart. Then, as a family, prepare a list of rules and laws that are a part of your household. Then write a paragraph explaining the importance of two or three rules. Please send the list and your paragraph to school for our class discussion.
>
> Sincerely,

FIGURE 14   Model Letter to Parents

HOUSEHOLD RULES AND LAWS

Rule: _____

Importance: _____

_____

_____

_____

_____

Rule: _____

Importance: _____

_____

_____

_____

_____

Rule: _____

Importance: _____

_____

_____

_____

_____

FIGURE 15   Household Rules and Laws

Lesson 11

People Solve Problems Together

Resources
- Pictures of volunteers joining together to solve local pollution problems
- Ballot box and ballot decision-making tree
- Junior Achievement materials on "Our Community"
  Junior Achievement is a non-profit organization designed to provide K–12 students with the skills to advance successfully in the business world. Its materials are available to schools that collaborate with Junior Achievement on a membership basis. The "Our Community" materials include a Decision Tree for use in addressing community problems using questions such as "What is the problem?", "What are the choices?", and "What are the results of each choice?" See: Junior Achievement. (1999). *Junior Achievement Guide for Consultants and Teachers: Our Community* (pp. 22–24). Colorado Springs, CO: Junior Achievement, Inc.

Children's Literature
DeRubertis, B. (1993). *Earth Day.* New York: The Kane Press.
McDonall, J. (1994). *Celebrating Earth Day.* Chicago: Children's Press.
Robinson, F. (1995). *Recycle That.* Chicago: Children's Press.
Wheeler, J. (1991). *Earth Day Every Day.* Edina, MN: Abdo and Daughters.

General Comments
Provide pictures or photos of families, including children, engaged in volunteer activities. Underscore the idea that people of all ages can make a positive difference in their community.

General Purposes or Goals
To help students: (1) realize that government cannot do everything; and (2) understand and appreciate the value of volunteerism as a means of providing community services and solving problems without adding to the size and cost of government.

Main Ideas to Develop
- Volunteering is the act of giving time and sometimes money to promote a cause, provide a service, or work to solve a problem without adding to the size and cost of government.
- Volunteering is one way to practice responsible citizenship.

- When enough people volunteer to solve a problem, the need for raising taxes to pay for the additional service is lessened.
- Government cannot and should not be expected to do everything for its people.
- Individuals can personally contribute time and money to help solve problems that affect members of the community.
- Volunteers work in their free time to help others in the community without getting paid.

Teaching Tips from Barbara

In the past, I have asked families to discuss and help select the nonprofit organization for our class to support. This generates much more ownership and participation when we launch the volunteer project. Look for ways to connect the project to other academic areas such as math or writing (e.g., counting the money collected, writing about why you are helping the organization).

Starting the Lesson

Begin the lesson by discussing the responses of the home assignment. Then ask students if they know what is meant by the phrase, "Earth Day is every day." Draw responses from the students.

Suggested Lesson Discussion

More and more people are working on their own to save the earth because they believe it is a very important thing to do. They are doing it voluntarily. Often they work in groups to help solve problems faced by the community—in this case, problems related to pollution. While many laws have been passed related to pollution, there are things that can be done in your neighborhood or community without more laws and without the need for more government regulations or services. The more services the government provides, the more money is needed to support them, with the result being higher taxes.

We will focus on *reuse* and *recycle*. [Show photos and provide explanations of real-life examples of volunteers who have joined together to solve local pollution problems.] Volunteers in your community might include students who bring their lunches to school in reusable containers and employees and students who put their waste into two bins—one for paper and one for trash like coffee cups or old pens and pencils. Even glossy paper, cellophane envelopes, and file folders can be recycled. People in the community, in their free time, work to keep the community clean. Volunteers do not get paid. They help in recycling projects; they pick up litter along our roads, and so on.

We will conduct a brainstorming session to come up with a range of ideas that our class as volunteers may engage in to fight pollution. [Ideas that might come out of the brainstorming: clean up the playground on a weekly basis, adopt a street or road (with adult supervision) to keep clean, write letters or create and post fliers or signs to encourage others to join the cause, create and manage recycling bins around the school, adopt a re-usable approach to lunch containers, collect and use recycled items for art projects, etc.]

[Once a satisfactory list has been developed, a decision-making tree (see Junior Achievement materials) or a voting strategy (using a ballot box) could be used to decide which volunteer project will be selected. Parental assistance is recommended for this activity. Ideally, the volunteer activity, with periodic debriefings, should take place over several weeks if not throughout the year.]

Alternative [After discussing Earth Day as one type of volunteer activity, brainstorm other possibilities (e.g., helping in a soup kitchen, collecting money for the local food bank, having candy and popcorn sales for the purchase of school yard equipment). The class should be encouraged to select a project that it is interested in and one that is important to the community.]

Activity

Have class members, using word cards as prompts (e.g., Volunteer, Voting, Government, Taxes, Responsible Citizenship, Pollution, etc.) role-play a presentation they would make to the parent-teacher association explaining the "what, why, and how" of their project. Guided discussion should follow each enactment.

Summarize

- Volunteering is a means of solving problems without adding to the size and cost of government.
- Government cannot do everything.
- Participating in a local cause can be personally rewarding and is an example of positive citizenship.

Assessment

Have students write letters to local government officials explaining how their class project using volunteers to help solve a pollution problem (or other selected project) helps the government with its services and potentially saves tax money. No money will be needed to pay for the service that the volunteers provide.

Note: The teacher should make a personal connection with the government official to ensure that a response will be forthcoming. It is important for volunteers to realize that their hard work and sense of civic responsibility are valued.

Home Assignment

Have students share copies of the letters to government officials explaining the class volunteer project with family members. Perhaps as a result, the family members will agree to assist on the project!

Have family members list any volunteering they do and explain how it is evidence of positive citizenship. Encourage each family to send the list of volunteering activities to school with the child so a class list can be compiled. The debriefing discussion will focus on all of the ways family members are helping the government by providing services without raising taxes.

Dear Parents,

Our class has designed a volunteer project to help our community. It is explained in the enclosed letter written to a local government official. Your assistance with our project would be welcomed!

Please discuss the project with your child. Then list any kinds of volunteering that your family participates in as part of demonstrating positive citizenship. Send your list to school with your child. We will compile a class list showing all of the ways that families help the government by providing volunteer services without raising taxes.

Sincerely,

FIGURE 16   Model Letter to Parents

Lesson 12

Government: Review

Resources

- Students' home assignments
- Students' journals
- Students' time lines
- Other student artifacts created during the unit
- Children's literature sources
- Photographs and pictures used during the unit
- Props for role-plays

General Comments

To conclude this unit, the students will invite fourth and fifth graders who have been studying about local, state, and U.S. government to serve as a panel of experts. This session will give the younger students an opportunity to experience authentic assessment and at the same time give the upper-grade students an opportunity to review some of what they have been learning and engage in some "reteaching" if necessary.

General Purposes and Goals

To provide students with: (1) an opportunity to revisit *selected* major understandings associated with government and laws that they have been exposed to during the unit; (2) the opportunity to share with others what they have been learning; and (3) a venue for acquiring assistance in clearing up misunderstandings about government and laws.

Main Ideas to Develop

Focus on *selected* understandings from the following list:

- A community is a place where people live, work, play, and share special times.
- People in a community work together, accomplish tasks, and achieve goals through cooperation.
- Members of communities are called citizens.
- Good citizens tend to be respectful, to be responsible, to think and act for the good of the community, and to be open to ideas of others that may be different from their own.
- Rules and laws are designed to remind people of their rights and responsibilities. They help people get along, keep things fair, protect individual and public property, and keep people safe.

- A community (township, town, suburb, city) is a place where people live and usually have many common needs and wants. Among them are community services.

- Many people work for the community.

- Community workers help make the community a better place to live.

- Different communities have different needs based on their location and size.

- Families pay money to the community. This money is called taxes. Tax money pays for the community services.

- A community (town, suburb, city) is a place where people live and usually have many common needs and wants. Among them is the need for rules and laws.

- Every township, town, or city makes plans and laws for itself.

- Usually the leaders of the community make the laws. Laws are rules made by the government that everyone in the community must follow.

- Leaders are elected by the people (of voting age) to make and enforce the laws.

- In some communities, the mayor is the chief leader. In other communities there are township boards. Other leaders help the mayor, manager, or board watch over the community.

- A state is made up of many communities.

- Citizens of voting age have the opportunity to elect leaders for the state.

- Our state government focuses on services such as higher education, recreation, state highways, a system of justice, licensing regulations, and others. The state government handles matters that affect people throughout the state.

- *Government* is defined as people running the country.

- The lawmaking branch of our United States government is made up of men and women from each state. They are called senators and representatives. They are also called legislators. Together they are known as the U.S. Congress. These men and women are elected by the people from the state that they represent.

- The leader of our government is elected by the people of our country who are of voting age. The leader is known as the president.

- Our president is George W. Bush. He lives and works in the White House. The president is elected by the voters in the United States to serve as the leader of our country. The president's position is voted on by the people every four years and the same person cannot serve more than eight years.

- The power of the presidency goes with the office. When George W. Bush leaves the office, the new president will have the power and Mr. Bush will be an ordinary citizen.
- In the United States, we have two major political parties: Democrats, who tend to want more services and more taxes to pay for them, and Republicans, who tend to want fewer services and fewer taxes.
- A person who runs for a government office (asks to be elected to a leadership position) is called a candidate.
- The candidate has a platform—a list of ideas that he or she supports. In speeches and printed campaign materials, the candidate explains what he or she wants government to do and why. On election day, voters decide whom they want to represent them and why. Candidates who receive the most votes win.
- The United States government makes the rules and laws that affect everyone in the United States.
- The United States government does many useful things that keep our country running smoothly.
- A lot of people work for the United States in an effort to make life better for its citizens.
- Voting is a method by which people choose among several alternatives.
- A democracy is a form of government in which people take an active role in the decision making.
- A ballot is the list of names and offices (and sometimes ideas about certain issues) on which voters make their choices.
- It would be difficult and confusing for people to try to live and work together with no rules or laws, no government.
- The earliest societies were small ones ruled by tribal leaders. Later, societies grew to become nations ruled by kings or queens.
- People came to America long ago because they were unhappy with their home countries. They came seeking liberties and happiness.
- At first, new settlers lived in colonies that were controlled by the king of England. But they wanted to govern themselves, so they declared their independence and fought a war against England to gain their freedom. They won the war and became a new country called the United States.
- The Declaration of Independence and the U.S. Constitution are important governmental documents that guarantee rights and freedoms to the people.
- Governments can be classified as democracies or dictatorships.
- Customs and beliefs (part of culture) are reflected in governments around the world.

- Government services are needed to do the things that the people cannot do by themselves.
- All governments in the United States (e.g., community, township, city, state, and federal) provide some services for people.
- To pay for the services, the government collects money from the people. The money is referred to as taxes.
- Volunteering is the act of giving time and sometimes money to promote a cause, provide a service, or work to solve a problem without making new laws.
- Volunteering is one way to practice responsible citizenship.
- When enough people volunteer to solve a problem, the need for making more laws or raising taxes to pay for the additional service is lessened.
- Government cannot be expected to do everything for its people.
- Individuals can personally contribute time and money to help solve problems that affect members of the community.
- Volunteers work in their free time to help others in the community without getting paid.

Teaching Tips from Barbara

Be sure to save the charts, pictures, and other artifacts from the lessons as you teach them. These will be valuable tools during your review. I found that the questions within the review lent themselves well to having students discuss their answers in groups. If possible, use high school or parent volunteers to help facilitate those discussions. A high school government class is a great place to look for help.

Starting the Lesson

Discuss the responses to the home assignment. In advance of the lesson, outline and prepare *selected* segments of the authentic assessments from *some* of the lessons (see Table 2). Selections might be based on difficulty experienced during initial teaching, lessons that seemed most important, lessons that yielded a depth of understanding, and so forth.

At the conclusion of the select mini-presentations, administer a short paper-and-pencil quiz. The panel of experts should also provide oral and/or written feedback regarding the *accuracy* of the presentations.

Summarize

- People everywhere have rules and laws that guide their daily activities.
- Governments make plans and laws.

- Governments provide us with services that we cannot provide on our own.
- Government services are paid for by the tax money collected from the people who live in our country.
- As citizens, we have rights and responsibilities. We are expected to manage our lives within the governmental structure of the country in which we live.

Assessment

Provide students with a ten-item true/false quiz. If the item is false, ask them to make it true.

1. False   Citizens have a lot of rights and no responsibilities.
2. False   We have fewer rules and laws than the people who lived long, long ago and long ago.
3. True   We in the United States have many freedoms and a say in our government.
4. False   Everybody can vote in local, state, and national elections as soon as they can read.
5. True   Governmental leaders in the local communities, states, and nation usually make the laws.
6. True   Families pay money to the government for the services that are provided.
7. False   The money that families pay to fund the community services is called an allowance.
8. False   The leader of your state is called an ambassador.
9. True   The state government provides money for schools, builds and maintains state roads, and provides a system of fairness and justice.
10. True   When the president of the United States finishes his term(s) in office, he leaves the White House and the newly elected president and his or her family moves in.

Check responses on site. Provide for reteaching as needed. As a class write thank-you letters to the upper-grade mentors who served as the panel of experts.

Table 2   Authentic Assessments

LESSONS	ASSESSMENTS
Lesson 1 What Is a Community? What Is Citizenship?	• Conduct a role-play accompanied by definitions and descriptions of key terms: community, rights, responsibilities, citizens.
Lesson 2 Community Services Provided by the Local Government	• Have students use a local map, pictures, and photographs to describe the local community services that are provided.
Lesson 3 The Local Government Makes Plans and Laws	• Have students use the *Local Government* booklets and the videotaped interview with a local government official to explain how the local government runs.
Lesson 4 State Government Handles Matters That Affect Everyone in the State	• Use a series of student-generated letters that they are sending to relatives and friends in other states explaining the features of our state government. The letters should list features of state government and tell which seem most important and why.
Lesson 5 National Government Handles Matters That Affect Everyone in the United States	• Have students report on their recent imaginary trip to Washington, D.C., and what they learned about the U.S. government and its connection to them and your community.
Lesson 6 Voting	• Have a group of students play the role of informing local citizens about voting: Who? When? How? Why? Students can use props and cue cards illustrating key ideas.
Lesson 7 History of Government	• Have students use a time line and pictures to tell the story of how government has changed over time. Make sure they include an explanation for the why.
Lesson 8 Governments Around the World	• Have students use a world map, globe, and pictures of children and families around the world to explain how their governments are similar or different than ours.

Table 2 (Continued)

LESSONS	ASSESSMENTS
Lesson 9 Functions and Services of Government	• Have children perform a skit with props to explain government services and how they are paid for. Provide a set of word cards that identify local community services.
Lesson 10 Functions of Government Regulations	• Have students retell the story of how children at your school directly or indirectly depend on rules and laws. Have them use props and word cards of key understandings to underscore the main points.
Lesson 11 People Solve Problems Together	• Have a series of role-plays to convey the value of volunteering and the realization that government cannot do everything.

Reflecting Back, Moving Forward

....

What roles do family members play in my development? How is my childhood different from those of my parents? How can we as children get rid of discrimination? What role can I play in influencing the choices my family makes regarding the goods and services it purchases? How does the government help my family? How can it be helpful to my family if I learn about budgeting?

Self-efficacy is a sense of empowerment, of being able to make a difference using what has been learned. It is a state of mind that says, "I can do it! I can contribute. I can decide. I can figure it out." Our experiences with these units have involved not only children but their families. We have been gratified with their response to the home assignments. In our interviews with parents, one overarching theme was their reports of "I can" statements by their children. We attribute this to four principles associated with self-efficacy that we threaded throughout each unit:

1. The content should be emotionally and intellectually comfortable for students so as to provide good places to start. (All children have prior experience with cultural universals, so no student is disenfranchised because of culture, socioeconomic background, or achievement level.)
2. The content should have potential for immediate application outside of school.
3. Home assignments should support students' transition from egocentrism to social engagement with family members and other children and adults.
4. The content and learning opportunities should develop students' awareness of their geographical and cultural contexts.

Childhood is a particularly good topic for making connections to other parts of the curriculum. For example, specialness connects to required lessons on diversity and character education. Several parents were especially curious about the information contained in the pledge that students had created and signed. One commented, "I never realized how hurtful little clubs that kids have could be. My daughter talked about feeling bad when other children formed a club for those who had Velcro tennis shoes. I never knew about it until we read the part in the student pledge that said, 'No clubs with limited membership.' I guess this is something our family needs to talk more about." Other parental responses included:

- "I enjoyed sitting down with my child to talk and reminisce about the day he was born. I showed him pictures and we talked about him as a baby. It was my favorite homework job from all year."

- "After the lesson about birthday celebrations around the world, our foster daughter got very involved in planning her own birthday party. She insisted that we have fairy bread and a piñata at her party. I enjoyed our working together to plan this special day for her."

- "I was thrilled when my son suddenly discovered the pitfalls of television commercials. I soon realized that this was connected to what he was learning in social studies. His knowledge carried over to our shopping trips. He takes special notice of the cereals we buy—and warns us the special offers probably make them cost a lot more."

- "When my child came home from school one day and suddenly was eager to practice piano, I knew it stemmed from an in-school conversation. Upon probing, I found out that as part of the childhood unit, she had been learning about individuals' interests and talents as entry points for avocations and careers. Obviously she really identified with the stories of talented children who had made careers out of their interests. I'm thrilled. For now, my daughter's attention to piano has added meaning!"

- "I was really pleased when my son decided to spend time with me on the 'Adopt a Mile' project. The conversation during last Saturday's cleanup was really interesting. He talked about a story that involved a boy and his family collecting and fixing old bikes for children at a juvenile home. He looked me straight in the eye and said, 'Gee, Mom, kids can make a difference.'"

The money unit is filled with intriguing connections that children have experienced superficially but have not yet grasped. For example, they are often passengers in the car when their families seek the nearest ATM machine and quickly return with a fistful of cash. Other times they witness a parent talking to the teller at the drive-through window at the bank. They hear talk about depositing money or withdrawing it but rarely ask, "So how does that work?" Given the desire of normal kids to acquire lots of stuff—and frequently asking, "Can I have . . . " or "Will you buy me a . . . ?"—it is not surprising that families were eager to have their children learn about money and how it impacts their lives. Because children are curious about it and some even collect currencies from other places, they too were instantly ready to learn about it and in fact exhibited lots of "I wonders" during the introductory lesson. One parent was particularly pleased that his son would learn about money. He said, "Recently I read that economics is rarely taught as part of elementary social studies and I think that's a problem. I'm glad to see it's a part of our school's curriculum." Other parent comments included:

- "My daughter came home and asked us about paying bills. I took out my bills and we talked about our family budget. I would love for our daughter to learn how to spend her money responsibly now when she's young instead of having to learn the hard way when she's older."

- "Our son used to constantly beg us for toys and treats whenever we'd go shopping. It used to be such a hassle. Since the money unit, he realizes that our money has to pay for so many things that he no longer begs at the store. In fact, last week he was helping me look for a bargain. I was amused—and impressed!"

- "As you recall, I was one of those parents who volunteered to accompany the class on the field trip to the credit union. The field trip revealed to me how much the students had absorbed during the class discussions. While the credit union employees had punch, cookies, and a penguin mascot waiting for us, it became perfectly clear that while the students appreciated these touches, they were more interested in information such as 'How much money will you pay me to keep my money here so that you can loan it to other people?'"

- "Paying taxes has created negative conversations in our family until this year. My second grader actually told me I'd better pay my taxes or she might not be able to go to school next year. She was sure she wouldn't have a teacher if the taxes weren't paid."

- "My son and I were shopping recently because he needed a new pair of gym shoes. Once we found a satisfactory pair, I pulled out my credit card and was ready to pay. To my amazement, my son looked up at me and asked, 'Are you sure you'll be able to pay the full amount when the credit card bill comes?' The salesman was blown away. I explained that they were studying about money in school."

Government seems, at least initially, to be quite a stretch for young learners because their knowledge is limited and what they do know is not organized and can be difficult to access. It usually centers on symbols and songs about America and some thin description of our national government, including its leadership. Once they got into our government unit, however, students became quite engaged—especially when they began realizing how much government affects their lives. Eventually, the unit became a class favorite. One mother commented that she was quite embarrassed when she realized that her daughter had thought a lot more about taxes—and in a positive way—than she ever had. Other parental comments:

- "Our daughter made a very personal connection between what she was learning at school and my disciplining her when she noted, 'Rules at home are just like laws that your parents decide to pass.'"
- "I got interested in learning more information about local government when my son knew the name of the township supervisor and even pointed out his picture in the newspaper. I knew I wasn't as involved in our local government as I should be."
- "This is amazing! These kids began seeing themselves as potential participants in different levels of government. During a sleepover at our house, I overheard two of the boys engaging in a very spirited debate about which job would be better to have in the future—justice of the Supreme Court or president of the United States. Finally, one of them summed it up by saying, 'If you were a Supreme Court judge, you could get the job for life and you could decide which laws were fair. But, if you were the president, you would be very powerful, meet lots of cool people, live in a big house, and someday have your face on a quarter.'"
- "Our daughter couldn't wait for us to sit down at the table and make a list of all the ways the government helps us. We were ashamed to admit that before she began studying this topic as a part of social studies, we hadn't seen the government as such a positive force."

- "Our daughter is convinced she can become the first female president. She's already trying to figure out what she needs to do."

Parents appreciated advance communication about completion dates for home assignments as well as specific directions about expected amounts of input. (One student told his parents that he had to interview at least a dozen people who had careers associated with money.) A few parents also voiced a desire for more material about the units in general, including the main ideas and the rationales underlying the home assignments to help guide them in expanding their discussions with their children.

Personal efficacy, family impact, and meaningful understandings have been the hallmarks of our experiences with these units. We encourage you to frequently revisit the big ideas drawn from the units to help your students explain life experiences and develop habits of thoughtful conversations about the world around them. Provide parents with lists of big ideas and provocative questions so they too may experience the luxury of helping their children make connections between book learning and real life, for example, by applying what they learned in school to a television program, retrieving data from the Internet to enhance a lesson, or discussing how things work at home and in the community.

References

Chapter 1

Brophy, J., & Alleman, J. (1996). *Powerful Social Studies for Elementary Students*. Fort Worth: Harcourt Brace.

Egan, K. (1988). *Primary Understanding: Education in Early Childhood*. New York: Routledge.

Evans, R., & Saxe, D. (Eds.). (1996). *Handbook on Teaching Social Issues*. Washington, DC: National Council for the Social Studies.

Good, T., & Brophy, J. (2003). *Looking in Classrooms* (9th Ed.). Boston: Allyn & Bacon.

Haas, M., & Laughlin, M. (Eds.). (1997). *Meeting the Standards: Social Studies Readings for K–6 Educators*. Washington, DC: National Council for the Social Studies.

Harris, D., & Yocum, M. (1999). *Powerful and Authentic Social Studies: A Professional Development Program for Teachers*. Washington, DC: National Council for the Social Studies.

Hirsch, E. D., Jr. (1988). *Cultural Literacy: What Every American Needs to Know*. New York: Vintage.

Krey, D. (1998). *Children's Literature in Social Studies: Teaching to the Standards* (Bulletin No. 95). Waldorf, MD: National Council for the Social Studies.

Larkins, A., Hawkins, M., & Gilmore, A. (1987). Trivial and Noninformative Content of Elementary Social Studies: A Review of Primary Texts in Four Series. *Theory and Research in Social Education, 15*, 299–311.

National Council for the Social Studies. (1993). A Vision of Powerful Teaching and Learning in the Social Studies: Building Social Understanding and Civic Efficacy. *Social Education, 57,* 213–223. [Also included in the NCSS 1994 Bulletin on Curriculum Standards for Social Studies]

National Council for the Social Studies. (1994). *Curriculum Standards for Ssocial Studies: Expectations of Excellence* (Bulletin No. 89). Washington, DC: Author.

Ravitch, D. (1987). Tot Sociology or What Happened to History in the Grade Schools. *American Scholar, 56,* 343–353.

Roth, K. (1996). Making Learners and Concepts Central: A Conceptual Change Approach to Learner-Centered, Fifth-Grade American History Planning and Teaching. In J. Brophy (Ed.), *Advances in Research on Teaching. Volume 6: Teaching and Learning History* (pp. 115–182). Greenwich, CT: JAI Press.

Chapter 2

Alleman, J., & Brophy, J. (1994). Taking Advantage of Out-of-School Opportunities for Meaningful Social Studies Learning. *Social Studies, 85,* 262–267.

Alleman, J., & Brophy, J. (1997). Elementary Social Studies: Instruments, Activities, and Standards. In G. Phye (Ed.), *Handbook of Classroom Assessment* (pp. 321–357). San Diego: Academic Press.

Alleman, J., & Brophy, J. (1999). The Changing Nature and Purpose of Assessment in the Social Studies Classroom. *Social Education, 65,* 334–337.

Barries, P., & Bernes, C. (1998). *Woodrow the White House Mouse.* Alexandria, VA: VSP Books.

Brophy, J., & Alleman, J. (1991). Activities as Instructional Tools: A Framework for Analysis and Evaluation. *Educational Researcher, 20*(4), 9–23.

Waters, K. (1991). *The Story of the White House House.* New York: Scholastic, Inc.

Introduction to Money

Berti, A., & Monaci, M. (1998). Third Graders' Acquisition of Knowledge of Banking: Restructuring or Accretion? *British Journal of Educational Psychology, 68,* 357–371.

Byrnes, J. (1996). *Cognitive development and Learning in Instructional Contexts.* Boston: Allyn & Bacon.

Schug, M., & Hartoonian, H. M. (1996). Issues and Practices in the Social Studies Curriculum. In M. Pugach and C. Warger (Eds.), *Curriculum Trends, Special Education, and Reform: Refocusing the Conversation* (pp. 106–122). New York: Teachers College Press.

Introduction to Government

Berti, A., & Benesso, C. (1998). The Concept of Nation-State in Italian Elementary School Children: Spontaneous Concepts and Effects of Teaching. *Genetic, Social, and General Psychology Monographs, 124,* 185–209.

Greenstein, F. (1969). *Children and Politics* (Revised Ed.). New Haven: Yale University Press.

Hess, R., & Torney, J. (1967). *The Development of Political Attitudes in Children*. Chicago: Aldine.

Moore, S., Lare, J., & Wagner, K. (1985). *The Child's Political World: A Longitudinal Perspective*. New York: Praeger.